MW00712235

THE INNOVATIVE CIO

HOW IT LEADERS CAN DRIVE BUSINESS TRANSFORMATION

Andi Mann
George Watt
Peter Matthews

technologies

CA Press

Apress®

The Innovative CIO: How IT Leaders Can Drive Business Transformation

Copyright © 2013 by CA. All rights reserved. All trademarks, trade names, service marks and logos referenced herein belong to their respective companies.

The information in this publication could include typographical errors or technical inaccuracies, and the authors assume no responsibility for its accuracy or completeness. The statements and opinions expressed in this book are those of the authors and are not necessarily those of CA, Inc. ("CA"). CA may make modifications to any CA product, software program, method or procedure described in this publication at any time without notice.

Any reference in this publication to third-party products and websites is provided for convenience only and shall not serve as the authors' endorsement of such products or websites. Your use of such products, websites, any information regarding such products or any materials provided with such products or on such websites shall be at your own risk.

To the extent permitted by applicable law, the content of this book is provided "AS IS" without warranty of any kind, including, without limitation, any implied warranties of merchantability, fitness for a particular purpose, or non-infringement. In no event will the authors or CA be liable for any loss or damage, direct or indirect, arising from or related to the use of this book, including, without limitation, lost profits, lost investment, business interruption, goodwill or lost data, even if expressly advised in advance of the possibility of such damages. Neither the content of this book nor any software product referenced herein serves as a substitute for your compliance with any laws (including but not limited to any act, statute, regulation, rule, directive, standard, policy, administrative order, executive order, and so on (collectively, "Laws") referenced herein or otherwise. You should consult with competent legal counsel regarding any such Laws.

All rights reserved. No part of this work may be reproduced or transmitted in any form or by any means, electronic or mechanical, including photocopying, recording, or by any information storage or retrieval system, without the prior written permission of the copyright owner and the publisher.

ISBN-13 (pbk): 978-1-4302-4410-3
ISBN-13 (electronic): 978-1-4302-4411-0

Trademarked names, logos, and images may appear in this book. Rather than use a trademark symbol with every occurrence of a trademarked name, logo, or image we use the names, logos, and images only in an editorial fashion and to the benefit of the trademark owner, with no intention of infringement of the trademark.

The use in this publication of trade names, trademarks, service marks, and similar terms, even if they are not identified as such, is not to be taken as an expression of opinion as to whether or not they are subject to proprietary rights.

President and Publisher: Paul Manning
Acquisitions Editor: Robert Hutchinson
Developmental Editor: Jeffrey Pepper
Editorial Board: Steve Anglin, Mark Beckner, Ewan Buckingham, Gary Cornell, Morgan Ertel, Jonathan Gennick, Jonathan Hassell, Robert Hutchinson, Michelle Lowman, James Markham, Matthew Moodie, Jeff Olson, Jeffrey Pepper, Douglas Pundick, Ben Renow-Clarke, Dominic Shakeshaft, Gwenan Spearing, Matt Wade, Tom Welsh
Coordinating Editor: Rita Fernando
Copy Editor: Jennifer Sharpe
Compositor: Bytheway Publishing Services
Indexer: SPi Global Inc.
Cover Designer: Anna Ishchenko

Distributed to the book trade worldwide by Springer Science+Business Media, LLC., 233 Spring Street, 6th Floor, New York, NY 10013. Phone 1-800-SPRINGER, fax (201) 348-4505, e-mail orders-ny@springer-sbm.com, or visit www.springeronline.com.

For information on translations, please e-mail rights@apress.com, or visit www.apress.com.

Apress and friends of ED books may be purchased in bulk for academic, corporate, or promotional use. eBook versions and licenses are also available for most titles. For more information, reference our Special Bulk Sales–eBook Licensing web page at www.apress.com/bulk-sales.

The information in this book is distributed on an "as is" basis, without warranty. Although every precaution has been taken in the preparation of this work, neither the author(s) nor Apress shall have any liability to any person or entity with respect to any loss or damage caused or alleged to be caused directly or indirectly by the information contained in this work.

*This book is dedicated to innovative IT leaders
who are already making a difference
to their businesses and customers, and
to those who are working hard to move past
keeping the lights on.*

Contents

Foreword

The role of the Chief Information Officer (CIO) has evolved ever since the first mention of the title over 30 years ago. Of course, the position of the IT leader has been around for as long again, although the job title has changed many times in the intervening years. While managing the IT function and resources, running efficient IT operations, and delivering reliable and consistent services were the core focus for early incumbents, achieving these objectives is merely expected of today's CIO. As IT has become more embedded in organizational processes and practices, and the conduct of business ever more digitized, the CIO role has expanded considerably. Today, because IT offers considerable potential as a source for competitive differentiation, many CIOs have been given the innovation mandate.

CIOs have always sought to innovate to reduce costs, to improve reliability and availability of systems, and to increase agility. Just look at the number of CIOs virtualizing their datacenters, automating IT service management, or moving their datacenters to the cloud. This kind of innovation is focused on the IT infrastructure: managing the technical legacy of past IT investment decisions. But this is only one kind of innovation—what I call "IT innovation of IT." I do not mean to denigrate this kind of innovation; it is vitally important. Where most CIOs struggle today is with "business innovation using IT"—that is, driving innovation in products and services, processes, business models, management, and customer experience.

One point is worth emphasizing: innovation using IT is less about the "T" and more about the "I." There are two ways to win with information: *exploration* and *exploitation*. Exploration is about discovering new knowledge from available information. This knowledge can be about customers, operations, competitors, or other unknown unknowns. Some of this information will be internally generated from operations, but an increasing volume will come from external sources such as social media, sensors, and third-party databases. This information will also be of a different variety from that traditionally stored in corporate databases: not just structured data, but increasingly unstructured varieties including video and Twitter feeds.

Exploitation is about seeking out opportunities to take advantage of information asymmetries; it is about making the invisible visible. These asymmetries arise when one party to a transaction, or interaction or potential transaction/interaction, has more or better information than the other. By identifying these asymmetries, an organization can leverage opportunities through the medium of technology to change both what it does and how it does it. Identifying innovative opportunities often rests on the interplay between exploration and exploitation. By generating new insights derived from exploring information, an organization may then choose to exploit any information asymmetries that may be revealed.

My research has found that most of the innovative ideas for using IT that come from the business side (as opposed to from the IT organization) tend to be for incremental improvements rather than real radical innovation. This "business-pull" innovation is generally limited by the business side's inability to envision new possibilities for doing things not possible without IT.

The potentially game-changing opportunities will usually emerge from "IT-push" innovation. These radical ideas can come from the CIO who has an appreciation of IT; understands the business, strategy, and competitive environment; and has the curiosity and entrepreneurship to identify these game-changing ideas. Of course, this may not be enough. To get traction for new ideas, the CIO must have credibility with his or her peers in the C-suite, the ability to communicate and influence, and the leadership capability to drive these ideas forward.

This book provides real guidance and practical advice for CIOs who seek to lead innovation using the IT in their organizations. It shows how IT can help drive value from innovation. It addresses the push and pull of IT innovation, illustrating how to innovate mindfully with IT, and it provides lots of examples and case studies. The authors also point to the structures and processes that have proved to work, as well as the organizational cultural demands to innovate successfully. There are sections addressing the risks associated with innovation and how they can be mitigated, as well as how to budget for IT innovation. There are numerous takeaways that won't leave you disappointed.

Professor Joe Peppard
Cranfield School of Management, UK

About the Authors

Andi Mann is vice president of strategic solutions at CA Technologies. With over 25 years' experience across five continents, Andi has deep expertise in enterprise software on cloud, mainframe, midrange, server, and desktop systems. Andi has worked within IT for global corporations, with software vendors, and as a leading industry analyst. He has been published in the *New York Times*, *USA Today*, *Forbes*, *CIO*, *ComputerWorld*, *InformationWeek*, *TechTarget*, and more, and has presented worldwide on IT strategy, innovation, virtualization, cloud, automation, and management. Andi is a co-author of the popular handbook, *Visible Ops – Private Cloud*. He blogs at http://pleasediscuss.com/andimann and tweets as @AndiMann.

George Watt is vice president of corporate strategy at CA Technologies. A transformative leader with more than 25 years of experience, George has spearheaded initiatives that have enabled organizations to simplify and automate their complex IT infrastructures, deliver new business benefits, and drive millions of dollars in savings and productivity gains. In the early 2000s George founded the CA Technologies Engineering Services team, responsible for protecting the company's intellectual property, managing the consolidated source-code repository, and providing automation and development tools. In this role George led the development of CA Technologies' own private cloud and enjoys sharing his lessons learned with others who are now venturing on a similar journey. George began his technical career as a systems programmer/sysadmin and systems engineer. He has held many leadership positions, leading technical and presales teams in Canada, the United States, and globally.

Throughout his career, George has delivered innovations such as a lightweight event management agent, a knowledge base for a neural network-based predictive performance management solution, and one of the earliest private clouds. Many of George's innovations are now available to CA Technologies customers as product components or features. He blogs at www.pragmaticcloud.com and tweets as @GeorgeDWatt.

Peter Matthews is vice president and research staff member in CA Labs at CA Technologies. Peter is based in the UK working as a researcher and coordinating research activity between CA's R&D laboratories and academia. He has more than 30 years of IT experience with leading-edge technology, ranging from mainframe programming and UNIX development to cloud computing and MIS research. Peter has leveraged his experience by participating in the CA Technologies corporate strategy team and leading groups investigating the influence of macro social, political, and economic trends on future technology. Collaborative research projects have been a major part of Peter's work with subjects as varied as service oriented architecture, requirements engineering, business process performance analysis, and value metrics for existing IT infrastructure. The latter generated a new research project examining the role of the CIO in a cloud-computing environment. Provisional results of this continuing project have been published by CA Technologies as a report, "Being the Boss." This and other projects have benefitted from Peter's frequent discussions with IT leaders on research and innovation topics. He is CA Technologies' representative on the Cloud Services Measurement Initiative Consortium, managed by Carnegie-Mellon University. He blogs at http://community.ca.com/blogs/innovation/default.aspx and tweets as @peterm57.

Acknowledgments

First and foremost, I wish to acknowledge the undying support of my darling wife, Heather Mann. Without your patience, wisdom, devotion, love, and much more, this book have been impossible, as would the better part of my success and joy in life to date. You are my love and my life, every single day.

I would also like to thank the many IT leaders who I have talked with, read about, and taken advice from over my many years in technology—whether in finance, logistics, entertainment, telecommunications, healthcare, government, service providers, or other industries; in my native Australia, my adopted USA, or across Europe, Africa, Asia, and Latin America; or in capacities as technology vendors, industry analysts, and media contributors: you are too numerous to name individually, but collectively constitute the source of the most important part of my contributions to this book.

To my co-authors George and Peter: you are brilliant, storied, and amazing people to work with. I can only bask in the reflected glory of your contributions, which are without doubt the best parts of this book. Similarly, thanks to all of my other amazing colleagues at CA Technologies who made this work possible, including Andrew Wittman, Jacob Lamm, Adam Famularo, Ron Collier, Jackie Kahle, Bill Talbot, and Katherine Demacopoulos.

Finally, I personally dedicate this book to my father, Brian Mann, who sadly passed away as we were writing this book; and offer my greatest thanks especially to my mother, Joan Mann, who still inspires me every day. You both taught me to be inquisitive but discerning, to challenge the status quo, to look beyond the obvious, to believe in myself, and always to strive to do new things in new ways. Whether at school or university, tinkering with personal computers, poring over crosswords and cards, cataloging decommissioned abattoirs, working night shift in datacenters, or visiting (and then occupying) executive suites, I owe you my life-long passion for thinking, learning, and leading. I love you and think of you every day, which thoughts never fail to buoy my spirits.

Andi Mann

I am fortunate to have been influenced by innovators very early in my life. They all played a part in this book in some way. Many of those were, of course, members of my family. My earliest memories of my love of innovation include my grandfathers, Albert Mombourquette and George V. Watt, both innovators in their own right. The latter also taught me the value of a patient second look when facing a problem, and how to begin facing any challenge with the belief that whatever *it* is, it *can* be done. My parents, Donalda and Everett Watt, taught me the value of hard work and the importance of honor and trust; all key to my success in innovation. My uncle Robert Watt and my cousin Leslie Dancses both inspired my interest in technology. Leslie was also my first business partner and witnessed the creations of the "Code Faeries" mentioned in the book first hand. To all of them, and to the many family members I have not named, thank you.

I have also been fortunate to work with many innovative people in my professional life. There are far too many to mention individually. The journey that leads to innovation is not easy, and making an innovative idea a business-value driver can be even more difficult. Thank you to the colleagues, team members, customers, and partners who were part of my journey. I look forward to the challenges we have yet to face.

To my co-authors, Andi and Peter, thank you for a great journey. I will surely miss our banter.

Finally, without the support of my children, James and Heather, and my wife, Lee Anne, it would not have been possible for me to write this book. To my children, thank you for being so patient and supportive those many evenings and weekends I spent writing. Lee Anne, I don't know how you endured my thinking aloud and the countless times I approached you with, "Hey, can you read this?" You all inspire me daily.

George Watt

I would first like to thank my wife Pat and my daughter Georgie for their generous support over the long nights and weekends locked in my room writing. I would particularly like to thank Pat for her patience and insight whenever I emerged to ask, "What do you think of this piece?" My daughter Georgie has patiently waited for me to finish writing to fulfill taxi duties and my wife Pat has frequently delayed dinner to suit my schedule not hers. Friends have also been supportive even when I vanished to work on a chapter during the Outcast's hockey tour.

Many of the ideas and comments in this book are the result of working with Professor Joe Peppard of Cranfield School of Management, without whom I would not have become interested in the role played by CIOs in innovation and business management. His kind support and the quality of his writing have been an example to me. I would also like to thank all my colleagues in CA who have enabled me to speak to and listen to senior IT management and given me so many good examples, particularly Terrence Clark, Gabby Silberman, Sarah Atkinson and Colin Bannister

To my co-authors Andi and George I have had a great time working with you, learned a lot and laughed a lot. It has been a pleasure collaborating with you both.

Peter Matthews

The Authors jointly wish to say thank you to Robert Hutchinson, Rita Fernando, Jennifer Sharpe, and the Apress team for your patience, guidance, and for keeping us on track. Without you this would have been a very different and much inferior text, if indeed it existed at all. Also our special thanks to Karen Sleeth and Connie Smallwood, our CA Press sponsors, Steve Versteeg our sponsor/reviewer, and Gabby Silberman our CA executive sponsor for giving us the opportunity, encouragement, and support to write this book.

Innovation Matters

The less things change, the more they remain the same.

—Sicilian Proverb

Why Innovate?

In 1986, 3.5 million people were inflicted with dracunculiasis.[1] This disease, commonly referred to as guinea worm disease (GWD), was then known to have infected people in at least 20 countries. The Drancunculus nematode or guinea worm—often referred to as "the fiery serpent" owing to the intense burning pain it causes—is a spaghetti-like parasite that grows up to a meter in length in the subcutaneous tissue of its hosts. Spread via contaminated drinking water, this disease impacts impoverished and disadvantaged people most. The disease itself is not usually fatal, although infections resulting from it can be.

Even when millions of people were suffering from this disease some groups within the affected areas of Africa and Asia were unaffected. This anomaly was perplexing to epidemiologists, since all people are susceptible to the guinea worm once it enters the body, and the unaffected groups of people were

---

[1] "Progress Toward Global Eradication of Dracunculiasis, January 2005--May 2007," Centers for Disease Control and Prevention, August 17, 2007, www.cdc.gov/mmwr/preview/mmwrhtml/mm5632a1.htm, retrieved on August 2012.

drinking from the same water sources as groups that were infected with GWD at much higher rates. How could that be?

Researchers learned that the people who had been unaffected would pour their drinking water through their clothing prior to consuming it. This prevented the parasite from entering their drinking water and left them largely without infection. This innovative use of an everyday item had spared these people not only from the painful disease, but also from the economic hardship that accompanied it. The story gets even better.

Since 1986, Dr. Donald Hopkins and a research team from the Carter Center (www.cartercenter.org) have leveraged that knowledge to create and deploy their own innovative programs, with amazing results. According to the Centers for Disease Control, there were only 391 cases of GWD in the first half of 2012,[2] and those working to eradicate it completely are on the cusp of success. The Carter Center's programs leverage the initial innovation—filtering drinking water—and they focus on keeping infected people away from drinking-water sources so that the worm cannot reproduce. Innovations of their own, such as small filter pipes that people can carry at all times so they can safely drink while on the move, have helped to deliver their incredible results.

If you were skeptical about the value of innovation, or about whether *you* could be innovative, hopefully this example will begin to convince you that innovation can happen anywhere. It can happen in a multi-million dollar laboratory, on the banks of a river, or in your own back yard. It can be discovered by anyone at any time. It can make an amazing difference in the life of the innovator and, as in this case, in the lives of many others.

Of course, not all innovation will have as dramatic an impact as this illustration. But some will. While the value of an innovation that eradicates a disease is obvious, the fact that an innovation does not eradicate a disease does not mean that the innovation is not valuable. Assuming that you are likely reading this using an artificial light source of some sort, or perhaps in the form of an e-book, you will not need to look too far for evidence. (If you're thinking, "Ha! I'm reading a printed copy using sunlight!"—you still have Johannes Gutenberg to thank for the printing press or those who came afterward and made improvements to mass publication.)

There are also Information Technology (IT) leaders who deserve of our thanks. IT leaders have delivered countless innovations that have improved

---

[2] WHO Collaborating Center for Research, "Guinea Worm Wrap-Up #213," July 16, 2012, www.cartercenter.org/resources/pdfs/news/health_publications/guinea_worm/wrap-up/213.pdf, retrieved on August 2012.

the lives of people in many ways—ranging from the convenience of the automated teller machine (ATM) to social media that has helped connect long lost friends and family to advances in organ donor matching and other areas of medicine.

The achievements of many technology innovators such as Charles Babbage, Herman Hollerith, and Steve Wozniak are well known. The contributions of others, such as Alan Turing (who made great advances in computing and broke the Enigma code) and Hedy Lamarr (the movie actress who co-invented frequency-hopping spread spectrum communications that served as the basis for Bluetooth and modern WiFi networks) are perhaps less celebrated.

Today's technology innovators have also delivered life saving advances. While visiting Parol, India, in 2009, Myshkin Ingawale witnessed the tragic passing of a mother and child due to post-partum anemia. He learned that anemia is simple to treat and that this tragedy would likely have been preventable had the local healthcare workers been able to diagnose the anemia. With a mission to "democratize healthcare" he built a portable-music-player-sized device (ToucHb) that can deliver a diagnosis in seconds, non-invasively, anywhere in the world. The University of Calgary's Faculty of Medicine created ResolutionMD, an iPhone and iPad based application that enables rapid, remote diagnosis of stroke with the same accuracy as a medical workstation.[3] In addition to innovators such as these there are countless unsung technology leaders and CIOs improving lives in untold ways, both large and small.

Fortunately, the pace of information technology innovation continues to be rapid. Advances in hardware, social media, cloud computing, and mobile computing are being delivered at a breakneck pace. Hardly a day goes by without news of an advance in one of those areas.

None of these advances happen without innovative people. Thankfully, it appears we are in the presence of a bumper crop of those as well. Take for example, 17-year-old Brittany Wenger, winner of the Google Science Fair 2012. Brittany created a "Global Neural Network Cloud Service for Breast Cancer" that combines the power of cloud computing and neural networks to deliver more accurate detection of breast cancer. Her noninvasive system delivered more than 99% accuracy in over 7 million trials.

Even from these few examples, critical lessons can be learned. First, innovation can and does happen everywhere. Next, innovation can come from anyone at any time. Third,—though far from last—as we saw in the case of the use of

---

[3] Marta Cyperling, "Stroke Diagnosis Using iPhone App Extremely Accurate Study Finds," University of Calgary Faculty of Medicine, May 9, 2011, www.medicine.ucalgary.ca/about/iPhone_medical_application, retrieved on August 2012.

clothing as a water filter, innovation does not require invention. We will explore of each of these further throughout the book.

Innovation Can Be Lost

Sadly, not all innovation is captured. Some is lost. Some is destroyed or sabotaged—intentionally or unintentionally. Sometimes people simply do not know what to do with an innovative idea when they encounter it. Each of these cases leads to the same, unfortunate outcome: opportunity lost, benefit lost, and competitive advantage lost.

Throughout this book, we will provide examples of various types of innovation from history, from current practitioners and IT leaders, and from our own experience. We will use each example to help you understand where innovation can be found and how to recognize it. We will also discuss how to foster innovation and how to capture it when it occurs. We will dispel some common innovation myths. And we will address one of the most critical aspects of innovation: how to ensure your organization fosters, and does not destroy, innovation and the innovative spirit of your team.

The importance of that last item cannot be overstated. Today many IT teams are suffering from a perception that they are not innovative. That they are too slow in their responses. That they are not nimble or agile enough to be a strategic weapon in today's business climate. That they are behind the times. That IT is where projects go to die. That they are the office of the C-I-No or C-I-Slow. These labels can be as much a cause as an effect, and this perception (or reality) must be addressed head-on.

Innovation Is Imperative

Businesses are putting such tremendous pressure on their IT teams to innovate because businesses that innovate thrive and lead. Netflix provides a striking recent example of the benefit of continuous innovation. Their innovative use of technology in support of a leading-edge business model completely transformed their industry. Businesses that do not innovate atrophy, become followers, or even cease to exist. One need not look further than Blockbuster for an example of what happens to those who do not innovate and advance quickly enough.

The need to innovate with speed is clear to most any business leader today. In order to be valued partners to business leaders, IT leaders must be capable of enabling innovation and innovating on their own.

Throughout the book, we will discuss innovation's challenges and opportunities, and what you can do if you find yourself a victim of the negative perceptions. IT teams have long been innovators, and it is time for them to reclaim their rightful title.

Much can be done to foster innovation, and strong leadership is a key ingredient. Innovative leaders can create environments that enable innovative teams to thrive. They can take action to ensure that the benefits of innovation are made real when it occurs. They can remove impediments to innovation. IT leaders who know how to recognize and deal with these critical items will be well on their way to building an innovative team and becoming an Innovative CIO.

Stories from the Trenches

Innovation in Action and Inaction

I will not follow where the path may lead, but I will go where there is no path, and I will leave a trail.

—Muriel Strode

Iron rusts from disuse, stagnant water loses its purity, and in cold weather becomes frozen; even so does inaction sap the vigors of the mind.

—Leonardo da VInci

Though there are many definitions of the word "innovation," for the most part they share several key characteristics. Most definitions of the term state that an innovation is the introduction of something new. They also generally agree that the "something" that is introduced can be a product, service, process, idea, technology—anything you can imagine. Another common characteristic is that they do not mention invention at all, or they state that though innovation may involve invention, invention need not be present for innovation to occur.

Understanding this aspect of innovation is critical. That is, innovation *may* involve invention, but innovation can also happen without it. Many times innovation occurs when someone—perhaps with a fresh perspective, no preconceptions, or no experience in a domain—sees an opportunity or challenge differently and applies an existing tool or process in a new way, context, or simply in a domain that differs from its common use. If a hard hat has ever spared you a splitting headache (or worse), thank Edward Bullard, an innovative thinker who realized that the helmets worn by World War II soldiers could serve another purpose.

Hopefully the previous example of an innovation in use will impress upon you how important it is to recognize, capture, and exploit all types of innovation. I recall playing with a doughboy-style hard hat given to me by my grandfather who worked at a steel plant. The metal hard hat had a substantial dent in its top, likely an indication that the hat had saved my grandfather from a serious injury.

So, it is imperative that you be on the lookout for all types of innovation, such as the following:

- Innovation in Use or Process
- Incremental Innovation
- Fortunate Innovation
- Deliberate Innovation
- Desperate Innovation

Innovation in Use or Process

Though frequently dismissed as not being innovative, innovation in use or process can deliver substantial value to a business. It is usually easy to implement and involves minimal training, often at minimal cost and with substantial returns.

In the mid-1990s, as a field engineer, I was assigned to help a very large corporation with the management of their distributed computing environment. The company offered a marquis online service, similar to the services offered by Google or Yahoo! today. With thousands of servers deployed, this company was challenged to keep their operation running smoothly and performing well.

Several teams had been unable to address this customer's three main challenges:

1. Key events of interest occurred on each of their thousands of servers.

2. The size of their challenge was beyond the scale of humans (their employees could not manage all of the events on every one of the servers).

3. State-of-the-art management software was designed for management servers as opposed to distributed application servers, had too large a footprint, and had too much of an impact on the performance of a non-management class machine.

We realized that the solution required a lightweight agent that could operate on its own and evaluate specific policies on each of the thousands of machines in the environment. It would also require central management and local autonomy and had to have a small footprint and acceptable performance. Simple. Except that nothing like that existed. (Solutions of this nature are commonplace today.)

In the end, the solution was quite straightforward. All of the components required to manage and respond to events, forward critical information to a central source (or multiple sources), "zoom in" on any "machine of interest," and deploy policy from one machine to many others were already present in our existing products. The challenge was not that there was insufficient functionality—there was too much functionality. That made the products too resource intensive for widely distributed machines. We removed superfluous components (such as user interface components only required for a central management function) until only those things that were absolutely required in order to accomplish the objectives remained. These components were repackaged and delivered as a very lightweight solution to the customer's problem.

None of the product's code was changed, though a few minor additions were created. In the end, a brand-new solution to a new problem in a new domain had been created through the innovative use and assembly of existing components. Subsequently, that lightweight management technology was added to product offerings and served as a competitive differentiator for quite some time.

If you were of the belief that advances in use or process cannot be innovative, perhaps the previous example will help you to think otherwise. If that example was unconvincing, consider the changes in the use of acetylsalicylic acid (commonly known as aspirin) from a pure analgesic (pain killer) to a key factor in the prevention of heart diseases and strokes. If you've ever used a GPS to guide you safely to your destination, you've been the benefactor of repurposed military technology. Examples of the benefit of this type of innovation are everywhere and yet it is still often under-appreciated.

Incremental Innovation

Incremental innovation is innovation's unsung hero. An incremental innovation can have just as large an impact on business value, quality of life, or revenue as any other type of innovation.

The March 2012 release of the third generation iPad provides a great example of incremental innovation. Around the time of its launch there was much written and said about how there were not really any compelling reasons for someone to upgrade from previous versions of the device. However, among these minor upgrades was the Retina display, which boasted 3.1 million pixels, four times as many as its predecessor. This display was purported to be the best ever for a device of this nature[1].

The Retina display made the iPad much more attractive to photographers, who could now see much more detail in their photographs, making basic photo editing a practical application for the device. This upgrade also opened up other new markets for the device that would benefit from the sharper resolution, such as medical imaging. Apple, always an adept marketer, branded the new version of the device as "resolutionary," and the third generation iPad with its incremental improvements sold three million units on the first weekend following its launch.

Sadly, incremental innovation is often perceived to be the runt of the innovation litter. Nothing could be further from the truth. If you offered to add a zero between the last digit of someone's paycheck and the decimal, you can be sure that employee would instantly be aware of the value of "incremental remuneration."

Fortunately, in addition to Apple, groups such as the Pharmaceutical Research and Manufacturers of America have discovered the value of incremental innovation. On their web site (Innovation.org), they state that innovation in their industry is often the result of a series of incremental improvements that together result in an overall improvement that delivers a significant impact. They also state that those incremental advances can result in better options for practitioners to deliver the best treatment to their patients.[2]

Opinions regarding the value of incremental innovation are beginning to change. In May 2011 at the "How Next Happens: Building our Economy Through Incremental Innovation" symposium, Roger Martin, Dean of the

---

[1] Though initially it was Apple's claim that the iPad 3 included the best display ever on a mobile device others, such as DisplayMate agreed: http://www.displaymate.com/iPad_ShootOut_1.htm.

[2] http://www.innovation.org/index.cfm/InnovationToday/KeyIssues/Incremental_Innovation

Rotman School of Management, University of Toronto stated that Canada's success and prosperity necessitate i t's welcoming incremental innovation.[3]

Be diligent in your pursuit of incremental innovation and reward and promote it when it drives value. When someone familiar with your product says "You know what would be great?"; "You know what would make this even better?"; or "I wish this had…" pay attention. Ask questions. They may have a fantastic idea for an incremental innovation, and they may not even be aware that they do.

Incremental innovations can also fail to live up to their potential when their benefits are not effectively communicated, which will be discussed later in this chapter.

Fortunate Innovation

Overlooking fortunate innovation or "accidental innovation" can also result in lost opportunity. This in spite of the fact that many of us know stories of this type of innovation that are interesting, fascinating, or even life-saving.

Sometimes fortunate innovation is simply that—just a fortunate turn of events that leads to a discovery. Thanks to a Petri dish that accidentally developed mold in Sir Alexander Fleming's laboratory, penicillin was discovered. As a result, countless lives were saved and Fleming and Ernst Chain earned the 1945 Nobel Prize. With similar good fortune, shareholders of the Kellogg Company can trace their fortunes to Will Kellogg leaving some cooked wheat sit too long when called to an urgent matter, accidentally inventing flaked cereals.

Sometimes fortunate innovation can be the result of frustration or can occur "in spite of" someone or something. Do you know the story of George Crum's creation of the potato chip (also known as "crisps" or "wafers")? Faced with what he considered to be an unreasonable patron who complained that his fried potatoes ("french fries") were too thick, he cut his potatoes wafer thin with the objective of infuriating the customer. Instead, the customer loved the new creation that became known as "Saratoga Chips," and Crum's disappointment about his failed attempt to frustrate the customer was likely quickly replaced by happiness at the income and infamy these chips bestowed upon him.[4]

---

[3] http://www.prnewswire.com/news-releases/incremental-innovation-essential-to-solving-canadas-productivity-problem-hnhii-122597858.html; http://www.agora-event.com/HowNextHappens/?p=1276&l=en

[4] The story of George Crum's Saratoga Chips is fairly well known. He was once featured as MIT's Inventor of the Week: http://web.mit.edu/invent/iow/crum.html.

What might be called "innovative humor" may also play a role in fortunate innovation. Several of the innovations we have been witness to have started with a humorous comment, often in the midst of a very long workday (week, month, . . .) or during intense brainstorming sessions. Thus, it is advised that you pay attention to at least some of those quips. During a brainstorming session I attended, someone made a one-sentence humorous comment during an all-hands session. In discussing the concept of data spaces, this employee quoted the television show *Star Trek* in parody and stated, "To boldly go where no byte has gone before." Later during breakouts where plans and campaigns were to be proposed one group used that comment as the inspiration for a space-themed program that became one of the line of business's most successful campaigns ever.

Deliberate Innovation

As strange and unusual as it may appear by now, at times innovation is deliberate. All right, so it's often deliberate or at least has a deliberate beginning. Deliberate innovation is what many people think of when they think of innovation in general terms. But deliberate innovation can also include aspects of some of the other types of innovation that have already been discussed.

With deliberate innovation, a person or group sets out to solve a specific problem or take advantage of a new opportunity with the objective of doing so in an innovative way. In many cases, one of these common approaches will be taken: trend deconstruction, brainstorming, patent and technology searches, reverse engineering (ethically), focus groups, preference modeling, feature evolution, or even the tried-and-true suggestion box. These more formal methods can be used in combination or, perhaps, not at all. Deliberate innovation can also be born of another type of innovation (commonly "desperate innovation") and then become deliberate innovation following a "Eureka!" moment.

In the mid-2000s, I was assigned by CA Technologies to lead a team challenged to address two key business issues: 1) Improve the quality of a suite of integrated products; 2) Decrease the time it took to bring those products to market. Our mission was to address those objectives through the creation of an integration, interoperability, and stress test lab. In the early days of the project, things were not going well. It was taking the team an entire week to run even the smallest of tests.

The assignment required the team to create computing environments that paralleled the very complex environments used by the world's largest corporations. As you might imagine, creating these environments required an enormous amount of effort. In fact, simply setting up a standard test environment took nearly an entire week. Sadly, this challenge was made more complex by the fact that the execution of such a test quite often invalidated the test environment. As a result, each execution of a specific test might require a complete refresh of the environment.

The team set out to purchase a solution, though they very quickly learned that (at that time) there was nothing that could satisfy their needs. Following a particularly frustrating call with one potential vendor who had been in full-on spin mode, I drew on a whiteboard a diagram of what was needed in what was more or less a rant. Once the diagram was complete, and at the peak of my passionate plea, I pointed to almost every box on the board and named a software component we already made that could provide the functionality we needed. I concluded the rant with this remark: "And we would just have to tie them together and create this self-service and reservation system and I'll bet CA would give us a fantastic price on all of those other components!"

The result of this deliberate approach (and the frustration) was that the team created one of the earliest private clouds. We did so years before cloud computing became mainstream, at a time when even the term was not commonly used.

If not for a deliberate resolve to address the solution—and an appetite for frozen yogurt—that cloud may not have ever been built. For you see, following the rant, the meeting quickly came to a close. Fortunately, the team had a habit of visiting the café for frozen yogurt regularly and would socialize in the team stand-up area while they enjoyed their treat. Later that day while doing so, they continued to discuss their challenge. All the while the solution sat forgotten, drawn on the whiteboard in that area. And then it happened . . .

"Wait a minute! This would actually work!"

A month later, an early version of the system was operational and two months following that two other teams had small versions of the system. By early 2012 that cloud placed more than 20,000 machines at this organization's disposal and has delivered millions of dollars in productivity gains, contributed significantly to the company's sustainability initiatives through reduction in consumption and carbon emissions, and resulted in millions of dollars in savings in equipment, real estate, and software. In addition, many of the tools, techniques, and processes developed for that project have been made available through the company's for-sale products and in their services.

It was through this project that I learned to keep a watchful eye out for innovation. Innovation can sneak up on you, and it will not always tell you it is there. If we had not had a yoghurt break that afternoon would we have missed our opportunity to leverage our innovation? Would we have missed out on its benefits? Thankfully we will never know. This is certainly proof that we must be constantly on the lookout for innovative solutions that present themselves this way. How many times has something like this happened to you and the result been a missed opportunity? Since the opportunities went unrecognized you may never know.

Similar to fortunate innovation, deliberate innovation can also be born of challenge or frustration. One of our colleagues once invented a graphical installable file system for an operating platform because several people told him it would be impossible to do so. It became a key differentiator of the product his team developed.

Desperate Innovation

Most of us are familiar with the saying, "Necessity is the mother of invention." There is nothing like having no other option but to succeed to drive an innovative solution. In fact, much of the great innovation that I have witnessed personally has come from some type of desperation. There is probably no better example of this type of innovation than "the mailbox" created to save the lives of the Apollo 13 astronauts.

As James Lovell, John Swigert, and Fred Haise made their journey to the moon, an oxygen tank ruptured and caused an explosion that blew an external panel off the spacecraft's service module. While there were many innovations necessary in order to bring the crew safely home to earth, the mailbox is perhaps the best known, possibly because of a 1995 movie that recounted the incident.

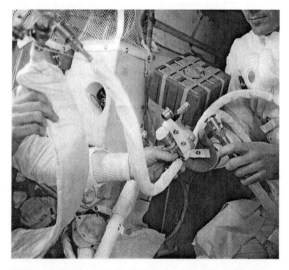

Figure 2-1. The "mailbox" (Photo courtesy of NASA)

As a result of the oxygen tank rupture, the three men were forced to occupy the spacecraft's lunar module for four days. This module had been designed to sustain two people for a day and a half and was not equipped with carbon dioxide–removing canisters with sufficient capacity to support the entire crew for that duration.

Another section of the spacecraft, the command module, did contain enough lithium hydroxide canisters to sustain the crew, but there was another problem. The command module canisters were cube-shaped, but the lunar module canisters were cylindrical. The NASA engineers were challenged to make a cube-shaped canister fit in a hole made for a cylinder using the very limited set of supplies that were present on the spacecraft. Three lives depended upon the successful completion of a true-to-life challenge to fit a square peg in a round hole.

The engineers and astronauts on the ground developed a way to improvise a connection using items that were available in the spacecraft such as tape, plastic, and cardboard. That astonishing group of people innovated to create the life saving device that became known as the mailbox, because it was necessary for them to do so.

Innovation Everywhere

Though we have only begun to scratch the surface in terms of types and sources of innovation, our hope is that the examples discussed in this chapter help sharpen your senses with regard to where to look for innovation and how to recognize it when it occurs. Innovative leaders must be able to recognize and capture innovation and to foster an innovative culture.

Why spend time defining innovation? In our experience, one of the most common things that can kill innovation is that it can simply be ignored or go unrecognized, even by the innovator. It seems that people often confuse innovation with invention, and only look for the latter. So, knowing what to look for is a necessary beginning.

So *Is* All Innovation Good Innovation?

It could certainly be stated that not all innovation is useful. We've all had those great ideas that, following an evening's rest, we realize are not of much use or are completely ridiculous.

This topic always brings to mind Michael Keaton's character, Bill Blazejowski, from the 1982 movie *Night Shift*. The consummate "idea man," Blazejowski had no shortage of "innovative" ideas. In one scene, he is lamenting the amount of effort it takes to make a tuna sandwich. As he walks down a hallway, his innovative gears begin to turn and he thinks that if tuna could be fed mayonnaise, then the time and effort required to prepare a tuna sandwich would be dramatically reduced. As the scene ends, he whips his voice recorder from his pocket at lightning speed and directs himself to contact a major tuna supplier about his idea.

Thus we can certainly concede that not all innovations will be of use in a corporate context. However, the creative process that produced even a useless innovation may itself be of benefit. It may help someone who has the potential to deliver useful innovative solutions to hone their innovation skills. Leaders must be deliberate in order to foster free thinking and an innovative spirit within their teams, even in cases where an idea has no practical application in your business context. Management and direction is obviously still needed (you cannot afford to have a legion of Bill Blazejowskis spending all day developing motorized yoga mats). It may be even more important to foster an innovative culture and atmosphere for younger team members. I will further explore this idea in Chapter 9.

Remember that an innovative idea that is not useful in the context of the innovator's "day job" may actually be extremely valuable in a different context or somewhere else in the business. Be diligent in keeping a record of those "useless innovations" because sometimes they eventually have a use. It is also possible that an innovative or inventive idea that has no application in your business could be extremely useful to others, which could present an opportunity for revenue through licensing or royalties or might be given freely in a philanthropic spirit.

Innovation Killers

Innovation can happen anywhere, and innovation killers are omnipresent. Some of the more common innovation killers include the following:

- Culture
- Organization
- The Perfectionist
- The Innovative Authoritarian
- The Protector
- The Downer Dog Pile
- Constrained Thought

- Timing
- Communication

Each of these can be as damaging as any other. A single person with the "innovative authoritarian" innovation illness (more later) can be as damaging to innovation as a dysfunctional "culture" or a lone "protector."

Culture

Echoing Peter Drucker's "culture eats strategy for breakfast" adage during a presentation to a group of aspiring leaders, Terrence Clark, general manager of the ecoSoftware group at CA Technologies, said "culture eats innovation for breakfast." He is correct. Too often, we have witnessed a corporation's culture devour innovation like Pac-Man devours those tiny dots in the classic arcade game. Some cultures are so skilled at this that, just as Pac-Man eventually learns it can also annihilate the other characters, those cultures can remove the innovative spirit from their people.

There are far too many aspects of culture that can kill innovation to enumerate them all here, so we will cover a few of the most common ones we have encountered.

Unhealthy Internal Competition

Unhealthy internal competition can be a major innovation killer. Yes, there is a place for healthy and functional types of internal competition; however, internal competition can also be extremely dysfunctional. Ironically, when internal competition becomes unhealthy, it can sometimes resemble a startup culture.

You may be thinking, "How can that be?" Often when we think of startup cultures, it is in the context of the positive—their team cohesiveness and "get-it-done" approach, effective and minimalistic processes, competitive spirit, and their ability to be nimble and adjust to challenges. But in the context of dysfunctional culture these, normally positive, qualities of a startup culture can be employed as tactics for one group within a company to compete with one another in unhealthy ways. In fact, quite often we have witnessed organizations within a company compete with one another much more fiercely than with their competitors. Having become smaller competitors with one another, they apply many of the strategies and tactics employed by startups to defeat one another. Competition of this nature is common following acquisitions.

When unhealthy competition exists precious resources that could be directed toward innovation are wasted. Quite often the internal strife created by the unhealthy competition can lead to inaction on the part of one or more of the teams involved, as their resources are focused on the competition and not on execution and delivery. In its worst form, it can slow the progress of, or even bring to a standstill, the execution of innovative ideas for all teams involved. It may even become an impediment to teams not directly involved.

Theft of Credit

A culture that permits theft of credit for accomplishments and innovation rewards undesirable behavior. Creative people will quickly learn no reward or pleasure will come of innovation. In fact, they may consciously or subconsciously associate innovation with negative consequences and outcomes. As a result, their innovative spirit will begin to atrophy, and they will innovate outside of the work environment or leave the company.

Failure to Acknowledge Effort and/or Accomplishment

Failure to acknowledge effort and/or accomplishment is a close cousin of theft of credit. In fact, they play well together. Acknowledgement of accomplishment is often the best kind of fuel for a person or team's innovation engine. The impact of a failure to appropriately acknowledge the contribution of a person or team can have a similar impact to permitting theft of credit for accomplishment.

Inconsistency in Rewards or Rewarding Failure

Inconsistency in rewards or rewarding failure can also suck the innovative spirit from a team or even an entire company. Often organizations provide rewards inconsistently or at a level not appropriate for the accomplishment, such as providing too high a reward for too little accomplishment or vice versa. For example, we know of a team that received a company's highest achievement award for a project they had almost completed. This project had cost tens of millions of dollars, was years behind schedule, had been delivered with less functionality than intended (in fact, with less functionality than the system it replaced), and the work was not complete at the time the award was presented to the team. This award caused many employees to scratch their heads.

At the same time, there were other teams that had innovated on their own and had delivered those innovative solutions on or prior to their deadlines and at or under their budget allocation. Those solutions had generated financial gains and competitive advantages for the company, but these teams had not been rewarded for their work. The leaders of these teams had not been expecting an award for their efforts, though they did admit an acknowledgement would have meant a lot to their teams. After the less successful project received the award, the leaders of the innovative teams had to work hard in order to maintain morale and to convince their team members that their own contributions were also appreciated.

Cliquetocracy

"Cliquetocracy" may be a new term to you, but we are confident that you have witnessed or experienced it. If you have ever seen or been part of an organization where the majority of the company's discretionary perks and benefits (e.g., society memberships, conference participation, honors, titles, awards) are given to a specific group and to those known to them, you've probably been in the presence of a cliquetocracy. A cliquetocracy rewards people for whom they know rather than what they have accomplished. Though there is an important nuance.

A cliquetocracy does not necessarily reward those they know only because they know them. They may have a very high standard for who receives these rewards. In fact, everyone who receives a reward or honor may be qualified to receive it, but that is certainly not always the case. This presence of a reasonable standard for recognition is what can make a cliquetocracy difficult to identify. Cliquetocracies are not always easy to recognize *because* those receiving the awards can be qualified, and even widely respected.

However, a cliquetocracy can make it impossible for those unknown to the clique at its heart to receive any of the company's awards or honors. What makes this innovation killer even more difficult to identify is that a cliquetocracy may not be a conscious initiative. It may simply be a bunch of well-intended people who happen to know each other, and the promotion of "those known" may be purely subconscious. The impact of a cliquetocracy can be profound, especially if they are well known and positioned in the organization, and if they have a great deal of influence.

Fear

Fear is one of the greatest culture-related innovation killers. This is often manifested in the form of fear of failure. If you've ever worked in an organization where you were only as good as your last failure, you know just how crushing this can be to creativity.

Managers with less mature emotional intelligence who ridicule "dumb" suggestions and ideas and who publicly flog a reasonable effort or opinion, often with the objective of making themselves "the smartest person in the room," are innovation assassins. These people are often adept at managing higher executives and can often use their culture of fear to ensure they receive promotions and accolades. In some cases, even those higher in an organization's hierarchy can be intimidated and aid such a manager's career advancement either intentionally or by their inaction. Furthermore, a culture of fear is in polar opposition to the "fail fast" approach used by many of today's most successful organizations.

"Culture Eats Innovation for Breakfast"

Terrence Clark's statement that "culture eats innovation for breakfast" does appear to be well founded. In addition to those we already discussed there are many other cultural elements that can have a negative impact on innovation. For example, we have all seen bad management practices or poor managers (at any level) have a negative impact on a culture. Tolerance and promotion of bad managers, and/or of some of the other innovation-killing personalities that will be discussed later in this chapter, can destroy a company if left uncorrected for too long. There are also cases where an industry or industry segment has common cultural shortcomings, often due to the latest industry fad in approach, management, or business discipline.

When companies have an innovation-killing culture, they will usually exhibit more than one of the types of innovation illness that we have discussed in this section. The effects of a dysfunctional culture include lost opportunity, irresponsible use of resources, poor morale, lost revenue, squandered competitive advantage, and exit of top talent. It can also impact the health and well-being of employees. Eventually people outside of a culturally challenged company learn of the company's maladies, which can result in difficulty attracting new employees, especially those who are highly sought after.

Organization

In the context of deterring innovation, organization is very similar to culture. However, certain aspects of organizational discipline are not culture-related and deserve a closer look because of their negative impact on innovation.

For example, a company can have a very healthy culture and not be capable of capturing and/or leveraging the innovation that their employees deliver. Lower-level and newer managers may not recognize innovation when it happens. If they recognize it, they may not know what they need to do in order to move the innovation toward its full potential. In addition, they may not know how to reward an innovative employee.

These things can destroy the innovative potential of an organization even in the simplest of cases, such as when employees create something innovative that will serve their own department or line of business. Innovation can be much more difficult for a lower-level or new manager to recognize when the innovation does not provide value directly to their team. For example, a less experienced manager may not be aware of the function and objectives of other groups and might be less likely to realize when something might be beneficial elsewhere.

Ironically, the opposite of this may also create problems. Surfacing too many innovative ideas, especially those that cannot help an organization to achieve its mission, can cause crucial and valuable innovations to be lost in the noise. We have participated in several innovation "jams" and competitions and in the delivery of systems to capture innovation. In the early days of some of these, there would be a deluge of ideas (hundreds of them) that were not at all related to any line of business. As a result, the people assigned to evaluate the ideas, themselves some of the company's most innovative people, were sentenced to hours of reviewing mind-numbing submissions, each of which had to be fairly evaluated and discussed.

The Perfectionist

As you may have predicted, perfectionists are those who set an unnecessarily high standard for anything they deliver. These individuals may be so much of a perfectionist that they will not show their innovations to anyone, or in some cases not even speak about them, until their standard has been achieved. That day may never arrive.

Even the best innovations can benefit from dialogue, brainstorming, and feedback. As a result, the perfectionist's innovations may deliver much less value, or be much less compelling or beneficial, than they might have were the ideas shared with others. In other cases, they may develop a "perfect" innovation that has no practical use or value.

In addition to killing or reducing the impact of their own innovations, perfectionists can have a profound impact on the innovations of others. For example, they can assume the role of the "protector" (discussed next) and apply their unrealistic standards to others. When the perfectionist is a manager or in a position of leadership, influence, or control, their impact can be far more damaging. As a manager, the perfectionist not only can recommend those high standards but also enforce them. So doing can lead to inaction or poor execution, or can kill the innovative spirit and morale of their team.

The Innovative Authoritarian

In the context of innovation killers, the innovative authoritarian can come in two flavors: "successful innovator" and "founder of the feast." The presence of either flavor results in constrained innovation and thinking throughout the leader's span of control.

The "successful innovator" is someone who has been involved in the delivery of one or more successful innovations. Due to previous success, this person has either been promoted or hired into an organization to drive the same sort of innovative spirit throughout that organization. Once established, these leaders begin to micro-manage teams, projects, and individuals. They constrain thought (more later in this chapter) and rather than reproduce the *environment* that made them successful innovators, they try to manage the innovation (in a sense, they attempt to reproduce their innovation). In some cases, their actions may be subconscious, but in others, they believe they are "smarter" than the members of their team.

Depending upon their span of control and influence, this type of management can destroy a team or company's innovative spirit. Truly innovative people will become extremely frustrated. The best of them will be among the first to leave. We have witnessed more than one such leader cause significant damage to an organization that in some cases took the affected company years to recover from. I had a programming professor with a similar blind spot. When the professor asked, "How would you solve the following problem?"—what he meant was, "How would *I* solve the following problem?"

The "founder of the feast" has a more specific blind spot. This person may have created a new product or service. As a result of this success, the "founder" has been promoted, and someone else is now responsible for the care and feeding of that particular innovation. Furthermore, the newly appointed leader of the team now responsible for the maintenance, advancement, and further innovation of the "founder's" creation now reports to the "founder."

Though it is the founder's responsibility to help set direction for the team, he is often subconsciously compelled to "strongly guide" the team and its new leader with regard to *how* each of the objectives must be accomplished. In reality, the creative freedom the founder had enjoyed and that enabled him to innovate is no longer available to the team and its new leader.

Had he been faced with the same environment, the founder would have been miserable and much less effective, perhaps ineffective. He has become the innovation killer, but likely has no idea that is the case.

I myself have been a "founder of the feast." I knew from the beginning it would be difficult, and that I would have a strong bias to have things done my way. That system was "my baby." I knew what it could and should become. So I told the new team leader he was free to cry foul, directly and without fear of repercussion, any time I started to do the work for him.

Even though I was conscious of this from the outset it wasn't easy. Early on there were some frustrating times for both of us. I didn't always catch myself, but he held me to my word and we are both thankful he did. In the end they added some amazing innovations that I am confident I would never have led them to.

The Protector

Protectors believe it is their mission to protect the company, and/or their team, from all things that might bring harm. While that "mission" is not by necessity an innovation killer, the protector manifests the mission in ways that can stifle the most innovative of personnel. They see only the downside of any proposal (from anyone). As part of a team, they can make it impossible to brainstorm, as they instinctively attack details of any proposal long before it is necessary or productive to do so.

As a stakeholder, the protector can unintentionally become a voracious resource consumer resulting in a significantly negative impact on productivity and morale. Not only will they not tolerate failure or experimentation, they will bring the heat of the organization upon anyone who does not pay homage to their demands. Often the protector exhibits the behaviors of a bully.

I had an encounter with a protector that may help to aid understanding. I had been away from my desk carrying out my duties. When I returned I noticed an instant message from [the protector]. At the same time I noticed an e-mail from the same person had just arrived in my inbox. The e-mail was a scathing account of how I had been unresponsive to [the protector's] needs and how our team was unfit to serve their organization. It had been sent to senior executives in both of our organizations. The e-mail was sent five minutes after the instant message.

Ironically, protectors can be so unpleasant to work with, and so potentially career damaging to others, the result of their involvement is often inaction by people unwilling or afraid to deal with them. When that happens it further aggravates the protector, who most often has no idea they are the root cause of their own frustration.

The Downer Dog Pile

The "downer dog pile" is one of the most fascinating and potentially destructive phenomena we have encountered. Most people have witnessed this innovation killer, and many of you have likely been active participants.

It often starts in a group setting following the statement of an objective or a creative idea. For a very short period of time, people contribute to the idea ("plus" it) and then someone states a reason why the idea won't work.

Sometimes someone will have a remedy to the first stated objection, but—whether or not that is the case—another objection or impediment is soon presented. Others follow until there is a deluge of impediments and a metropolis of innovation-killing, energy-consuming walls.

It becomes a bit like the gang tackle that is often bestowed upon the winning goal scorer at a sporting event. The objective of the gathering has somehow changed from making something new happen to finding reasons why it can't be done as participants metaphorically pile barriers on top of one another. Though the dog pile is a metaphor the person responsible for the idea may feel somewhat like they are actually being gang tackled. At this point the team's objective has shifted from promoting to destroying their idea. Or so it would appear.

We have witnessed many cases where those with an execution bias and/or passion for solving problems (i.e., puzzles) became very excited about an idea. Sadly, this early buy-in often manifests itself in a way that creates the impression that they are not supportive of the idea or worse, that their intent is to ensure its demise. How does their positive intent come to be perceived as unsupportive? In an attempt to help advance the idea, their execution and puzzle-solving biases activate and they immediately begin to think about how the new idea or objective could be accomplished. Unfortunately by the time someone asks them a question, they are five phases into mental preparation and thinking about how to overcome a potential obstacle they feel they may encounter later on. Sadly, it is this potential roadblock that is often surfaced when that person speaks or is asked a question, long before it needed to be addressed, and before it had been thought through completely. This can have the unintended consequence of initiating a downer dog pile. In addition, it can send the wrong message to the others, especially if senior businesspeople are present.

This "thinking aloud" is potentially destructive and can often have the unfortunate side effect of "sucking the energy out of a room." People can become exhausted dealing with what appears to be a barrage of questions or "artificial roadblocks," and this can contribute to an IT organization's reputation of being the "Department of No" or the "Office of the CI-No."

I had a "life-changing" encounter with this combination morale and career killer when I was invited to participate in a 360-degree review with a senior business leader and his team. The exercise was intense, though very positive. We sat in a circle and those present took turns receiving feedback from everyone else. We had performed a written 360-degree review prior to the session, so we were somewhat prepared for what we were about to receive. But not really . . .

When it came to my turn, the feedback was generally very positive with one exception. Over and over again, from people in vastly different positions with vastly different backgrounds, who had vastly different personalities, I heard the same thing. I was "*that guy.*" I was the lead dog on a downer dogsled. I was crushed. That was not *who* I was, though it certainly was *what* I was. Not only did I know that this was not my intention, I knew it was a potential career killer. And it certainly must have been limiting my effectiveness.

It turns out that I was the person who, when asked about a new initiative about which everyone was excited, was five steps into implementation in my mind and when asked about it posed a question about a possible constraint. Fortunately I was able to discover that during the exercise, and the difference it has made to my effectiveness has been remarkable.

Constrained Thought

It can be extremely difficult to realize when a person or team is suffering from constrained thinking because they are usually unaware of it. It is not easy to recognize one's own biases, especially since they are often subconscious. The symptoms of constrained thought can be the same as those described for a person or group possessing the innovation-killing qualities of "The Protector" that was discussed earlier. (Yes, it is possible for either a single person, or a group of people collectively, to develop some of these innovation illnesses. You can have a "downer dog pile" of one, or a group acting as a protector.)

Constrained thought is manifested by applying constraints from existing systems, processes, and disciplines to a newly proposed innovation. Quite often, perhaps even most often, these constraints are irrelevant.

Constrained thought is often exposed when a young employee or someone new to a domain solves a problem that was declared "unsolvable" or innovates in an unexpected way. In our experience, the reason this happens is that the new or young employee was not aware of the constraints, so she was not bound by them. Consider the recent trend of cloud computing solutions that actually attract new customers by offering them *less* functionality than the "traditional IT" or "on-premise" systems they replace. Many people would reasonably assume that consumers of their service would not agree to such a thing. Yet they have, and they have done so in large numbers.

I have had personal experience with constrained thought at a team level. Leading innovative teams, and trying to create innovative leaders, this was something that we had to manage constantly and actively. There were a lot of very creative and energetic people on the team yet they often fell victim to constrained thinking or the downer dog pile, especially during brainstorming.

What's crazy is that we often didn't realize it was happening. We had to train ourselves to be diligent in listening for it.

Timing

The timing of the development of something innovative may be one of the greatest innovation killers of all. The very nature of innovation often means that the innovator has developed an understanding of a problem or opportunity ahead of others. In the beginning, it may be extremely difficult for others to understand the value of the innovation, or even the innovation itself. Not all innovators are great communicators, and fewer are able to communicate with people from other disciplines. (Communication is the next innovation killer we will discuss.) This only serves to exacerbate the issue.

More than once we have heard that innovation takes five to seven years to catch on, and to be truly understood by others. While this may not be a precise rule, we have personally witnessed innovations that were not understood or accepted, or that were not accepted as relevant in a specific domain for many years prior to their becoming mainstream. For example, the cloud computing example mentioned earlier in this chapter was not initially widely accepted as something of value outside the team that created it. The team had to diligently pursue ways to communicate its value.

Another example that might resonate more with your personal experience is the acceptance of the Automated Teller Machine, or ATM (also referred to as an Automated Banking Machine or "Hole in the Wall"). Certainly in the industrialized world, there are very few people who do not use an ATM regularly. In fact, I remember when the ATM was introduced to my hometown. The primary industries in this remote city were fishing, coal mining, and steelmaking. Many people were required to work shifts that prevented them from visiting a bank during their hours of operation. When the first ATM was brought into the city, it was as if you could see a groove in the pavement leading from the other banks to the one with the ATM, as customers swarmed toward its convenience.

What might surprise you is that this event occurred more than 20 years following the introduction of the ATM. In fact, New York City was home to an ATM (then called a "bankograph") in 1961[5]. In the 1960s ATMs were removed shortly after their introduction due to lack of customer acceptance.

---

[5] An article entitled "Machine Accepts Bank Deposits" introducing the Bankograph appeared in *The New York Times* on April 12, 1961.

Communication

Even the greatest innovations have no future—and will deliver no value to a business or to humanity—unless someone is capable of communicating their value to those who can benefit from them or bring them to fruition. Norville Barnes, the character played by Tim Robbins in the 1994 movie *The Hudsucker Proxy*, provides a lighthearted example of this type of challenge. Throughout the movie, Barnes repeatedly displays a hand-drawn circle and states only that the item is for children. This is often greeted with confusion or ridicule. Later the viewer learns that Barnes has invented the hula-hoop, which generates behemoth revenues for "Hudsucker Industries."

Unfortunately in the real world, the result of such "skilled" communication is rarely success. Often the result is that an innovative opportunity is lost forever. If the innovator is not discouraged by the fact that others cannot see the benefits of their innovation, the consequence is often a lot of personal "pain and suffering", and a great degree of frustration, as they try again and again to convey the virtues of their innovation without reward. This kind of interaction can result in extremely unfortunate outcomes, such as tension or conflict in the workplace, open hostility, or the end of a career.

Other communication challenges can also kill innovation. One symptom of a communication challenge we frequently encounter is the "we've already done this" response. Certainly there are cases where a proposed innovation has been attempted in the past and is known to be an unsuccessful approach. That is not what we are referring to here. Often when the response to a proposed innovation is "we've already done this," the people making that evaluation have made assumptions about the proposal, frequently before an explanation or proposal has begun. This can be the result of differences in vocabulary, especially among technology professionals. It can also be the result of bias based upon current events and projects.

Good communication is critical to the success of an innovation, not only while obtaining initial support for the innovation or in the early stages of its implementation. In order to maximize the value of an innovation, superb communication is likely a necessity throughout its entire life. Changes in personnel, leadership, corporate mission, or priorities can result in the need to revisit the benefits of an innovation. And, of course, "budget season" is a perpetual driver.

Three years following the introduction of the cloud computing system mentioned earlier in this chapter, communication to new and key stakeholders became critical to the survival of the initiative. Though the team managed to keep the initiative alive that year with increased support and funding, it might be overstated to classify the communication as a success. The following year there was an even greater crisis. It was following that stressful episode that a lesson had been clearly learned—communication must be proactive and continuous, even when the benefits of an innovation are compelling and quantifiable.

Face It Head-on

There is most certainly no shortage of innovation killers, and they can be viral. Sometimes many players in an industry suffer from the same malaise, resulting in an epidemic of one or more of the previously described innovation illnesses across an industry or segment. Often this is because the implementation of a poor solution can sometimes give the appearance of positive results in the short term. After all, there's nothing like short-term success for the nurturing of short-term thinking.

Other systematic causes of innovation atrophy are at least as concerning. For example, Harvard professor and innovation expert Clayton Christensen has recently stated that he believes that the way business schools are teaching their students to measure success through the "pursuit of profits," and the metrics they teach and promote, are having a detrimental effect on innovation in certain geographies.[6]

Thus, given the information in this chapter, it should now be clear that being an innovative leader is simple. (We'll remove our metaphoric tongues from our cheeks now.) Of course it isn't simple, though you should not let these innovation killers discourage you. Awareness of these is a necessary part of the journey toward becoming an effective leader. Discipline, diligence, vision, thick skin, and the information in this book will set you on course toward becoming an Innovative CIO.

---

[6] Steve Denning, "Clayton Christensen: How Pursuit of Profits Kills Innovation and the U.S. Economy," *Forbes*, November 2011, www.forbes.com/sites/stevedenning/2011/11/18/ clayton-christensen-how-pursuit-of-profits-kills-innovation-and-the-us-economy, retrieved on March 2012.

Innovation Is Not the Only "I"

The Other I's in CIO

"I notice," said the duck, "that you talk with only one of your mouths. Can't the other head talk as well?"

"Oh, yes," said the pushmi-pullyu. "But I keep the other mouth for eating— mostly. In that way I can talk while I am eating without being rude. Our people have always been very polite."

—Hugh Lofting, *The Story of Doctor Dolittle*

Business and IT leaders long for the "glory days" when IT was heralded as a business value leader. It is widely believed that those days are, to a great degree, far behind us. There has been much discussion of late about how CIOs and IT leaders must become more innovative, and even more discussion about how they are failing to drive innovation for their businesses; in some cases even becoming barriers to innovation.

The perception that even successful IT teams are no more than a cost center and a drain on business is prevalent. IT is often thought of as a "necessary evil" rather than as a strategic asset.

Pushmi-Pullyu

The existence of an IT innovation drought is a widely held belief, and in many cases a reality. What may be surprising is that business leaders may be as responsible for this drought as their IT colleagues—perhaps even more so. A recent study[1] concluded that information technologies deployed since 1995 have positively impacted profits more than other investments, such as marketing or development. In addition, the study concluded that the impact of IT investments have an even greater positive impact as industries become more competitive. The study suggests, as we believe, that IT teams can overcome this innovation drought and make significant, strategic contributions to their businesses.

Paradoxically, those same people who want CIOs and IT leaders to be spend more time on innovation quite often put tremendous pressure on them, and on the IT team, to focus on other mundane operational tasks. To further complicate matters, the complexity and size of today's technology environments are such that simply maintaining those operations can consume all of an IT team's capacity and budget.

Like the two-headed "pushmi-pullyu" ungulate interrogated by Doctor Doolittle's duck, today's CIO is under constant pressure to move in different, often opposite, directions. While some of these pressures can help CIOs to be innovative, others can impede innovation.

The I's Have It

To state that senior IT leaders and CIOs are under a tremendous amount of pressure is to state the obvious. Not all pressure, however, is bad. Some types of pressure can inspire and drive innovation. Others can free up resources or create additional time that can be directed toward innovation—what we refer to as "increasing the innovation time surplus." Therefore, today's IT leaders must be able to identify which of these pressures are healthy, and focus on creating an environment that fosters and leverages those healthy pressures. In addition, IT leaders must also be aware of which pressures are unhealthy, and quickly identify and address those.

We refer to these pressures as "the other I's" in CIO. This is partially because it has become *en vogue* to replace the word "Information" in "Chief Information Officer" with other words beginning with the letter "I." In some cases, they are terms of respect, as in "Chief Invigoration Officer." In others, such as "Chief Immutability Officer," they are quite the opposite. While some of these make for a better pun than others, each has an important impact on the performance of today's technology leader.

---

[1] Sunil Mithas, Ali Tafti, Indranil Bardhan, and Jie Mein Goh, "Information Technology and Firm Profitability: Mechanisms and Empirical Evidence," January 2012, http://papers.ssrn.com/sol3/papers.cfm?abstract_id=1000732, retrieved on March 2012.

In the sections that follow, we will examine some of the I's that we most commonly encounter, both harmful (I-Negatives) and helpful (I-Positives).

I-Negatives

First, consider the I's that often work in opposition to innovative activities. These "I-Negatives" can stifle or quash innovation and even careers:

- Inbox
- Intermediation
- Impenetrability
- Investment
- Innovation
- Inarticulacy
- Intelligence
- Infallibility
- Interloper
- Immutability

Inbox

If you have an e-mail account, and today most people have more than one, then this I-Negative may need no explanation whatsoever. Think of the large number of e-mail messages you receive every day. Now imagine how many a senior IT leader receives—operational reports, vendor and stakeholder requests, personnel and people management messages, complaints, misunderstandings, and the occasional (or not-so-occasional) "throw someone under a bus" message. These are but some of the messages a senior IT leader receives daily. Several of these messages contain no value at all (though they must be read in order to determine that to be the case), others are simple and can be dealt with quickly, and many contain detailed documents that must be read and evaluated.

Rarely, if ever, are any of these raindrops in the e-mail deluge related to something that will drive new and innovative business value.

Now consider the amount of time that must be spent processing these messages. When I was a senior manager as a provider of IT services, a "light" e-mail day for me was at least a hundred messages. Most days brought more, and many days brought hundreds. Not to mention the four digits of e-mail insanity that greeted me following a vacation or a few days away from the office. Consider the amount of time processing this much e-mail takes. If it were to take only two minutes to read, process, and respond to each of the hundred messages, nearly three-and-a-half hours would be required solely for e-mail every day. We have also witnessed people taking several evening hours to carefully craft an e-mail to address an issue that could have been addressed via a ten-minute conversation.

Out-of-control e-mail can also serve as a warning of destructive cultural issues, such as a lack of trust. These issues can themselves destroy innovative spirit. We have been a part of teams where the use of e-mail as a weapon was their greatest talent. This phenomenon can be even more prevalent in cross-functional teams.

Have you ever witnessed an e-mail snowball fight? In dysfunctional teams, e-mail is often used as a way to throw work at other members of the team—often when the sender believes the recipient of the work will be unable to respond. It only takes one rock-laden snowball to the head before the recipient realizes he needs to build a snow fort of his own. Once that occurs, e-mail itself becomes the mission, and the team is working all hours on their e-mail defense and offense.

This has become such a widespread issue that stories of major corporations taking what might be considered drastic measures to address it are becoming public. For example, Volkswagen shut off access to corporate e-mail after business hours. The CEO of Atos plans to eliminate e-mail altogether by 2014 in favor of other methods such as social media and instant messaging. He also suggests that employees might adopt other radical forms of communication like face-to-face conversations![2]

Email driven productivity losses are sometimes touted as the result of today's always-connected, mobile, social world. However, the actions of these two leaders are not a new phenomenon. We know of a manager who, in the 1990s, disabled the corporate e-mail system between the hours of 10 a.m. and noon and again from 2–4 p.m. every business day because he thought people were not talking to one another enough. They weren't. I was also witness to an e-mail battle royal between two people who had no idea they sat two aisles apart in a cube farm. Once they were introduced to one another, it took only a few minutes speaking together to resolve the issue they had been working on via e-mail for so long.

---

[2] BBC News, "Volkswagen Turns Off Blackberry Email After Work Hours," December 2011, www.bbc.com/news/technology-16314901, retrieved on March 2012.

BBC News, "Atos boss Thierry Breton defends his internal email ban", December 2011, www.bbc.co.uk/news/technology-16055310, retrieved on March 2012.

So whether you believe out-of-control e-mail to be a symptom of a dysfunctional team or an innovation killer in itself, the bottom line is that an out-of-control e-mail culture can certainly take away valuable, scarce time from innovation. It can also poison a team's morale, destroy *esprit de corps*, and leave team members too stressed and exhausted to be innovative.

Intermediation

"Disintermediation" is a word that has come to strike terror into the hearts of IT teams and especially IT managers, who often associate it with "rogue IT", loss of control over their organization's technology, and loss of internal IT jobs. In fact, it has been our experience that "intermediation" can be far more damaging than disintermediation.

Our use of the word "intermediation" in this context refers to situations where IT exercises too much control. Sometimes this is because IT teams feel they have a duty to protect the company, and the only way to accomplish that is to control everything. Other times it is because they believe the people whom they serve do not have enough knowledge about technology. In some cases, intermediation happens because a leader or team feels they are "smarter" than those whom they serve (more on this later in the chapter). Often it is a passive-aggressive tactic aimed at job preservation. Whether the motivation is noble or selfish, the impact is damaging.

Many, perhaps most, IT teams can frequently be found discussing how the pile of requests they are receiving from their stakeholders is representative of much more work than they could possibly perform. So ironically, by trying to preserve their role in everything IT-related, they are missing a tremendous opportunity to free capacity for innovation.

I learned this lesson firsthand when I was responsible for running a private cloud for many years. In this role, I was fortunate to lead one of the most service-focused teams I have ever had the pleasure of serving with. However, they learned the hard way that being service-focused, one of their greatest strengths, could also become their greatest weakness.

Due to their service focus, the team felt more or less duty-bound to fulfill every request from their customers themselves. The result was that the team took on much more work than they were capable of performing. As a result, 40- and 50-hour weeks quickly turned into 60- to 90-hour (sometimes more!) weeks.

With hours like that, your team can quickly begin to burn out and the quality of work delivered can rapidly become, at best, mediocre. As a result, team morale is jeopardized. Eventually this approach also results in setting unachievable or unsustainable expectations with the stakeholders. Together, it is a recipe for spectacular failure. A team's propensity for "intermediation" is something that must be monitored constantly.

Impenetrability

When overwhelmed by the pressures they face, IT teams will often reduce the amount of direct contact they have with their customers. The broadcasting term "going dark" is often used in reference to such a withdrawal of communication.

Going dark may or may not be a conscious response by the IT team. Questions like "Why don't they just get out of our way and let us do our job?" can be an indicator that a team is adopting this I-Negative. The rationale is often a belief that they (the IT team) know what they're doing, whereas the stakeholders (often "nontechnical" people) do not. Furthermore, IT teams can believe that if they didn't have to spend so much time explaining things to their customers and stakeholders, they would have more time to spend providing service to them: "We would be done by now!"

Impenetrable teams often see no value in spending time dealing with stakeholders, at least until relevant tasks are complete. They cannot understand why stakeholders need so much attention or information (that they would not know what to do with, would not understand, etc.). They perceive investments in this type of work as large, intrusive, of no value to the business, and offering no contribution to the end product or objective.

Technical teams often perceive requests for such information as a lack of trust, and they can be quite insulted by it. This is where the great irony lies. As a team adopts the impenetrable posture, stakeholders perceive them as having intentionally gone dark. The longer the technical team's lack of communication persists, the more concerned the business consumers become. The stakeholders' concern is not necessarily because they do not trust the team, at least initially (though trust issues can be as much of a cause as an effect). Rather, it is often because they lose visibility into things they require in order to fulfill their own professional duties. For example, the delivery of a piece of technology may be a key element in the delivery of a new customer-facing service. As a result, the sales team may need to know the delivery date in order to produce revenue forecasts and plans for training, and the marketing team may need to develop advertising and promotional campaigns.

So, the more underground a team goes, the more anxious their stakeholders become. The more anxious the stakeholders, the more active they become in requesting information and updates. This vicious cycle creates ever-increasing tension for all, resulting in animosity, loss of respect, loss of trust, or even in the stakeholders engaging another team or external service provider. In the worst cases members of the team that went dark could lose their jobs, or their careers can severely, or permanently, damaged.

This I-Negative can definitely be a symptom that a team is inefficient or disorganized. However, this I-Negative can also be found in teams who are very skilled in the other (usually technical) aspects of their work.

Investment

Investment in existing systems, processes, and technologies may be the greatest and most well-known pressure facing technology leaders. When many people think of this type of pressure, they commonly think of investments that were made, perhaps over a period of many years, in key business systems that remain critical to a company's operations. In some cases, those systems may be outdated and no longer capable of delivering the required business value. But for others, they are adequate and continue to drive value. Either way, systems of this nature often require an enormous amount of time, effort, and expense just to keep them up and running.

In cases where the existing systems remain viable and deliver good business value, IT leaders have many options to counteract this I-Negative. Successful IT leaders often speak of their use of "edge innovation." Edge innovation is symbiotic innovation. It involves creating new solutions outside the core of existing business processes and leveraging those existing business processes to enhance the new solutions. This type of innovation certainly has its advantages. In cases such as this, the "legacy" solution, instead of being an innovation inhibitor, can be an innovation accelerator. With larger enterprises, edge innovation that leverages existing systems can deliver an advantage that smaller competitors would find difficult, perhaps impossible, to replicate.

Mobile check-depositing services are a great example of this type of innovation. These services enable account holders to use their mobile phone to take a photo of a check. The check is immediately deposited into their bank account, managed by the bank's "legacy" systems, all without a visit to a bank or even sending the check via mail afterward. Such a service provides new, innovative business opportunities to early adopter institutions by providing increased service and convenience to their customers.

IT leaders must be careful not to allow their thinking to be constrained by existing investments and systems. Existing systems may not be suited to today's requirements. They may, however, present a tremendous opportunity to innovate. Unfortunately, IT leaders are sometimes reluctant to replace or modify existing systems. This may be because of the business risk involved, their inability to deliver a compelling business case even though one exists, or because the leader or team is comfortable with the existing systems and does not want to change in order to keep things comfortable.

Another common reason is fear that the team who created the existing system (often the same team evaluating its replacement) does not want that system to be seen as a failure—their failure. Be aware of this treacherous trap. It is well-known that technology changes, and at times changes with unbelievable speed. This is not a new phenomenon.

As lauded and useful as the Pony Express was for its customers, it was state-of-the-art for only 14 months (April 1860 to October 1861). The fact that it was short-lived did not mean it was not of value while it existed. However, the fact that it once provided value did not mean customers should continue to use it following the introduction of the telegraph.

IT leaders must have the courage to ask whether technology that they, or anyone else, implemented in the past—even the recent past—remains relevant and effective. They must constantly evaluate whether existing investments still deliver compelling business value, and whether there are alternatives that would be business value justified. We have experienced this ourselves.

While operating a cloud service, I was faced with an environment in which technology and best practices were changing with amazing speed. Sometimes we would make a decision to develop and implement a technology that was not available anywhere or from anyone. Six to twelve months later, there might be a host of providers offering off-the-shelf services that addressed the need for which we had developed that solution. Often these new providers offered their new solutions for less cost than our internally developed solutions (since it was now their core business).

With maximizing business value as our barometer, sometimes it even made sense to leverage external services in cases where the cost of those services was the same, similar to, or even higher than the cost of developing them ourselves. There were also times when it made sense to leverage external services even though the solution we could have developed internally might even have been "better" than the one we purchased. When either of these options was chosen it was usually because so doing enabled us to allow our internal talent pool to focus on innovation and on initiatives that would deliver higher business value. Value only we could deliver.

It is critical to not become too emotionally attached to what you have created. That is not always easy, and it requires conscious consideration.

Dealing with these investment related issues requires a very balanced approach. On one hand, you should not adopt new technology for the sake of new technology. But on the other, becoming emotionally attached to technology or solutions well past their "best before" date is also the wrong approach. Your focus must remain on the business value delivered by the solutions and on the greater business strategy.

Today's technologies also provide an opportunity for a hybrid approach. For example, consider mammoth legacy applications, some of which have existed for decades. These can be extremely expensive to maintain. They can also be very expensive and risky to modify, in some cases requiring many months, or perhaps more than a year, for even the simplest changes. These simple changes can cost tens or hundreds of thousands, or even millions of dollars. There are now opportunities for these applications to be decomposed and for portions of them to be modernized—to take advantage of new opportunities, to better prepare them for changes where they will most likely be required, or to prepare them for edge innovation—while leaving core functionality in place.

The investment I-Negative certainly places a lot of conflicting pressure on technology leaders, perhaps more than any of the others. What can make matters worse is that in many cases, even though existing investments contribute a great deal of value to a business, some business leaders may not attribute that value back to the IT team. In other words, the IT team will not even "get credit" for the, sometimes substantial, value those systems bring to the business.

Innovation

Confused? How could "innovation" be an I-Negative in a book about being innovative? Here's how. Not all innovation will be of value to your company. Even good and valuable innovation may not be relevant to your organization. Given that time is a finite and scarce resource, leaders must be sure to devote their time to relevant innovation. (I suppose this I-Negative could be "irrelevant" innovation.)

This I-Negative may not be as obvious as it appears. It is easy to get caught up in something new and cool, even if it has no relevance whatsoever to your company.

For example, I once worked with a very senior technical leader who had a great new idea that he could not let go of, even though it was not related to the business. He continued to pursue this idea in spite of the fact that a conscious decision had been made not to go into that line of business. I watched this leader deliver the same presentation at least four times, though it was not actually on the agenda for any of the meetings in which it was presented. Each meeting was fairly well-attended and included senior people, so the company spent quite a bit of money to have people sit through each of the presentations. It's not that this new idea wasn't interesting or even useful. It simply had no value or relevance to the company's business.

Irrelevant innovation can consume resources at any level of a company. Managers of teams or people caught in this trap must address irrelevant innovation, but they must also be careful not to crush a person or team's innovative spirit when a situation such as this arises.

Managers must also be capable of realizing when they are presented with an innovative idea that may present a new business opportunity, but may also appear irrelevant to some. In those cases, they must ensure the idea is presented to the appropriate people or groups, in the appropriate context, so that a conscious business decision regarding whether to enter a new business or market can be made.

Not every manager will be inherently capable of either of these. Newer or first-time managers are even less likely to possess these skills. Therefore, it is critical that new and junior managers receive explicit coaching on how to foster innovation. It is likely that they will be among the first to learn of most new innovative ideas since they interact with the largest portion of the workforce every day.

Inarticulacy

All right, so it may be unlikely that an inarticulate person could rise to the level of CIO. In that sense, this I-Negative applies universally. Leaders, even technical leaders, must have the ability to express themselves clearly and to communicate their vision and goals to their team. This is, perhaps, the more obvious aspect of this I-Negative.

However, there is a nuance to this I-Negative that is worthy of further explanation. It is possible to be articulate in the context of the IT team and still be perceived as being completely inarticulate by business people, senior managers, and key stakeholders—especially when those senior executives do not have a technical background. We have witnessed too many cases where great ideas that were poorly communicated to senior executives came to an abrupt end, sometimes taking a career or two with them. As the senior IT leader takes the floor during a business-led or business-focused meeting, the ballet of eyes rolling back in heads and the storm-force gale of frustrated exhalations make us think that sometimes the selection criteria for a senior

IT leadership position is to be the technical person who annoys their business counterparts the least—"the best of the worst," if you will.

Senior technical people must have the ability to communicate with business people using "their language." In other words, they need to demonstrate the value of their proposals using business terms, keywords, and context that are timely and relevant to their audience. In addition, they need to avoid some of the most common errors we see technical people making when speaking to senior managers. I recently published a paper that offers some simple strategies to help technical people, at any level, communicate with senior managers.[3] The following is an excerpt from that paper:

When communicating with senior executives and managers one should consider the following:

1. Less IS More—Start with the Most Important Point (Begin at the End)

2. Consider What Is Most Important to Your Audience

3. Tell the Time, Not How the Watch Works

4. Use Questions to Empower the Audience and Confirm Less IS More

5. Practice Your Message, Anticipate Questions (The Rule of Three)

6. Write a Script

7. Reduce Your Footprint

8. If All Else Fails . . . Tell Your Story, Your Way . . . Backward

9. Have Your Backup (Sometimes More IS More)

10. Only Wide Receivers Should Go Long—Stay On, Or Under, Time

1. Less IS More—Start with the Most Important Point (Begin at the End)

The most important thing to remember when speaking to senior managers is to begin with the most important point. Some might say "begin at the end." In some cases this may run counter to our culture or "to our being." We have been trained to educate. To lead people to arrive at our conclusion by sharing

---

[3] Excerpt from "When Techs Talk to Execs" by George Watt, May 2009. Reprinted with permission.

some history and leading them through the points that brought us to the point ourselves. To build a case.

It is my experience that senior executives think in exactly the opposite way. They want first to understand the value of a proposal or solution . . . before they invest time in exploring it.

With that in mind it is important to begin at the end. If your proposal will result in $7 million in savings, then let that be the first thing you share. Use an impactful statement such as "Our project is ahead of schedule with 92% of relocations complete" or "Our recent training program has resulted in a $4 million productivity gain."

Think of it in these terms: each executive has a light above their head with a pull-chain switch. When you begin your conversation or presentation the light is on. Their hand is on the chain. Your initial mission is to gain their interest and get their hand off the chain. (You have two minutes. Maybe.) You need to answer the questions: "Why should I listen to this person?" "What's in it for the company?" "What's in it for me?"

State the purpose of the meeting (e.g., to obtain approval for . . . , to provide an update on . . .), request permission to proceed, say thank you, and then open with an impactful statement.

2. Consider What Is Most Important to Your Audience

Beginning with an impactful statement (i.e., getting right to the point) is important. The statement must also have relevance to your audience. If you are speaking with more than one executive, be sure to consider whether all of the executives you are speaking with have common interests. If they do not, make sure to consider adding the relevant "and" to your impact statement. For example, speaking to a sales executive and the Chief Sustainability Officer you might offer an opening line of this nature in order to capture their attention: "I am pleased to report that our project added $2 million to our top-line revenue and reduced our carbon footprint by 450 tons."

3. Tell the Time, Not How the Watch Works

I recall leaving one of my first-ever customer visits as a field engineer. A customer had asked me a fascinating question. I had never considered the problem or solution the customer had asked about. It was very challenging, and I was excited because I had thought of a very good solution to the problem on the spot. The customer had asked a question in the form of "Can your product [do this]?" I wove a tapestry of technological wizardry that would have made the most talented rug makers jealous. My answer had to be at least five minutes in length. The meeting went very well. On our way out of the building, Paul, the sales executive, put his hand on my shoulder and said, "George, sometimes the answer is just 'yes.'"

That is more often than not the case with senior executives. They want the short answer. If they want an explanation they will ask for one. If you find yourself uncertain you can offer one: "Yes. Would you like to know more?" "Yes. Would you like me to explain how?"

Imagine if you asked someone what the time was and they began with an explanation of how the crystal in their watch vibrated at a constant speed . . . By the time they got to the time, you would likely have forgotten what you had asked them. Most of us have been on both ends of a conversation like this.

Senior executives are typically under tremendous time constraints. In my experience they are grateful to and appreciate very much people who can get to the root of issues quickly.

4. Use Questions to Empower the Audience and Confirm Less IS More

A common trap that people trying to practice "less is more" can fall into is rushing through too quickly. Ironically it is possible to offer too little. It is therefore good practice to ask confirming questions, especially if you have summarized something large, critical, or complex. For example, when showing a detailed project plan you might state something such as, "This is our plan. We are on time and within budget. Do you have any questions?" When showing a process flow diagram you might state something such as, "Here is our customer intake process. Would you like me to step through it for you?"

Asking questions of this nature adds a small pause to allow your audience to digest your material or statement without adding too much of a delay or disruption in the flow of your conversation or presentation. It is a good idea to keep in mind the fact that these senior executives are where they are for a reason. They likely have a wealth of experience and are typically very good at digesting a large amount of information quickly.

Asking questions of this nature also helps to confirm whether you are delivering relevant information and shows respect for the authority of the senior executive.

5. Practice Your Message, Anticipate Questions (The Rule of Three)

It may be a statement of the obvious to note that anyone who will be presenting something to senior managers should rehearse their presentation. However, what we often fail to remember is that almost every interaction with a senior manager is a "presentation" of a sort. A meeting in an elevator or a brief encounter in the café can be every bit as important as a formal presentation.

It is important to "carry with you" the executive summary for your important projects. Have that "we have completed 92% of relocations and reduced expenses by $2 million" summary in your head at all times. When asked a question, think for a moment about the reason for the question. "What about my project would be of most interest to a person in this position? To this person?"

When preparing for a meeting or presentation, it is also beneficial to view things from the senior managers' perspective and try to anticipate questions they may ask. For example, if preparing for a presentation ask yourself what questions may be asked about each and every slide, and about the presentation or topic overall. Then prepare answers, in executive summary form (less is more), for each of the questions. It is amazing the difference this can make in the level of confidence you will have in yourself, and the executives will have in you in return.

The rule of three: the first time you present something to a senior manager (or anyone, really) should be at least the third time you are presenting it. Practice at least twice as if you are with the executives. Even if you are alone, stand, gesture, and anticipate and respond to a few questions. That will help you to set the message and flow and is likely to make you much more comfortable during the actual event.

If you can find someone willing to participate in your practice and to give you feedback then do so. If you do so it is strongly recommended that you follow the rule of three and rehearse prior to your "live" practice session. That should help make the session even more effective.

6. Write a Script

Once you have your message refined, it is almost always worthwhile to write it down. Writing it will not only help you to refine the message—it can also often help set the message clearly in your mind.

Include not only your message or presentation, but also the questions you anticipate along with the answers you would give. Having a written practice

Q&A can dramatically improve your ability to answer questions succinctly. The act of writing the Q&A can also help you to identify key items that may have been left out of the main body of the presentation, or even items that should be removed.

It is fine to refer to your notes during a presentation. If you are presenting in person, reading the entire presentation directly from your notes is likely ill advised. If you are presenting via teleconference, you may be able to use your notes more actively. Some people are able to read an entire script during a teleconference and deliver an effective presentation. If you are not confident that you are one of those people then it is recommended you not do so, or that you practice with someone who will provide honest feedback.

Your script may also be of great value if ever you are asked to speak about the topic at a time you were not expecting to.

7. Reduce Your Footprint

If you have time to review your notes or slides, take the key points and try to restate them in fewer words. Changing the grammatical voice of a statement can sometimes help. Less is more, and the more you practice this the better and more effective your message will be.

Begin by reducing the key points. Time permitting, move to secondary points and the answers you prepared for the questions you anticipated.

8. If All Else Fails . . . Tell Your Story, Your Way . . . Backward

If you have been trained to build a persuasive case—to "tell a story"—it may be very difficult for you to begin at the end. If this is the case, try writing your story the way you would normally write it. Then take the end of the story (e.g., "and we saved $15 million") and make that your first statement or slide. Keep the story line; you may need it. Just begin with the most important point.

In many cases this may be the only way to prepare an executive summary. There have been cases where I have spent hours preparing a presentation with many, many slides only to realize that most of the detail would be of no interest (at least initially) to the senior executives. After some rework, those presentations become 3–5 slides and 10–15 minutes in duration. Some of the most effective presentations I have delivered lasted 10–15 minutes, even though they covered large and complex projects that lasted many quarters.

Preparation is paramount. The shorter the presentation, the more important the preparation.

9. Have Your Backup (Sometimes More IS More)

It is important to note that the fact that you may lead with something very brief, or you may have a brief presentation planned (3–5 slides, for example), does not mean the executives will never be interested in details. The point of this paper is not to state executives never care about details nor that they are incapable of digesting them. Nothing could be further from the truth. In some cases the senior managers you are speaking with may wish to get into the details. You might state "This is our process. Would you like me to step through it?" and receive the response "Yes, please."

Thus, though you may not plan to present the details you must be adequately prepared to do so.

In these situations you may also need to put some of the other strategies into practice. For example, if more than one senior manager is present, it may be the case that only one of them is interested in the details. Though there is no magic formula, in these cases a well-considered question can often make your presentation more effective. For example, when asked to dive into the details you might ask, "Is that something of interest to everyone or would you prefer I cover this with you alone following the presentation?" A question of this nature can help keep you from situations where some key executives lose interest while you go through details which they either have no interest in or do not understand. Caution is critical, and your question must be asked respectfully, especially if you feel there is someone present who may not have the background necessary to understand the details. Please be careful not to be perceived as patronizing.

10. Only Wide Receivers Should Go Long— Stay On, Or Under, Time

This may be one of the most important items to consider. The calendar of the most senior executives is typically an insane tapestry of logistics. It is important to stay on, or under, the time allotted. Under is best. If you have 30 minutes of an executive's time and you can get your point across in 10, then do so. Practice hitting that time target. That will leave some time for possible late starts and for questions.

If you begin that 30-minute meeting on time and finish in 10 minutes, the senior executive will very much appreciate your getting to the point and respecting their time. That will dramatically increase the likelihood you will get more of it when you need to.

Intelligence

Leaders suffering from the intelligence I-Negative often fall into a classic trap. In many cases, they became senior IT leaders as a result of their personal intelligence and/or creativity. This can lead to a well-intended, though perhaps subconscious, tendency to try to solve every problem themselves. This tendency can have some fairly obvious consequences. For example, leaders can unconsciously take learning or growth opportunities away from their employees. Furthermore, a leader with this I-Negative may be repeatedly preventing innovations from being discovered. At the very least they will never know what their employees may have accomplished if left to solve problems on their own. In worst cases, leaders can send a morale-crushing implicit message that they do not trust or respect the members of their team.

Regardless of the impact on the team, the result of this I-Negative is often that the leader takes on too much work and/or responsibility. This overload often leads to burnout and a decrease in the quality of the leader's own work, which often cascades throughout their team.

Infallibility

A more destructive form of the intelligence I-Negative also exists. Extreme "Chief Intelligence/Infallibility Officers" often feel, in fact often strongly believe, they are always "the smartest person in the room." Because of this trait, they either intentionally (usually) or unintentionally demean the ideas and contributions of others. In its worst manifestation, those ideas sometimes find their way back to the organization later (sometimes many months later) as "great new ideas" from the same "Chief Infallibility Officer" who killed the idea when it was originally proposed.

There have been spirited debates regarding whether or not these people actually realize they are revisiting the ideas of others, almost always (OK, always) without attribution to the originator—not even as someone who "inspired" their thinking. In reality, that "how" does not matter. The outcome is unforgivable, and the impact is the same.

Interloper

In the previous chapter, we discussed a number of innovation killers. You may have noticed that many of them were related to human personality traits. People with these traits can place an enormous amount of pressure on an IT leader. Not all of this pressure is bad and not all is malevolent. However, dealing with it can be time-consuming and mind-numbing.

Several types of interlopers can attempt to insert themselves into innovative processes. In some cases, their agenda may be destructive, such as when they want to take or share credit for new ideas and innovation that they had no real part in. Or they may be skeptical about the innovation and concerned that it might be bad for the company. To be clear, in the latter case the negative aspect is often related to their approach or tactics. This is not a suggestion that a proposed innovation should never be questioned.

Others will become involved with the best of intentions. They may find the innovation exciting or simply be service-minded and wish to help. In the end, the result is very often the same. IT leaders can become consumed by the new idea, or overwhelmed by the sheer volume of activity they have to deal with, if they do not realize this is happening to them and respond to it correctly.

IT leaders must also take care to recognize when this type of meddling occurs in the context of their operational responsibilities. This type of lost time is not only an innovation-related issue. Time lost due to this type of interaction—even in the context of "keeping the lights on"—is taken directly from the innovation time surplus.

Immutability

Though this is, perhaps, a fairly obvious I-Negative, it is certainly worth mentioning and cannot be ignored. Today's IT leaders need not only be willing to accept change in the form of new technologies (i.e., advances in mobile computing, social media, cloud computing), they also must be willing to accept new ways of communicating and working with their stakeholders and with younger workers (now often referred to as "Millennials").

In addition, today's IT leaders must learn to accept successful approaches to innovation that are different from their own, even if their own approaches have been successful.

I-Positives

Not all pressure is negative. True creative tension can be inspiring. Challenge can be exciting and energizing. We refer to the I's that can help foster innovation and/or counteract some of the I-Negatives as the I-Positives. These include the following:

- Instrumentation
- Innovation

- (dis)Intermediation
- Improvement
- ITIL , ITSM . . .
- Independence/Initiative
- Instruction
- Invigoration
- Integrity

Instrumentation

Innovative technical people love to spend their time creating reports. As I remove my metaphoric tongue from my cheek, I can recall my own experience of requesting new reports while leading technical teams developing and operating a cloud computing solution. The sighs. The eyes on the ceiling. The body language. Every time I asked for a report, it was as if I had told a child I was going to take his puppy away. There were so many other cool things to be done . . . and those were "actually valuable."

It is quite common that innovative technicians, and even their leaders, cannot see the value in instrumentation or transparency with stakeholders. The irony is that the time it takes to stop and create this type of instrumentation is often rapidly recovered. Each and every time someone uses a report or dashboard is an instance when someone in the technology team did *not* have to spend time retrieving data, creating a report, or answering a question. These requests often occur frequently, so proactive creation of instrumentation can very quickly create a time surplus that can be directed toward innovation and other, more interesting, work. Furthermore, investments in instrumentation pay off ad infinitum. Leaders and teams who are not proactive in their communication with customers and key stakeholders also are subject to whatever perceptions, good or bad, that customers have about them. Here are some of the most common, damaging perceptions:

- Your service is awful.
- My team does not use your service.
- Your service has little (no) value to the company (to my team . . .).
- Your service is less modern than [the name of an external service].
- Your service is out-of-date.

- Your service is more expensive than [the name of an external service].

Consider, for example, the first perception, "Your service is awful." If a stakeholder's perception is that your service is awful and you are not measuring your service, then your service *is* awful. In reality your service might be perfectly acceptable, or even very good. Yet that will not matter because your customers feel differently and you have no data to engage in a meaningful, fact-based conversation with them. If, however, you are collecting meaningful data, you might find yourself in one of the following three situations, any of which would result in a much more productive conversation with your stakeholder:

1. You review the data and determine the service truly is bad. You acknowledge this failing, supply some supplementary information, identify the cause, and share your plan of action.

2. Your reports demonstrate the service of interest is actually performing well. Even though that is the case, you acknowledge that you are concerned because your stakeholder is not satisfied. You engage with the stakeholder to determine the root cause of their dissatisfaction (even if the cause is simply perception.) In such cases, it may be your stakeholder's engagement model and/ or your communication scheme that is in need of repair.

3. Your measurements detect that a service is about to suffer. You take action to address the cause before it impacts your customer. There is no conversation necessary. You meet your SLAs.

Good instrumentation not only helps improve operational efficiency, it can also dramatically increase the confidence and trust stakeholders have in your organization.

When a team does not possess good operational reporting, they can pay dearly for it. Every request for information becomes ad hoc. Often these requests are the result of someone voicing one of those previously mentioned statements of perception in a meeting of senior managers. If not addressed, statements in this context can have results as dramatic as the complete dissolution of a service or team. Due to this, we have witnessed these ad hoc requests resulting in a full-on, full-time fire drill for one or more employees that took them off productive work for one or two days, or more. Sadly, due to the time constraints involved, these reports are often created in such a way that they are useful for only the request at hand. Thus, the next time a request of this nature is received, the fire drill begins again.

It can be worse. Add one of the innovation-killing personalities discussed in Chapter 2 to this context and creating these "one-time" reports can become an innovation killer on its own. In fairness to those caught in this trap, it is not always simple (perhaps even possible) to realize this is happening to you while you are in the middle of it. The additional workload and accompanying frustration can be an effective disguise.

Not only can transparent and proactive communication to key stakeholders and senior managers result in a better relationship with them, increased trust, and increased confidence in your team, it can also result in the creation of a significant amount of time for innovation ("proactive" being the keyword). The value of proactive stakeholder communication is becoming much more widely recognized. Many businesses are creating "trust" sites that can be visited by their stakeholders (in some cases by anyone) at any time. Through these sites, customers always know the current state of their services, and in many cases they can view historical status as well. Trust.salesforce.com is one well-known example of a successful trust site you can visit to see this type of proactive, transparent communication in action.

To this point we have focused on measurements of service. It is also key that IT leaders be capable of articulating the value their services bring to the business. (See also the "Inarticulacy" I-Negative mentioned earlier in the chapter.) In order to do so, the *value* of services must also be measured and shared. Measuring items of this nature ensures that IT leaders are able to communicate their value to business leaders in *business* terms. (e.g.: "Orders have increased by $2 million in the month since we implemented the new search facility.") This can be extremely beneficial during budget discussions. In addition, these measurements can also serve as an indication that a service should be re-evaluated or replaced as its value begins to diminish. This key benefit of value measurement is often overlooked.

Effective leaders are proactive in their reporting and transparent with their customers and stakeholders. This approach to stakeholder engagement results in better service to the stakeholders, higher levels of trust, and often a substantial increase in the innovation time surplus as a result. It is worth noting, however, that measuring the wrong things or ignoring signs from "outside the measurements" can be a path to misery.

Innovation

This entire book is about becoming a "Chief Innovation Officer". While (obviously) we will not reproduce the entire contents of the book in this section, we would be remiss not to include "Innovation" in our list of I-Positives. In addition, we want to reinforce one key point.

Being a "Chief Innovation Officer" is not only about your own track record of innovation or about being innovative yourself. Sure, that can be part of it. However, your own creativity may not be the most important key to your success. Innovative leaders must also be able to harvest innovation from their entire team. Furthermore, even if the CIO is the most creative and innovative person in their team, "we" (the CIO and the team) will always be able to accomplish more than "I" (the CIO). This is something to keep in mind whether you are someone who aspires to be an innovative IT leader, or someone who decides which people are assigned to those leadership positions.

(dis)Intermediation

Previously, in the "Intermediation" section, we referred to disintermediation in the context of an IT team's customers creating and acquiring services without involving the IT team. While this is certainly one type disintermediation, disintermediation can also be a strategic weapon. Disintermediation, when applied intelligently, can act as a force multiplier for an IT team.

What may be surprising is that removing oneself from the service equation, done properly, can also result in a more satisfied customer. Odds are that you have experienced this as a consumer, though you may not have realized the reason for your satisfaction. This personal experience may help illustrate this point.

Believe it or not, there was actually a time when people had to check out of hotels. Face to face. At that time, I was a field engineer and traveled more or less every working day of the year (and then some). I rarely spent more than a day or two in one place, so several mornings each week I would wait in line, luggage in hand, waiting to settle my bill. This process was unpredictable, though it was likely to take at least 10 or 15 minutes at the best of times. Often it took longer. Since I had to be certain I would arrive at my customers' premises on time, I had to schedule a half-hour for checkout each morning of a departure.

Think about that—a half-hour, two to five times every week. In a single year, this represents approximately 50–125 total hours set aside to accommodate hotel checkout. But then came "zip-out checkout," "no hassle checkout," and many other similar services. These services allowed guests to have charges automatically assigned to their credit cards and either checkout via their television or by picking up a receipt from a slot in the lobby. It is obvious that these services have evolved, and most hotels offer an even simpler automatic checkout today. Guests need only visit the reception desk if there is a problem with the bill (in my experience, a very rare occurrence).

So, what's the big deal? It certainly was not that I did not want to speak with the hotel agents. In fact, I knew most of them very well. Think about what this meant to my time—30 minutes two to five times a week of my personal time was again mine. What a huge gift! Even at two checkouts per week, this would result in more than 40 hours of personal time returned each year. (It was likely twice that.) It also meant a much more predictable schedule. Checkout was no longer a factor in whether I would be on time for a customer visit.

With these checkout options, we have a much better service and the hotels have a much more efficient operation. Of course, we are all aware that this type of positive disintermediation is not limited to rapid checkout services. We happily and willfully select positive disintermediation every day through services such as online shopping, self-service retail checkout, and automated banking machines.

Disintermediation can be used as a strategic weapon—both for IT and for the businesses they serve. Recently, I used positive disintermediation (OK, self-service) to deliver better, faster service while giving my team more time to focus on high-value activities like further automating our environment. It also enabled them to be more nimble and more responsive to our customers.

(Incidentally, we realize we took a bit of literary license including "(dis)" with this I-Positive. This word has such strong currency we thought it important to use it.)

Improvement

Often improvement can be the forgotten victim of innovation. New and/or innovative approaches are often applied in an information technology context to make existing processes more efficient. However, in many cases the processes that they improved are no longer relevant, resulting in an efficient, irrelevant process.

In some cases, the overall process may be somewhat relevant, though with modification could be made more efficient. For example, a process might be automated, without changing the process itself, and result in a reduction in execution time from one week to three days. That may be heralded as a great success (greater than 50% improvement). However, it may later be revealed that minor changes in the process itself in combination with the automation (perhaps made possible by the automation) could reduce the process to a matter of minutes. We and our colleagues hear of these situations regularly.

Something far worse can also happen when processes are automated. If that process is no longer relevant (no longer best practice, made incorrect by the automation, etc.), the "wrong" process can be automated. As a result, bad things happen far faster than they would have ever before been possible.

Process improvements can contribute greatly to the innovation time surplus. Opportunities for process improvements often present themselves while other things, such as process automation, are being attended to. Be on the lookout for those opportunities. In addition, changes made while automating an existing system's processes can result in changes to the overall business system itself. Failing to update processes accordingly can result in missed opportunities to deliver additional business value and missed opportunities to create time for innovation. Worse, the impact of a failure to update processes when necessary can negatively impact a business' bottom line through the delivery of inaccurate information or the automatic execution of an incorrect action—that is, doing the wrong things with great efficiency.

ITIL, ITSM . . .

Plenty has been written about the Information Technology Infrastructure Library (ITIL), IT service management (ITSM), and other frameworks and maturity models. A detailed discussion of these is certainly outside the scope of this book. However, this type of discipline or best practice can be extremely beneficial and is certainly worthy of mention. The benefits of their implementation are similar to those mentioned in the "Instrumentation" and "Improvement" sections of this chapter. These frameworks provide a prescriptive approach to achieving these benefits.

One of my teams once implemented a Change Advisory Board (CAB), an ITIL concept, to help deal with stakeholder engagement issues (some of which were mentioned previously in the "Instrumentation" section). The results were very positive. In fact, in the early days the simple fact that the CAB had been established was a source of stakeholder satisfaction. The result was a happier stakeholder base, better aligned system improvements, and much less time spent explaining implementation priorities to stakeholders. This measure also helped build stakeholder trust, which also resulted in less time spent in confrontation and/or with "nervous" stakeholders.

Care must be taken because not all aspects of these frameworks and models are universally beneficial. It is important to understand the value each aspect of the system will bring. Being too literal or pedantic in implementation or implementing "too much" (i.e., irrelevant aspects) can diminish their value. It is even possible to derive negative impact from them if they are approached or implemented incorrectly. In some cases, it will be possible to adopt specific techniques without adopting an entire system, bringing benefits without baggage. If you choose specific aspects of these disciplines early in an implementation, you can then recognize and enable their benefits early while keeping the burden and cost of implementation low.

Independence/Initiative

Innovative IT leaders must support the independence and initiative of others. Those others are often referred to as "rogues." If you are thinking, "But I thought one of our main objectives was to eliminate rogue IT"—you are not alone. Certainly it would be ideal if your technology team could anticipate all future needs of your consumers far in advance and provide perfect solutions for them ahead of those needs. Unfortunately, that seldom happens and it is likely that every senior IT leader will encounter some form of rogue IT.

Our advice: Embrace the rogue! Often concepts and ideas, and sometimes entire solutions, created via rogue IT can deliver substantial value. Great ideas can come from anywhere, and it makes sense that often "anywhere" represents a group of people who work closest with the systems, processes, products, and customers each day of their career. To ignore these solutions or cast them away on principle is to potentially squander great opportunity. Technology leaders must be confident enough to embrace ideas of this nature, to help foster them and make them real, to apply their knowledge and resources to ensure the solutions' success, and to properly attribute the ideas to their source.

The presence of rogue IT can also serve as a warning. The proliferation of rogue IT can be an indication of a problem-ridden IT department. Certainly that is not always the case. At times, ideas just happen where they happen. There is no malice aforethought. Other times the consumers (the rogues) are simply not aware that the IT group can help them in certain ways and develop their own solutions out of "desperation." The point is that it does not matter how the idea came to be. If an idea or innovation can add value to your business, does its source really matter (as long as the source is ethical and morally sound, that is)?

Thus there are benefits in embracing rogues once they are encountered. Moreover, those who do not embrace rogues risk driving them further underground. An anti-rogue policy can result in the addition of risk to a company's information assets, as the rogues may or may not know how to address key foundation disciplines such as security and data recovery. In some cases, they may not even be aware of these key requirements.

Instruction

As has been mentioned previously and in multiple contexts, one trap senior IT leaders can fall into is becoming too involved in detailed execution. This can be a completely subconscious action, especially when the work itself is exciting and engaging. It can also be a result of some of the innovation killers discussed in Chapter 2. It is often well-intended as a show of solidarity: "I am willing to get my hands dirty too."

An IT leader working shoulder-to-shoulder with their employees is fine in moderation. In fact, it can be an effective way for the IT leader to learn more about the team and vice versa. In our experience, such a display of support and camaraderie is often greatly appreciated when work is unpleasant, such as when a team is moving to a new location or cleaning a facility.

However, IT leaders must be careful not to take all of the exciting opportunities—the fun work—away from their teams. When they do so, they squander opportunities for the personal growth of their team members. So doing can also result in a negative impact on morale, or at the very least a missed opportunity to have a positive impact on morale. Furthermore, IT leaders who do this—whatever their motivation—can often take on too much detailed work and lower the overall quality of the work associated with their "real job" as a result. Alone any one of these effects can be detrimental to a leader's or team's performance. Combined they are the building blocks for a spectacular disaster.

Some of the most effective IT leaders we have encountered have mastered the balancing of these forces. They are great coaches who know when to step in and when to provide direction. The balance is usually heavily weighted toward the latter. They are masters at asking great questions to help guide team members to the discovery of solutions, as opposed to giving them the answers. The result of helping their team to grow is a more passionate, excited, higher performing team—a team with a higher level of trust and mutual respect. And their team's results show it.

Invigoration

Invigoration is another aspect of the CIO as "coach." Surprisingly, it is one that is commonly overlooked. At times, IT leaders are so consumed by the volume of work that faces them, the day-to-day pressures, and all of the other I's, that they do not deal with energizing their teams and maintaining and improving employee morale and engagement. Some do not know how. It is critical that IT leaders at all levels learn the skills necessary in order to invigorate their teams.

Much has been written about boosting morale and creating amazing team spirit. We will not restate what can be found there, though we do believe this aspect of being a great IT leader is critical and could not omit at least a mention of it. Invigorated teams are much more likely to be high-performing teams. The higher a team's level of performance and efficiency, the more likely there will be additional time for innovation, and the more likely the team will have a culture that can take advantage of innovation when it occurs.

We believe that clear vision and good communication are key elements in the achievement of an invigorated team. Team members must have a clear picture of the vision they are trying to achieve, their objectives, and how they contribute value to the greater organization, to its broader objectives, and to its customers. IT leaders must be capable of articulating their vision and objectives, and they must be passionate about their mission. Engaging team members in these ways will not only increase the likelihood that the team will achieve or exceed their objectives, it will also likely result in the team's leader having more personal time to spend on innovation and higher value activities.

Integrity

Integrity is a critical I-Positive. Though we believe this is critical on principle alone, those with integrity receive tangible benefits that will help in the context of innovation. Those who have demonstrated a high level of integrity can often accomplish things at much greater speed than their counterparts.

When IT leaders are trusted by their stakeholders, often the time it takes to convince them to try something new is greatly reduced. For example, the stakeholders know the IT leaders will be diligent in their invention, forthcoming with all risks and mitigation plans, and quickly admit failure when it occurs. When IT leaders are trusted by their peers, they can co-opt their assistance with the creation and implementation of new ideas, sometimes even when their peers are not convinced of the value. When IT leaders are trusted by their team, delivery speed increases.

Shifting the Balance

One of life's certainties appears to be that there will always be opposing forces, positive and negative, related to almost everything we do. That has certainly been our experience with innovation. The key is to shift the balance heavily in favor of the positive items. In the case of innovation, a discussion of balance often takes the form of a conversation about the amount of investment directed at "keeping the lights on" (sustaining operations) vs. the amount directed toward innovation. This is an epic struggle according to most IT leaders we speak with. Simply knowing where to begin can be difficult to figure out.

Increasing the Innovation Time Surplus

Recognizing the I's discussed in this chapter is a key early step in the journey toward shifting the balance toward innovation. IT leaders must be able to quickly identify which pressures can have a negative impact on innovation (I-Negatives), which can have a positive impact (I-Positives), and what to do to reduce I-Negatives and increase I-Positives. Shifting the balance can also increase the innovation time surplus, as less time is spent on low-value activity. But there is another balance in need of shifting that is often overlooked.

Lowering the Price of Admission

We all have our own personal biases. We have some things we like to do and others we prefer not to do. We all have our passions and apathies. We encounter these every day of our working lives. The passions are easy to deal with. We rush to those. What about the tasks we would rather not perform? Some managers discount the latter with phrases such as "That's why they call it a job." I refer to this part of the job as "the price of admission."

People join a team so they can do what they love to do. What they care about. What energizes them. Everything else they do comprises the price they pay to be a member of the team. But effective managers and leaders recognize that it is their duty to lower the price of admission for their employees.

Lowering the price of admission begins with knowing—truly knowing—every member of your team. In order to lower the price of admission, you must know what each member of your team loves and what he or she dislikes. You will quickly find that each team member will have different likes and dislikes. Some will love being creative and working in "whitespace." Some will be extremely uncomfortable with this way of working and will love back office or administrative-type tasks. That's where you can find the magic.

As a manager and a leader, your job is to assign responsibilities equitably to those most likely to enjoy them but also to set realistic expectations. There will always be some price of admission. The key is to keep it as low as possible and to distribute the "fun things" equitably.

Setting employee expectations appropriately is critical as well. Try sharing this analogy with your new team members. Explain there will always be a price of admission but that you are committed to working with them to keep it as low as possible. Only say this if you mean it. It is a commitment that will earn or destroy their trust in you.

When you lead this way you must be realistic. Explain that sometimes the price will be higher. Then do your best to keep those times to a minimum. By making your team members aware of your commitment they will be able to help you to keep the price of admission low by making you more aware of their often-changing likes and dislikes.

Of course, as leaders we need to be careful to assign responsibility to those capable of succeeding. It has been our experience that passion and performance are often correlated. We also need to be mindful that we may have to take team members outside their "comfort zone" in order to help them with personal growth or to prepare them for advancement.

With those provisos, we have found that shifting the balance of work to lower the price of admission was an extremely useful strategy that helped improve team performance and increase trust and mutual respect. We also found that the larger a team, the better chance we had at creating a very low price of admission.

4

Business Innovation vs. IT Innovation

What Is the Right Focus for an Innovative CIO?

The authors of this book have met with many IT senior managers and CIOs over the years. Technology and innovation are frequently the main topics of these meetings. Our discussions are usually triggered by some new technology, news, or practice in which the CIO is interested. This is sometimes mere technical tire-kicking and light relief from our day job. On other occasions, it is a more serious discussion about the impact of implementing the new stuff. While these technology discussions are fun and impart some useful information, we must consider if they are the right type of discussion to encourage an innovative approach to business across the whole organization that the CIO works for.

Chris Curran[1] reviewed a Price Waterhouse Coopers study[2] that found only 25% of surveyed CIOs were interested in or engaged in external innovation. Curran explains that external innovation is innovation external to the IT department. Specifically, external innovation is innovation of the business and customer domain. In a separate finding, Curran also notes that the other 75%

---

[1] Chris Curran, "Business Innovation or IT Innovation?," CIO Dashboard, October 2010, www.ciodashboard.com/leadership/business-innovation-or-it-innovation, retrieved on May 2012.

[2] Chris Curran, Tom DeGarmo, John Sviokla, "4th Annual Digital IQ Survey," pwc, 2010, www.pwc.com/us/en/advisory/2011-Digital-iq-survey/key-findings.jhtml, retrieved on May 2012.

of CIOs were involved in innovation of existing IT. The findings of a recent survey by CA Technologies[3] support those reported by Curran. The CA survey recorded that only 16% of surveyed CIOs were involved in the organization's strategy discussions. Figure 4-1 shows that the majority of CIOs surveyed said they are either never or only infrequently involved in developing the organization's strategy.

Are CIOs Involved in Their Company's Business Strategies?

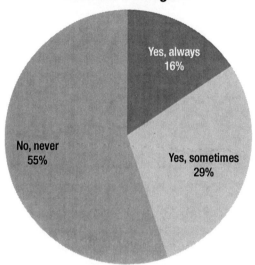

Figure 4-1. This figure shows the results of a CA Technologies survey where 685 CIOs were asked this question: "Are you involved in helping to define and agree the business strategy of your organization?"

Both studies indicate that the majority of CIOs tend to be inward-looking,[2] focusing on the IT department rather than the business and the customers. For example, CIOs often see internal IT innovation as a major part of their role. Conversely, they may be under external constraints from senior leaders in their organization to keep their focus on IT. Those external constraints may result from a company leadership view that CIOs have nothing to contribute to organizational strategy. In this same CA survey, CIOS were asked why they thought they were not involved in their organization's strategy. The highest number of respondents answered that CIOs have a technology-focused role.

---

[3] "The Future Role of the CIO," CA Technologies, October 2011, www.ca.com/us/collateral/white-papers/na/The-Future-Role-of-the-CIO-Becoming-the-Boss.aspx, retrieved on May 2012.

The following is a list of reasons given for non-involvement ranked in order of most to least frequent answers:

- My role is seen as a technology-focused role.

- I am not a member of the senior leadership team.

- I lack the appropriate skills to be involved in those discussions.

- IT is seen as a cost of doing business.

- IT is not seen as central to the direction of the business.

- I am only ever consulted about the technical deployment of any strategies in discussion.

- I have a poor relationship with the CEO.

- The management team does not recognize the contribution that a CIO could bring to strategy discussions.

The respondents to this question were the majority of CIOs who self-identify as never being involved in organizational strategy. These answers show that many CIOs see themselves either as technology-focused or as not having the requisite skills to take part in organizational discussions.

Given these results it is natural to ask: what is the right domain for an innovative CIO? Would your company benefit from your being a CIO whose innovations are IT-focused or business-focused?

Which Is the Most Difficult to Achieve: Business Innovation or IT Innovation?

When we discuss innovation with CIOs, one topic often recurs: the relative difficulty of generating either business innovations or IT innovations. CIOs see themselves as having limited time and resources to engage in innovation and often assume that these resources would be better focused on the IT domain, not the business domain. The IT domain is where they are on familiar ground, but there is pull to join the 25% of CIOs mentioned by Curran who are innovating externally. The decision about which direction to go in may depend on the relative difficulty of the two types of innovation.

To gauge the level of difficulty, it is best to ask an initial question about your company's target marketplaces. The value of IT-focused innovation tends to be greater in a technology-based, online company rather than in the more traditional nontechnology companies. The level of difficulty in achieving an IT innovation in an online business is also generally far less than in a more traditional business. In an online business, the benefits of IT to the business are generally understood and accepted. In a more traditional, less technology-based business, it may be easier to gain acceptance for a business-focused innovation instead. In a traditional business, IT is usually less visible to people outside the IT department as an enabler of innovation. This view is more likely because staff outside of IT are usually not familiar with thinking of IT as an innovative tool and as a business support tool. Therefore, we can conclude that the type of market the business is engaged in will have a significant impact on how acceptable and credible an IT-led innovation will be.

Creativity

Creativity is at the heart of innovation. It has already been mentioned in Chapter 2 but here we will discuss it briefly as a component of business and IT innovation. Innovations come from people thinking creatively. Studies have shown that people who are considered highly creative have many more ideas than people who are not considered highly creative. It is generally accepted that everyone is creative and has creative potential, tapped or untapped. Even if you are considered as a person of low creativity, you have the potential to innovate, although you may not produce as many innovative ideas as a highly creative person. As a CIO, you must tap into the creative potential of your staff.

Innovation requires creativity but it also needs your domain expertise. Domain expertise is an asset your employees have that may overcome any creativity shortcomings and often stimulates business and IT innovation. You don't need to be highly creative to be innovative if you have domain expertise. As a CIO, you should ask if you and your staff have a lack of business domain expertise that is hampering a move to external innovation.

Creativity helps to generate ideas, but creativity can be stifled by routine. For example, the creativity of children reduces as they get older and move into full-time education.[4] Creative adults can also find that their creative muscles are atrophied by repetitive or boring work, lack of recognition, etc. In Chapter Two, we talked about innovation killers. These innovation killers often do their work by stifling creativity as well as reducing the enthusiasm for innovation. We will look at ways you can encourage innovation in later chapters. But for now, it is worth asking if your department and your company are endeavoring to stimulate creativity or whether work and management

---

[4] Sir Ken Robinson, "How Schools Stiffle Creativity," Published by TED Talks, 2009, http:// articles.cnn.com/2009-11-03/opinion/robinson.schools.stifle.creativity_1_talk-college-degrees-education?_s=PM:OPINION, retrieved on May 2012.

styles are encumbering creativity and innovation. This is discussed more fully in Chapter 10.

A creative staff is more likely to think of new products or processes, but innovation is the combination of thinking of something new and putting it into practice. Having a lot of ideas does not necessarily make for an innovative CIO or an innovative business. It is the combination of ideas and—most importantly—the drive to implement useful ideas that generates innovation.

Business Cases for Innovations

Business innovation and IT innovation generally will require funding and approval by the senior leadership team. In all but the most trivial departmental innovations, a business case is the best way of moving from an innovative idea to an implementation for the business.

Sadly, IT departments do not have a good reputation when it comes to business cases. John Thorpe[5] quotes a Cranfield University study where 38% of respondents claim that business benefits are exaggerated in business cases. It can be inferred that a business case has only one purpose: to gain funding and has no value beyond that. The failure to deliver the benefits forecast in a business case can create an atmosphere of mistrust between the implementation team and the approvers. In many business cases with IT innovations, they are well-explained in technology features but not so in business benefits terms. While the IT benefits are clear, the claimed business benefits may be fudged or simply misunderstood.

To credibly suggest business innovations, it is not enough that you have great technical skills. These technical skills need to be matched with an understanding of the business domain and how technology fits into that domain as we explained in Chapter 3. The credibility of the business case will depend on how well the business benefits are articulated and measured. Furthermore, CIOs should not shelve the business case when approval is given but focus on reporting progress on both the technical innovation and, more importantly, the progress toward the business benefits being delivered. This will require an understanding of the business process changes that the IT innovation will support. Business cases must be developed with care if they are to be influential in promoting innovation and securing the necessary funding.

IT departments often believe that business innovation is difficult and IT innovation is is seen as your comfort zone. This should not be an excuse for remaining one of the 75% of CIOs who stick to internal IT innovation. An

---

[5] John Thorpe, "Lies, Damn Lies and Business Cases," The Thorp Network, July 2009, www.thorpnet.com/2009/07/lies-damn-lies-and-business-cases/, retrieved on July 2012.

innovative CIO will be looking for business innovations and working to overcome the obstacles to creativity, innovation throughout the organization, and the articulation of business benefits for those innovations.

CIOs Are Always on the Leading Edge of Technology

Discussions about innovation with the IT department frequently focus on new or leading edge technology. All CIOs are under a constant bombardment of e-mails, phone calls, press releases, and marketing material about the "next big thing." It does not matter if the new technology is "bring your own device" (BYOD), big data, or cloud computing—the pressure is there.

To gain an understanding of the influence and evolution of leading edge technology, we looked through the web site of Gartner, a respected IT industry analysis company, and specifically reviewed their hype cycle press releases. The term "hype cycle" is attributed to Gartner and describes new technology in terms of its adoption from the first breakthrough to the adoption of a fully productive implementation. The Gartner press release of 2006[6] indicated that quantum computing was at the breakthrough stage, social networking was just coming to the peak of its hype, and smartphones were entering the productive phase. In 2008,[7] cloud computing, video telepresence, and green IT were all cited at the top of the hype cycle. In 2011,[8] cloud computing was still in a similar position at the top of the hype cycle, and big data also made an appearance at the top. All of these are technologies that may reasonably be on a potential CIO shopping list.

This may be a superficial analysis, but it illustrates issues that CIOs face all the time. CIOs are expected to make sense out of the technologies that are new or emerging within the context of the company's own IT and business context. There is an expectation that CIOs understand all the new technologies and can predict and know how to plan for which technologies will be important to their company in the future.

The CIO may also feel pressure coming from staff members from both inside and outside IT to consider newer technologies as possible catalysts for innovation. Employees will have their own preference for technology and

---

[6] "Gartner's 2006 Emerging Technologies Hype Cycle Highlights Key Technology Themes," August 2006, www.gartner.com/it/page.jsp?id=495475, retrieved on May 2012.

[7] "Gartner Highlights 27 Technologies in the 2008 Hype Cycle for Emerging Technologies," August 2008, www.gartner.com/it/page.jsp?id=739613, retrieved on May 2012.

[8] "Gartner's 2011 Hype Cycle Special Report Evaluates the Maturity of 1,900 Technologies," August 2011, www.gartner.com/it/page.jsp?id=1763814, retrieved on May 2012.

what it can do for them. This preference is more pronounced in the IT industry. In the IT industry, there is a core belief that technology staff love new technology. Technologists are frequently seen as favoring the new and shiny technology just because it is new and shiny. Whether these assumptions are true or not doesn't matter, but in any sizeable organization there will be many differing opinions about the relative merits of emerging technologies. The different opinions often map on a one-to-one basis with the number of technologists.

The burden of the CIO is increased by the inclusion of legacy IT systems. As discussed in Chapter Three, the term "legacy" describes systems that may have been implemented from a few to many years ago. These systems run a significant part of the core business processes. A CIO who plans to replace these systems will need a very convincing justification; however, it will most likely be necessary to replace them eventually. Many legacy systems have evolved over time and still perform well, supported by the "if it's not broken don't fix it" mantra.

Most CIOs would love a clean slate with no legacy systems. They would prefer to be able to specify and deliver business process support using the latest proven technologies. But that is a luxury that few are allowed except in emerging businesses or economies. Some of these legacy systems have been implemented a long time ago but are still considered vital to the organisation. The mainframe systems that were implemented years ago are still used to run large corporations. Once a system has been implemented and proven, it usually stays in place until external forces generate a need for a replacement strategy.

The CIO role is also largely that of maintenance of the status quo; CIOs are expected to keep the lights on, with everything having to do with IT and maintenance of IT working smoothly. As we have discussed, this is in addition to the expectation that they be conversant with new technology and its potential place in their IT strategy. CIOs will have to sell their strategy to senior leadership who may have differing views of the value of the technology and its place in the IT strategy. CIOs also have to include legacy systems in their plans against a background of the momentum of new technologies and the associated vendor marketing and sales campaigns.

CIOs need to be able to discriminate between new, leading edge technologies that present an opportunity and new technologies that are cool toys. Selecting the clear signal of an opportunity from all of the noise of marketing hype is difficult but we discuss some ways of making that selection in Chapters 9 and 10. For the moment all we need to say is that the CIO should consider the following points:

- New does not equal good. New technology is not always good technology. In the world of confectionery new recipes for old favourites have not always been successful.

- Technology should not be the key driver in considering an innovation. IT is an enabler and sometimes a catalyst, but the focus must be on the business and innovation for the business.

The innovative CIO should evaluate all their prospective IT innovations against the value for the business.

Innovation Is Quantifiable

To be justified in a business case, innovation needs to be quantifiable to the extent necessary for approval. Some innovations may not need the formal structure of a business case, but they still need to be quantified and justifiable if there is a cost involved. There are two ways of justifying a project: the inward IT example and the external business approach. The internal IT example is focused on introducing efficiencies and cost savings through more effective use of IT and new technologies. The external business approach is focused on business benefits that will accrue from implementing new technology.

IT innovation needs to have a clear value statement that should be expressed in business terms. The communication of value is one of the more important functions of a CIO and should be approached with care and the right language. Let's consider the example of Service Oriented Architecture (SOA).

In 2005, there was a vogue for SOA that has increased over subsequent years. IT departments began to adopt SOA because the technology enabled functionality to be expressed as reusable services rather than as blocks of code, modules, or subroutines. The service interface was a function call that had input values and output values, while the functionality and code of the service was hidden. The reuse of services yields a "code-once-use-often" model of development. The attraction for an IT development shop is the lowering of costs resulting from using a component-based approach to constructing applications. An internal IT justification would describe the potential for cost and time savings in development. The developers would only have to code a component, not insert new code within a complete application. IT would also see cost savings in testing, with the component being tested rather than the whole application being tested. Delta testing would be much faster than testing all aspects of an application. These cost-saving features, accompanied by an increase in application quality from reusing tried-and-tested components in an application, are the main technology features of SOA. Although this is a simplistic representation and does not discuss the effort needed to create a truly reusable component, it indicates the common arguments for developing a SOA-based approach to new projects, particularly in application maintenance or conversion. There may also be an enthusiasm for SOA within the IT staff, generated by SOA's place in emerging Web 2.0 technologies. As we have said before, new and leading edge technologies often excite technologists.

A justification for the implementation of SOA would have to be made in a business case. If this were an IT-focused business case, the current cost of application development, the technology implications of moving to a reusable code base, and the cost reduction and quality potential of service reuse should be emphasized. The reaction of the leadership team of the company to an IT feature–led business case would be muted at best.

Many IT projects have promised much and delivered little and there are still regular reports of project failures[9]. To overcome the stigma of failed projects, we should consider the way SOA would be justified using a business benefits approach. It is interesting that the criteria most frequently used to measure a project's success or failure are those of the IT justification: on time, on budget, functionally correct, etc. Business cases for an IT project seldom measure success on business metrics such as cost of business change or benefits realised.

A hypothetical case of an organization that has many legacy technologies can be used to illustrate the different approaches. These are frequently large departments established over a long time, such as the taxation department of your favorite country. This department may have applications written in an old established language like COBOL and may have been originally developed 20 or 30 years ago. The human resources that can understand and maintain these types of applications are rare and declining in number. There is a well-documented demographic time bomb ticking under legacy applications.[10]

Reducing the cost of maintenance and re-engineering the applications may seem like a valid proposal to a CIO. Reducing the reliance on declining resources and cost reductions could also seem an attractive prospect but brings nothing obvious to the business and may also contain an element of risk. Proposing the innovation as an IT cost- and resource-saving measure aligns the innovation with the IT requirements and may be difficult to justify.

---

[9] "Recession Causes Rising IT Project Failure Rates," CIO, June 2009, www.cio.com/article/495306/Recession_Causes_Rising_IT_Project_Failure_Rates, retrieved on May 2012.

[10] Joe McKendrick "Mainframe Skills Shortage Worsening" Insurance Networking News 2012 http://www.insurancenetworking.com/blogs/mainframe-skills-shortage-jobs-30039-1.html, retrieved on October 2012.

To help with the justification, it is wise to pick a rather obvious area that might benefit. Taxation applications are at the mercy of legislators, and they are sometimes difficult to implement because of changes to the law that require extensive changes to the application. Many taxation legislators demand the tax changes to be implemented as quickly as possible with no errors.

Typical large taxation application source code would need to be opened, the source code modified, and then the whole application retested. Developers familiar with the applications would take time to locate the areas for code changes, make the changes, and rebuild the application. Developers less familiar would take even more time. Once the application had been built, it would need to be tested as a whole. Once the whole application had been tested and any problems found and fixed, which would involve retesting of the whole application, it would be ready for deployment.

As we have said, starting a proposal with the technical and resource reasons for application decomposition would place this business case squarely in the IT domain. Instead, start the discussion with business managers with these questions: "What if we can show you how you can respond to legislation changes in hours and days rather than weeks and months? Would that be interesting to you?" Most revenue department business managers would reply, "Yes, how could you do that?" From there you can describe briefly the tools that you would use to achieve the business solution. In this way, you concentrate on the solution and its benefits rather than the tools. Implementing application decomposition using a SOA approach and the features to be implemented are the concern of the IT department, not the business management. The business department is interested only in the benefits described and the delivery date that will enable them to be more agile in responding to business and legislative requirements.

The confidence in business case justification of innovations in business benefit terms would rise with continued success. To ensure that the focus of a business case is in the business benefit area and not the IT tools, CIOs need to use a repeatable process that focuses on the business innovation rather than the IT implementation. This is often not the case in business cases developed by the IT department, where the emphasis is on the IT changes and assumes that business managers will be able to understand the effect the IT changes will have on business environments.

Is This Invention or Incremental Innovation?

The differences between invention and innovation have been discussed in earlier chapters. IT is capable of generating business innovations, but is IT capable of delivering business invention or creation? This question can best be answered by considering the source of ideas for an invention or an innovation. Many CIOs have demonstrated an entrepreneurial spirit, but are they capable of creating or inventing a whole new business?

Innovative ideas tend to come from some stimulus leading to a new idea that builds on other innovations. It may be an *incremental change* in IT that opens up new possibilities. Organizations such as Amazon and Google are using existing infrastructure and spare capacity to start a new business. The innovation comes in the form of a new line of business using incremental change by putting existing IT metrics and spare capacity to use. Inventions are seen as much more "blue sky" thinking.

Innovation, creativity, and invention are often considered almost interchangeable terms, and we often hear people discussing inventors and innovators as special people who have a moment of enlightenment. As we have said earlier, anyone in business can be innovative to some degree. Many tools and techniques can be taught to develop innovative behavior. There are even university degrees in innovation and creativity.[11]

One technique that is often used to stimulate creativity and innovation is brainstorming. This has been discussed in Chapter 2 in a secion on Fortunate Innovation. We extend that discussion to include critical brainstorming. Quite often these are fun exercises, where people gather in a room to discuss a topic and are told it is a brainstorming session. Most people follow some general rules for running brainstorming sessions, such as the following:

- No idea is wrong; all ideas need to be recorded.
- Anyone can put any idea into the mix.
- There is *no discussion* of any idea until the exercise is completed.
- The exercise of idea-gathering should be nonjudgmental.

There are more formal rules used by consultancies, but these general points are understood by most people involved. Before instituting brainstorming

---

[11] City University, London, www.city.ac.uk/courses/postgraduate/innovation-creativity-and-leadership, retrieved on May 2012.

sessions, there are some points to consider from work done by Charlan Nemeth.[12] Nemeth created two groups that were given general brainstorming rules. One group was given the additional rule to debate ideas as they occurred. The other group just had brainstorming rules similar to those we just listed. The findings of the study were that the group that had discussion of ideas, and even criticism in their rule set, produced more creative ideas than the group without discussion in their rules. This should be implemented with caution, to avoid a tendency to move from a critical review of an idea into a Downer Dog Pile as we mentioned in Chapter 2. CIOs should consider extending innovation brainstorming with discussion of ideas as a means to improving the yield of relevant ideas generated.

Generating innovation in the IT department is not too difficult if you consider the amount of new and emerging technology that is often discussed, but the innovative urge may be driven into unproductive areas. CIOs and their staff need to spend time discussing the business with people outside the IT department if they are to generate business innovation. An understanding of the problems and challenges faced by the business people can help direct innovation outside of IT. An understanding of the markets that the business operates in and the corporate strategy will also help direct thought toward business strategies.

CIOs also should not be seduced by stories of innovative companies like Google allowing employees to spend 20% of their time thinking about innovative opportunities and new technologies. Just giving people time to be innovative does not generate innovation. The corporate culture has to change before this strategy would yield the level of innovation that would deliver a return on the investment in time. For example, CIOs could start in small ways by suggesting conferences or workshops for staff to attend. This is often a good motivator and has the added advantage that the attendees get some downtime for thinking outside their normal work environment.

The main point is that you and your employees need to speak to a wider variety of people inside and outside the company, read from an eclectic reading list, or just socialize with others. These have the potential to produce a "liquid network of ideas," a term coined by Steven Johnson in his book *Where Good Ideas Come From.*[13] A liquid network combines the connectivity of a dense network and the plasticity of a liquid. Each new idea changes the shape of the network, while maintaining the density of the network. This takes advantage of people and ideas that come together and interact. Johnson

---

[12] Charlan Nemeth et al, "The Liberating Role of Conflict in Group Creativity: A Study in Two Countries," *European Journal of Social Psychology* 34 (2004): 365-374.

[13] Steven Johnson, *Where Good Ideas Come From* (New York: Penguin, 2011).

theorizes that often an innovation comes from a few people having part of a good idea, but until they come together in a network there is little value in these half-baked ideas.

Becoming an innovative CIO means getting out of your office. Ideas don't come sleeting in through the window or leaping from the page. I am suggesting that CIOs add interaction with others to the strategy for exploring ideas. The real innovations tend to come when you leave your department and your comfort zone to communicate your ideas. It is important to listen to other ideas and consider a combination of ideas to mold them into game-changing innovation for the organization. Incremental innovation can yield real competitive advantage to an organization, but a game-changing idea can revolutionize an organization.

Business Innovation Requires an Understanding of the Corporate Strategy

To step outside the IT comfort zone, one of the first things to do is become acquainted with the overall corporate strategy. We are not implying that you have not read or understood the corporate strategy. We are saying that you need to understand it in more detail than a paper or a presentation will tell you.

Your first task is to discover the corporate strategy. There is an assumption that there is one, but if you are not sure, now is a good time to ask the question and show that you are more interested in the company than bits and bytes. Other questions then should follow. If there is a strategy, have the company leaders reviewed it recently? Have they looked at new directions and growth? Is there something in the strategy that generates an idea? These are the questions to ask of the strategy team to determine where IT can fit into the strategy more seamlessly. As we have noted earlier, CIOs are often given challenges to deliver IT support for business process changes when a strategic decision has been made. It would be smarter to anticipate the challenges by participating in some or all of the strategic decision-making.

Once you are familiar with the corporate strategy, now is the time to look at how it is produced. Is this something that happens in meetings that you are not invited to? Figure 4-1 showed that this is likely. Also take notice of the people attending these meetings: are there any you can talk to informally? Does the CEO encourage free discussion, or is the CEO an autocrat? This is not a treatise on climbing the corporate ladder or how to play office politics, but it is important that the CIO be aware of the business direction and can review this to find new business opportunities.

To find these opportunities, first establish how the corporate strategy process works. Sometimes this may come as a shock. Many years ago, I was summoned to a corporate strategy meeting for a company that is no longer in business. You will not be surprised that it failed when I tell you that the venue for the corporate strategy discussion was the bar of Rigby's Pub. The strategy outlined was as outrageous as the location of the discussion, and I formed the conclusion that I needed to leave the company.

Most strategic discussions start with gathering information—creating a knowledge base for discussion. The focal point for the IT department and the CIO is to represent the technology landscape in that knowledge base. There are many ways of accomplishing this task. One of the most common is to adapt the innovation funnel to look at technological innovation. Figure 4-2 is a rudimentary representation of a funnel for technologies based on the general acceptance of this metaphor. The funnel shape is used to indicate a refinement of understanding of technologies and the selection of relevant technologies as their potential becomes better known. The advantage of this type of graphic is that it is easily understood.

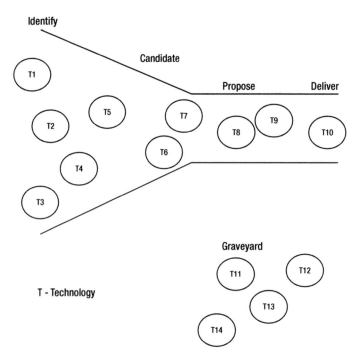

Figure 4-2. This figure is an example of an innovation funnel showing the graveyard and progress of ideas.

In this figure, technology innovations are represented by T1, T2, etc., and they are identified and included in the "identify" part of the funnel. This part is where all the technologies that may have potential for the company are first recorded. More information is gathered for technologies in the "identify" stage, which will allow an evaluation of the technology potential and the relationship of that technology to a desired innovation. After passing the evaluation, the technologies may be moved to the "candidate" stage, where more intensive investigation will take place. It is at this stage where any prototyping may take place. The next stage in Figure 4-2 is the "propose" stage. At this point, the technology is seen as sufficiently mature and understood well enough to be considered for development and subsequent delivery to the business.

Many entries are moved from the funnel section to the "graveyard" once they have been evaluated. The "graveyard" items are in the limbo of ideas that may need to be referred to but that have no place in the active part of the company's innovation funnel. It is where you keep track of technology and business innovations that are not moving on to the next stage within the funnel. Its main function is to be a repository of knowledge about what technologies have been rejected. The funnel concept works because it visually demonstrates the focus on smaller numbers of relevant ideas to reach those that are critical to the organization. Many organizations use the innovation funnel as a tool for communicating only the technology landscape; however, it is possible to use this for innovations in general. In the case of general innovations, you need to decide on the mix of technology and business.

As you can see from this figure, all of the ideas are considered as technology-based ideas. Would these be interesting in a business context? Perhaps the "techno-babble" will just reinforce the notion that IT and the CIO have nothing to say that is business-related. To modify this view, it is important to include business context to each of the technologies. For example, you could classify each entry according to the potential benefit to the company, the time frame in which it will impact the company, and the line of business it may affect.

When reviewing the corporate strategy, there are a few pointers to indicate how IT can relate to the corporate strategy. For example, a corporate strategy that focuses on growth by increasing your organization's market share or entering new markets can indicate opportunities for new technology that will support growth. This can be a fruitful area for innovation.

A corporate strategy of maintaining the value of your organization in a stable market would have a different effect on technology. A value-based strategy would require a continued focus on technology costs. In these circumstances, a CIO can develop a strategy that evaluates innovative ways of cutting costs.

Any organization that intends growth or stability will keep a close eye on costs, but in a growth strategy, cost management has to be allied to investment in growth. In this circumstance, an IT strategy that focused on agility and speed of delivery would gain more credibility than a cost-cutting argument.

CIOs Need to Understand the Context in Which the Company Works

Developing a business strategy cannot be done in a vacuum. To paraphrase John Donne, "no company is an island." There may be, for instance, a good idea for the next product or initiative that will generate corporate growth. In many companies, evaluating the good idea by looking at the market, your product's place in the market, and the expected impact on the market would be considered enough. In some businesses, this statement may be true, but the increasing globalization of business demands a broader view of the influences that can affect your market. One thing is certain—markets today have increased potential to broaden out from their physical location to a national or international market. The effect of the Internet on markets has been massive. Few organizations with a public interface ignore the Internet. While this has an expansive effect on your potential market, it also brings national and international influences to bear. These influences may generate revenue and profit, or they may depress the potential advantage of your innovations.

A good example of the influence of market conditions can be found in the competitive world of greetings cards production. Supermarkets and other volume outlets expect major discounts without compromising quality. The production costs in Europe are comparatively high, leaving only a small margin. We know of an executive involved in this market and who decided to move production from Europe to China, and this move gave a significant cost advantage for production. The use of the Internet to communicate designs and orders facilitated the move. The context that was used was the comparative production costs across the world. A continual review of the global context of card production resulted in production being switched from southern China to northern China to counter increasing costs in southern China. This executive even has a plan to move production to another country if the cost base increases in China. This example makes a good case for having a worldview of business strategy.

Many factors should be considered when building an understanding of the context for decision-making:

- World political situation

- Economic pressures
- Disruptive technology
- Security
- Physical constraints
- The ability of staff to deliver
- The availability of staff to deliver
- Business transformation

While this is not an exhaustive list, these are most of the factors that organizations consider when making decisions in a global marketplace.

As a CIO, your role may be to implement the business strategy, but implementation cannot be done without understanding the context within which you make the implementation decisions. Consider this example: I was a part of the creation of a backup data center for a Middle Eastern organization. I discussed the resilience and recovery strategy with the stakeholders and they were clear that they needed a backup strategy, including a new data center for a hot fail-over to fulfill their business requirements.

The location was the problem. We discussed other major centers in the country. Anything smaller than a city would not have the power generation capacity to cope. One city looked perfect in our view until we discussed this with the mayor of the city. He was delighted that we would place the facility in his town but asked if we were aware of the city's problems with earthquakes—the city was on an earthquake fault and had frequent tremors. This information changed the cost and risk profile of the project to unacceptable levels. We finished the project by locating the data center in Dubai, thousands of miles away. The context of the location had not been considered originally during the business justification. Therefore, the costs in the business case were understated because the original planners had considered requirements without understanding the wider context.

It may not be possible to accurately predict chaotic events that would alter the context of an innovative decision, but there is a need to consider all the predictable possibilities that may have an influence on decisions and minimize the risk.

New Market Opportunities

Once you have considered how to innovate, immersed yourself in the corporate strategy, and considered the context for your decision-making, the next step is to look into new markets. How you identify and exploit new markets is a constant requirement for an innovative CIO.

Some help may come from your study of the corporate strategy. The strategy may identify adjacent markets to your own. Amazon's expansion into music and DVDs was able to exploit those markets because they were adjacent and very similar to the book market. The book market has a similar low-cost/high-volume product structure as in the entertainment space and needs only a few changes in the sales techniques to open up a new area. It is worth considering adjacent markets whatever line of business you are in. If you are in a metal pressing company, is it such a big leap from servicing the building industry with door hinges to servicing luggage makers with suitcase hinges? Market adjacency may be one of the easiest innovations to implement. Consider if there is new technology that can help you exploit that adjacency.

New technology, tools, and techniques may also enable you to enter a market that had been previously closed to you due to the lack of technology at an earlier time. The world of soccer may not seem to be a natural market for high technology solutions—except in the commoditized markets of exercise machines, health care systems, and administration systems. The proliferation of data from exercise machines and health monitoring meant that the fitness of soccer players was frequently measured with a few parameters that gave a "good enough" indication of their aerobic fitness. If that measure of fitness is allied to the ability of an experienced coach, a more comprehensive view of the players' health can be gained. Despite large amounts of data being available, it was difficult to analyze and draw conclusions until the advent of commercial implementations of artificial intelligence (AI) analysis and machine learning tools. Once these tools had been used in commercial grade applications, a new application of AI and predictive analytics opened up for soccer clubs and their suppliers.

New markets may also be found in new geographic or demographic areas. As the emerging economies develop, they represent new markets for goods and services. They also represent a challenge due to their different cultures and societies. The competitive world of fast food illustrates how these challenges can result in winners and losers. In China, Kentucky Fried Chicken (KFC) has approximately three times as many stores as McDonald's. This is despite McDonald's dominance of the US market.[14] One of the main reasons for KFC's dominance is that KFC has adapted its menu far more to the Chinese market than McDonald's. KFC China is a Chinese organization, as opposed to

---

[14] Kim Peterson, "Why the Chinese Love KFC," MSN Money, February 2011, http://money.msn.com/top-stocks/post.aspx?post=ac5d659b-e9c3-4c48-af96-dbb228c62039, retrieved on May 2012.

McDonald's in China, which is an American organization that is operating in China. To take advantage of new markets geographically, you will have to consider cultural differences and localization. This may mean acquiring new skills and techniques. In the case of KFC, they made changes to product, marketing, sales, and management strategies. However, you need to be sure that you can make money entering a new geography before considering if the required changes are needed.

Demographic opportunities are also an interesting challenge for CIOs. My daughter cringes when I use (she says misuse) teenage terms to sound "cool." Often the only people who can successfully enter and exploit a teenage market are young people who understand teen groupthink. This should not prevent you from engaging with a younger, more tech-savvy audience for your projects, but you may have to make some changes to your methods of delivery of products and your interface.

A good example is the rise of the smartphone. Go into any phone sales outlet and you will have considerable difficulty in finding an old-style feature phone— almost all the offerings are smartphones. Without going into the complex techno-social reasons for this, you can see that smartphones are treated differently from mobile phones by their users. These users spend more time accessing data and information than they do talking on the phone. In the US, smartphone growth among the young is in the high double digits and less so in the middle-aged range. The youth market is a great market to tap if you can, but your strategy has to be focused on the interface, applications, and services that you can offer this group, not just on putting up an HTML5 interface and saying "my stuff runs in a smartphone browser." Young smartphone users are discerning and want intuitive specialized interfaces.

To fully exploit this new market, you may even have to invest in some new skills and thinking. Gamification, discussed more fully in Chapter 6, is one of the techniques for modifying products and interfaces for the smartphone.[15] Gamification turns simple applications such as to-do lists into an adventure quest, with game-like interfaces and paradigms. While this may not appeal to late adopters and curmudgeons, it resonates with the younger demographic who are welded to their smartphones and may constitute a new market opportunity for the organization.

---

[15] Natasha Singer, "You've Won a Badge (and Now We Know All About You)," *New York Times*, February 2012, www.nytimes.com/2012/02/05/business/employers-and-brands-use-gaming-to-gauge-engagement.html, retrieved on May 2012.

Out-of-the-Box Thinking on Existing Markets

Now that you have done some work understanding strategy, context, and looking at adjacent new markets, it's time to think outside the box. Ask yourself, "What assets and skills do you have as an organization that can lead to new markets and new businesses?" A classic out-of-the-box new business was the entry of Amazon into the cloud services market. As we have already mentioned, Amazon started slowly in the online book retail trade, expanding into the music and DVD business. Amazon's entry into Kindle eBooks was an adjacent market that depended on new technology—eInk—that was not available earlier. In this instance, Amazon was not really thinking outside the box. It was a bold decision that created a new market and engendered some rivals, but it was a technology extension of existing business—books online rather than on paper.

Amazon's use of spare IT capacity to create an entry into cloud computing services has gained them entry to a domain that originally dominated by technology companies and was a far more out-of-the box direction. Google, EMC, Microsoft, etc. were the leading technology companies that provide cloud computing services. Companies who already have a large technology base dominate this market. This market now includes Amazon. They converted that existing stake in technology to launch their business into a new business opportunity: selling and developing solutions for technologists. Amazon sold books and other retail goods, not technological services. Their entry into a completely divergent business area was something that could not have been predicted. Amazon's presence disrupted the market and caused some concern among the "traditional" cloud computing vendors. While the internal decision process and idea creation is not known, it can be surmised that Amazon's spare capacity was needed to handle peak demand and forced them to look at initiatives such as virtualization to maximize the use of their expensive technology. From there, it was a short step to considering their internal solution as a cloud computing solution. The real out-of-the-box thinking was to externalize their technology by making their internal virtualization solution into a product that can be used by people outside Amazon.

How can this lateral thinking be applied to your organization? You should consider what assets you use as part of the existing business. Is there an area of expertise that you could market differently? Even if you are CIO of a manufacturing company, you may be an expert in customer services and customer interaction. These are skills that you may be able to sell to other organizations who have a requirement for your expertise. Warehousing companies may have expertise in supply chain management and RFID management.

Can this be applied to another market? Do supermarket chains keep track of their staff locations? If there is a spillage in one area of the store, the best person to start the cleanup may be closer than the janitor. Where is the logic of contacting a cleaning employee in the rear of the store when another employee is nearer and can ensure that customers are not in danger of slipping or tracking the spillage? Is supply chain location management something that you can introduce to increase customer satisfaction?

RFID tagging and expertise in managing goods in transit may be transferrable to tagging employee badges. Add the RFID tag to a pager and cell phone and you not only know where that employee's device is in the store, but you can contact them. Does your organization operate in a market that has a bad customer relationship profile? Are there skills in your internal IT customer management that can be transferred to your company's customer base? An increase in customer satisfaction ratings may increase marketing and sales for the company as a whole.

These are examples of questions that can stimulate incremental innovation and adjacent market thinking and might even generate the next big corporate innovation.

Creating IT-Aware Business Leaders

So far in this chapter, we have been discussing how IT leaders can use the corporate strategy as a way of understanding the relationship between business and IT. We have also encouraged you to develop an understanding of the potential for business-led innovation in existing and new markets. In our opinion, there is a need for CIOs to develop a "business brain" if they do not have one at the moment. It is equally important for all IT leaders to develop their ability to educate business leaders on the potential for IT to enable business innovation.

Tools like the innovation funnel can present technology innovations in a business context and are easily understood by business leaders. Communication between the IT leadership and the business leadership is discussed in more depth in later chapters. Communication of innovation has a dual purpose. The first purpose is to help other members of the company to understand the work that is being done in the IT department to build business innovations. The second purpose is to increase the business organization's understanding of the potential of IT to deliver business innovation. We are not advocating formal education or training, but guidance for business leaders on technologies, their values, and their potential for innovation. You could find yourself developing a free flow of information and discussion between IT and the business, leading to a much stronger innovative culture in the future.

IT Innovating IT Is Not Business Innovation

You have made the decision to become an innovative CIO, and now you are considering your options. It does not matter if that decision is forced on you, or if you are taking this step yourself. Your first consideration is the type of innovation you will foster. Let's revisit the two studies that we considered at the outset of this chapter.

Chris Curran tells us that 75% of CIOs consider only internal IT innovation.[16] This myopia comes from the pressure in the business to keep the lights on and keep the costs down. As we agreed earlier, this might have an effect on the bottom line by keeping costs low and improving margins, but this is not the main contribution IT can make to the growth and success of the business. Gaining flexibility and time-to-market by swapping existing technology for new technology may be important to the IT department, but it is never going to create the next million dollar line of business. Keeping the lights on and cutting costs may build your reputation as a great IT guy, but where does that lead you? If you want to grow as a member of the executive team or move into another senior role in the organization, you will need to do more.

The CA Technologies survey of CIOs had two purposes.[17] Very often people make assumptions without testing them by asking questions. One assumption is that a CIO who reports to the CEO will be senior enough to be involved in all aspects of the business, including the corporate strategy. The survey results showed this to be a false assumption.

The second purpose was to ascertain the views of CIOs around the world regarding a career move from IT to becoming the CEO. The survey indicated that many CIOs had the necessary skills to make the switch to CEO, but that the opportunity was not always there. Not all CIOs are seen as business people with an IT specialty, which is indicated by the relatively small number—16%—who are involved in forming the business strategy.

One hypothesis the survey tested was that changes in the role of the CIO were accelerated by cloud computing. The hypothesis further assumed that

---

[16] Chris Curran, www.ciodashboard.com/leadership/business-innovation-or-it-innovation.

[17] "The Future Role of the CIO," www.ca.com/us/collateral/white-papers/na/The-Future-Role-of-the-CIO-Becoming-the-Boss.aspx.

the focus of cloud computing on business rather than on technology may encourage more CIOs to regard themselves as suitable for the top roles.

The survey answers were used to develop a white paper outlining the potential of CIOs to become CEOs. The most significant conclusion is that many CIOs lack the opportunity to externalize their skills to customers and partners. It may be that the skills and qualities of the CIO are not being communicated to the senior leaders in the company. This is a double problem. Poor communication may result in the CIO being excluded from customer and partner interaction. It may also indicate that the senior leaders in the organization do not believe that the CIO has anything to offer in the corporate strategy discussions.

To overcome these negative attitudes, CIOs must take stock of the corporate strategy and ensure that the IT strategy is in step with and supports the corporate strategy. In addition, innovative CIOs must identify and bring forward opportunities that may not be seen by less technology-based leaders in the company. These opportunities can be incremental or game-changing, depending on their scope. Discovering these opportunities is difficult and sitting in the IT department and talking "geek" will not accomplish this goal. The innovative CIO is looking outside the IT department, examining the market that the company exists in. We are not advising that you neglect the IT market, but try and match the events and new technology in the IT market with events and changes in the corporate market. This approach, along with an understanding of the context of world and market events, will enable CIOs to pan for the gold of business innovation.

IT innovation of IT is not something that will make your name as an innovative CIO. IT innovation of the business will lead to business growth and profitability. The innovative CIO has the potential to transform IT from a stable fulfilling a demand to produce a faster horse to an organization that builds the best sports car.

5

Pull and Push

The Sources of Technology Innovation

Bringing together business and IT to create and deliver technology innovation should be a combined effort. No one area of the business should have supremacy, but rather all areas of business—including IT—should work together to stimulate growth and competitive advantage through new innovation.

Central to this approach is the notion that *anyone* can be the key to great innovation, especially when it comes to groundbreaking new ideas (as opposed to incremental innovation). After all, if a lowly patent clerk like Albert Einstein can end up generating some of the most innovative and impactful new ideas in the history of science, then there is no reason why IT leadership, or even business leaders for that matter, should be the sole holders of the keys to innovation.

Nevertheless, it is still important that the innovative CIO—as the informed technology leader and expert advisor—comes forward to *enable* the entire business to innovate, while also stepping up to the challenge to *drive* the IT department to innovate directly.

This means working with business leaders (and their teams) to unleash their capacity for innovation, helping them come up with new ideas that they can ask IT to deliver: the "business pull" of new technology. It also means that IT should come up with new ideas and propose them to the business: the "IT push" of new technology. Just as we have shown in Chapter 3, IT push of technology can surely deliver business impact, but innovation is a two-sided coin, and both sides are heads—much like the pushmi-pullyu!

So while IT leaders and their staff cannot (and should not) be the sole drivers of technology innovation, it is likely they are the most connected and informed about the potential for business innovation driven by technology. This puts the innovative CIO in a unique position to assist and drive both the business pull and the IT push of new technology opportunity.

This chapter will explore how the innovative CIO can contribute in both of these approaches to innovation—the business pull and the IT push—while working with counterparts in other business units, including marketing, finance, sales, product development, human resources, legal, and others.

The Business "Pull"

For some IT leaders, the effect of the business pull of technology innovation is not just painfully obvious, but also obviously painful. This new era of business-adopted technology and innovation has been a wake-up call, especially for IT organizations that have grown up through an old school era when they "owned" the technology budgets and decisions.

Increasingly we are seeing the business units as key technology adopters, especially driven by demand for consumer-oriented technologies (e.g., social media, smartphones, cloud, tablets). Indeed, in many companies non-IT employees are adopting these technologies faster than IT staff can respond. These IT consumers learn about new technologies in their personal life, not from IT. Then they bring these devices to the workplace, regardless of whether IT supports their choices or not.

The inability of IT to keep up is proven in reports on technology budgets. Since the global economic downturn of 2008, IT leaders are reporting that traditional IT budgets are remaining flat and forcing a cost-conscious approach to IT spending. However, overall technology spending is actually increasing, and quite significantly.

For example, in a recent survey of CIOs, research firm IDC found that the majority were expecting their budgets to decrease or remain flat in 2012 compared with their budgets from 2011.[1] Yet IDC was still predicting that worldwide IT spending in 2012 would increase by 6% over 2011 spending in constant currency.[2] This is almost twice the 3% global GDP growth predicted by Goldman Sachs for 2012,[3] and more than double the World Bank prediction of 2.5% for the same period.[4]

---

[1] IDC, *The CIO Agenda for 2012 and Beyond: A Look at CIO Sentiment and Priorities*, Document No. 233098, February 2012.

[2] IDC, *Worldwide Black Book Query Tool, Version 2, 2012*, Document No. 236347, August 2012.

[3] Jan Hatzius, "Outlook 2012," Goldman Sachs, December 2011, www.goldmansachs.com/our-thinking/global-economic-outlook/outlook-2012/index.html, retrieved on May 2012.

[4] Andrew Burns, Theo Janse van Rensburg, *Global Economic Prospects, Volume 4: Uncertainties and Vulnerabilities*, The International Bank for Reconstruction and Development/The World Bank, January 2012, http://siteresources.worldbank.org/

The clear implication then is that business units outside of IT are directing a larger percentage of technology spending for the company, leaving IT leaders with a smaller and smaller share of the pie. And indeed, CMOs are recruiting external agencies for digital marketing, marketing automation, social media programs, and more. CFOs are using cloud services for accounting, finance, and ERP. Sales leads are buying tablets to enable their sales teams to be mobile, agile, and connected, and they are using cloud-based CRM and SFA systems to support them anywhere in the world.

The rapid rise in this business pull of innovation has also significantly affected the ability of IT to support innovation. With little extra in the way of budgets or personnel to match the increase in technology adoption, not only is IT unable to react fast enough to deliver the technology innovation the business demands, it cannot even adapt fast enough to support the technologies that the business is already adopting for itself.

As business units and business owners run increasingly faster in their adoption of new consumer-driven technologies, IT struggles to keep up with even the most basic level of support—connecting to the network, assisting with security and privacy, or enabling e-mail connectivity.

As a result, when it comes to the business pull of technology, the entrenched approach to IT appears to be holding business back from innovation. We need to turn that equation on its head, and get IT back to a trusted position of helping the business to drive and adopt technology, rather than fighting against it. This means IT departments need to move away from the old school approaches that are holding them back.

Overcome the "Old School" Approach

IT departments have put in place many traditional approaches to empower the business "pull" of technology innovation. Unfortunately, they often have the opposite effect.

For example, one attempt by IT to enable business pull is the traditional service desk or request management system, an online system where business users can request new product upgrades, application developments, new device purchases, and other technologies. This is often integrated with a defined catalog of available (approved) technology services. IT staff monitor, prioritize, forward, and/or respond to each request as best they can (typically with a number of restrictive policies).

INTPROSPECTS/Resources/334934-1322593305595/8287139-1326374900917/GEP_ January_2012a_FullReport_FINAL.pdf, retrieved on May 2012.

These service desk and service catalog systems can be very positive engines for soliciting innovation—especially when coupled with other enabling capabilities such as ideation tools, agile development planning, and automated cloud service deployment. However, many catalog-based systems are used to impose a restrictive or exclusive approach, which turns them into gating mechanisms instead.

The first gate or barrier is often technical—a lack of data fields in the ticketing or catalog system to accommodate new technologies. With most of these systems, IT enters the range of "allowed" or "approved" services. Business users can only select from these approved services when they require new technology.

Such systems also can be slow to progress through the multistage approval, acquisition, and provisioning workflows. Worse still, users may discover that they cannot even order an item they want only after they have already completed most or all of a lengthy workflow.

This exclusive catalog approach also suggests IT has de facto control over technology adoption, exercised as control over the "approved" technology catalog. Catalogs can also solidify or atrophy over time as no one bothers to remove or update out-of-date entries. Obsolete or unavailable technology remains available to order, duplicates proliferate, and newer entries pile up.

This approach is not business-focused, it is not service-centric, and it inevitably reinforces the perception of IT as the "Department of No."

In some ways it is also inherently anti-innovation. A restrictive request/catalog system by definition only offers services and technologies that already exist and have already been tested and approved by IT. The result of such a restrictive approach to service request systems is that they are simply barriers when business users want new, innovative technologies.

No wonder business units go around IT to sign up for cloud storage, buy a new tablet or smartphone, or even adopt a new Point-of-Sale (POS) system! When the new generation of consumer-styled tablet devices first started appearing, one large US healthcare organization's service request system was set up to allow users to only order existing devices (various desktops, laptops, and smartphones). No options were available for ordering tablets. IT did not see these as business devices, so they were never added to the service catalog.

This exclusionary approach stifled business users' requests for these innovative new tablets, and all the new opportunities they would enable. So doctors, nurses, administrators, and executives went around IT and bought tablets anyway (and connected them to the corporate network), with no standards, policies, or security rules.

The problem is not necessarily inherent in the systems themselves. Rather, it is typically in the processes that business and IT are tied to in using such systems. A good service request system, tied with appropriate process and other supporting technology, can actively serve business innovation by linking in capabilities for new technology adoption with "known-good" services.

Another standard approach that can slow innovation is for business and IT to conduct annual strategy meetings together, to set technology decisions and budgets for the year (or more) ahead.

This approach can have value for innovation if this annual process acts not only to establish long-term strategy, but also to establish ongoing review. Reviewing progress annually—or more—can give organizations early warning when technologies show a faster uptake than predicted. Of course, the further out you predict the less accurate you will be, but more frequent reviews will enable more confidence in the long-term strategy.

However, this approach is typically at odds with the sometimes explosive nature of innovation. While there is definitely a need to consider and deliver long-term planning, with technology moving so quickly this approach is no longer adequate to encourage rapid innovation.

For example, just days after Apple released the first iPad, adoption exploded. According to Apple's own reports

- By May 3, 2010, just 28 days after its introduction, the company sold its millionth iPad.[5]

- By the end of that first quarter, it had sold 3.2 million units in total. In the second quarter, it sold an additional 4.1 million units.

- In just one year following the initial release, Apple had sold almost 20 million iPads (see Figure 5-1).

- By the time Apple released the third generation of this device, it would sell over three million units within the space of just three days.[6]

---

[5] "Apple Sells One Million iPads," Apple Inc. Press Release, May 2010, www.apple.com/pr/library/2010/05/03Apple-Sells-One-Million-iPads.html, retrieved on May 2012.

[6] "New iPad Tops Three Million," Apple Inc. Press Release, March 2012, www.apple.com/pr/library/2012/03/19New-iPad-Tops-Three-Million.html, retrieved on May 2012.

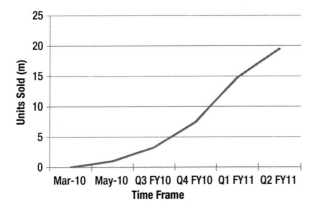

Figure 5-1. This figure shows the iPad unit sales in the first four quarters after its release.[7]

An annual planning meeting held in February 2010 would have failed to accommodate this phenomenon. A rigid annual business plan would have been unable to leverage the opportunities for innovation that such a revolution made available. New engagement apps, greater workforce mobility, new consumer interactions, and more would simply go begging.

Similarly, the adoption rate of the social network Twitter was both exceptional and rapid, especially between 2009 and 2010, when it grew from 2.5 million tweets per day to 35 million tweets per day—a one-year growth of 1,400% (see Figure 5-2).

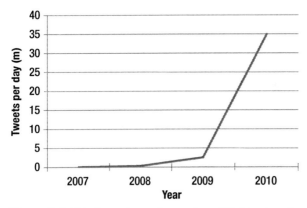

Figure 5-2. This figure shows the number of Twitter tweets per day from 2007–2010.[8]

---

[7] "Apple Inc. Unaudited Summary Data," http://images.apple.com/pr/pdf/q310data_sum.pdf, http://images.apple.com/pr/pdf/q410data_sum.pdf, http://images.apple.com/pr/pdf/q111data_sum.pdf, http://images.apple.com/pr/pdf/q211data_sum.pdf, Apple Inc., retrieved on May 2012.

[8] "Measuring Tweets," http://blog.twitter.com/2010/02/measuring-tweets.html, Twitter, retrieved on May 2012.

A tech strategy set annually would not be agile enough to react to the opportunity this growth presented—to connect with customers, influencers, and others in a completely new medium with a fundamentally different personal attachment, and to leverage that for a new and innovative inbound marketing strategy.

With such a rapid rise in new technology adoption, even a biannual approach to technology evaluation and strategy planning is well behind the innovation timeline, leaving you scrambling to catch up at the next planning session, or struggling to adapt to dramatic interstitial strategic changes.

Not only this, but with an annual planning approach, when you factor in the time between strategy plans *and* the time it will take to execute on each new technology strategy, you will unavoidably be anywhere from a year to 18 months or more behind your more agile competitors.

Clearly, such old school approaches are no longer sufficient to enable the business pull of new technology innovation. Start by knowing your own house. Conduct an audit of existing "enablement" systems and processes, and see if they really are helping or hurting your innovation efforts.

Adopting a "New School" Approach

The new school CIO takes a much different approach to enabling other business areas to "pull" innovation from technology. Such new approaches are more consultative, more cooperative, more timely, and more aligned both to real-time business needs and to real-time technology innovations. These new approaches also equalize the power to say "no" to new ideas—and the power to say "yes."

So, how does the business know which services to pull? How do business leaders find out about the new technologies that might be available to them?

To promote business pull of technology, one key starting point is the democratization of knowledge. Former US Secretary of Defense Donald Rumsfeld put it this way in a now-famous 2002 news briefing:[9]

> There are known knowns; there are things we know we know. We also know there are known unknowns; that is to say we know there are some things we do not know. But there are also unknown unknowns—the ones we don't know we don't know.

---

[9] Donald Rumsfeld, "DoD News Briefing - Secretary Rumsfeld and Gen. Myers," US Department of Defense, February 2002, www.defense.gov/Transcripts/Transcript. aspx?TranscriptID=2636, retrieved on May 2012.

These "unknown unknowns" especially apply to the business pull of innovation too. Business leaders are limited in their ability to apply new technologies to business innovation by the limits of what they know about the technologies available. They can only innovate within the set of "known knowns"—those technologies that they already understand.

For them there is a world of "unknown unknowns"—that vast set of new technologies they have never even heard of, and which they would not even know well enough to ask about. Such business leaders simply cannot pull technology innovation into their business needs when they do not have the knowledge of what is possible.

This is where technology leaders such as the innovative CIO need to be more proactive. By breaking down the barriers to knowledge of new technology opportunities, the innovative CIO not only can *allow* but also positively *encourage* business leaders to innovate with technology themselves. You can help teach business leaders about technology, expose them to new opportunities, and be their trusted advisor.

For example, periodically brief your peers in the business—from the C-level down—on new and upcoming technologies to help them form a starting point for potential innovation opportunities. Initiate regular innovation or technology workshops with your business peers. Look at implementing the innovation funnel (see Chapter 4) as one of the ways of articulating technology potential on a regular basis, talking with business leaders about the status of entries in the funnel.

This approach also addresses those CEOs who are inveterate headline readers, and who, left to their own devices, are prone to "management by magazine." They see a headline about a new technology, or some new capability in which a competitor has invested, and start asking what their company is doing to catch up. This is exacerbated when there is little communication between them and the CIO.

Encourage your team to also take up this commitment to regular communications with their business peers. Remember that great new ideas can come from anywhere, not just from senior managers.

Acting as a trusted advisor to the rest of the C-team, the innovative CIO can provide technology awareness. And by extension, the entire IT department can help to nurture technology adoption by the whole organization.

You and your team are ideally positioned to work actively with business peers to explain to them the latest ideas, the newest technologies, upcoming capabilities, and potential opportunities—all with the purpose of enabling them to see and understand for themselves how these technologies can drive business innovation. Do not just teach, lecture, and inform—workshop together with your peers and their reports to drive innovation as a team.

Consider holding such workshops on both a regular and ad hoc basis. You can certainly plan such sessions ahead of time to cover relatively slow-burning technology changes, such as virtualization or cloud computing. But for explosive opportunities like the newest device release or the latest social networking development, a rapid response and immediate briefing may be a better and timelier way to keep your business peers informed.

Incorporate formal knowledge management (KM) systems to make the sharing of knowledge institutional, rather than a gating function in itself. You can buy extensive KM systems off the shelf, but they do not need to be overly complex or expensive. Start with something very simple, even just a shared notebook on a shared drive or a common folder for filing documents and pages on new technologies.

For just a little more complexity, you can have a much better system. Install a common innovation wiki, using one of many different open source wikis, allowing both IT and business users to collaborate on sharing knowledge about new technologies, what they could be used for, and which part of the business could benefit.

Extend a basic wiki with a collaboration service, or include other tools to foster innovation such as project management, content management, instant messaging, or resource management. You may evolve this service to a sophisticated system that connects and aligns business with IT through real-time business-connected ideation; knowledge; portfolio; project; and service management systems that include all of these capabilities and more.

This new approach to a democratization of information will help you to establish knowledge sharing about new technologies and new opportunities as a corporate-wide value, not just an individual value.

Beyond this democratization of knowledge, IT must also *act* as part of the business, to be *considered* as part of the business.

For example, as the technology leader and trusted advisor to the business, you need to actively consider the business interest of new technology innovations and whether IT should "own" these, or whether IT can better enable business users to own the technology themselves. The old school approach, of course, was that IT owned (and therefore controlled) all the new technology. The new world of consumerization now enables business users to directly select and deploy technology themselves, both from internal and external sources.

For example, business users can go out and buy their own tablets and start using them for work right away. Perhaps more impactfully, they can also "pull" innovation directly from third-party cloud service providers, such as sales managers signing up their teams to use online CRM and SFA systems, marketing managers signing up their teams to use web-based marketing services, or finance managers deciding to migrate the company accounts to a pay-by-use financial management service.

In an old school approach, the CIO may have taken steps, even draconian ones, to retake control of technology adoption and stamp out this "rogue IT" that threatens the standardized process. In the new school approach, this is entirely unacceptable.

To achieve the status as trusted advisor, the innovative CIO must take a more balanced and business-centric approach. In some cases, this will mean doing more than merely tacitly condoning such rogue IT, but explicitly supporting it, and even actively encouraging it. Active interest in integrating and supporting new technologies, such as consumer devices, will also generate goodwill and add to the likelihood that you will be seen as a trusted advisor.

This is not to say that rogue IT does not create problems, especially with security, privacy, cost, and efficiency. However, it is the role of the new school CIO to focus on and resolve those problems, rather than stamp out these rogue practices entirely. For example, try encouraging business users toward one cloud service over another to stabilize budgets or leverage purchasing power, or implement tools or processes that prevent unauthorized data use and/or leakage when using cloud services or consumer devices. The key is to figure out what business users are doing, why they are doing it, and how you can help, rather than simply reacting and shutting it down.

The innovative CIO therefore must also be intimately aware of and driven toward real business goals. The whole business (IT included) must work together to take advantage of new technologies in a way that makes sense in context of the overall business goals. IT must also learn about the business goals—what really matters, where the priorities are, and where the problems are.

A key skill for innovative CIOs is the ability to listen with open ears as advocated by former Amgen CEO Kevin Sharer and IBM CEO Sam Palmisano. This means to listen solely to comprehend and to understand what your business peers are trying to achieve—without trying to critique or object or convince them of anything.[10] This is part of the required organizational change

---

[10] "Why I'm a Listener: Amgen CEO Kevin Sharer," *McKinsey Quarterly*, April 2012, www.mckinseyquarterly.com/Governance/Leadership/Why_Im_a_listener_Amgen_CEO_Kevin_Sharer_2956, retrieved on May 2012.

to foster innovation—in the structure, culture, skill sets, and more—and no doubt requires a new level of technology education, training, mentoring, and knowledge sharing throughout the organization.

Another way to engage the business pull of technology innovation is suggested by Monte Ford, former CIO of American Airlines, in Chapter 3 of our stablemate publication, *CIOs at Work* by Ed Yourdon (Apress, 2011). Ford discussed how American Airlines required employees to work in the IT department for a few months so that they understood the technology and issues and processes in order to better use that technology. This level of commitment may be unrealistic for your organization, but the core idea makes a lot of sense.

Exposing your counterparts in other business units to new technologies through closer technology education will help the whole organization to understand and use technology better. IT can be an ideal partner to help the organization understand what is possible and what is not, to improve their processes at all levels, and use this understanding to drive innovation through business pull.

Going one step further, IT can also actively offer the rest of the business technology options that it *can* pull, and promoting these to other business units. To assist in this mission, a well-designed and maintained service catalog is key—an online catalog of "known good" technology services that business users can order for themselves, supported by processes flexible enough to accommodate "unknown good" innovations.

A service catalog can offer a wide range of out-of-the-box services, such as Linux-Apache-MySQL-PHP/Perl/Python (LAMP) stacks for developers, Computer Aided Design (CAD) software for engineers, fully configured client images, collaboration services, cloud service leases (public or private), and even physical device orders (tablets, smartphones, office equipment, etc.). It can also include automation to deliver the services, to accelerate workflows for process and approvals, and include chargeback mechanisms for accounting. And it can have flexible workflows that can accommodate exceptions and alternatives to satisfy even unexpected requests.

As mentioned earlier, using service catalogs to restrict technology adoption *can* inhibit innovation. However, when they are used to deliver a *baseline* of accessible technologies, innovation will be stimulated. This is especially true if the catalogs are kept up-to-date and if users can easily request additions to the standardized services, even if on a trial basis."

In other chapters we will explore additional ways to improve business pull for technology innovation, such as the following:

- Using new agile development techniques to improve response to service requests. (Chapter 6).

- Helping to *adopt* existing new technologies and practices such as Near Field Communications, big data, etc. (Chapter 6).

- Helping to *adapt* to existing consumer technologies such as social and mobile (Chapter 7).

- Fostering other capabilities to enable intentional business-driven innovation (Chapter 9).

The IT "Push"

Of course, technology innovation is not all about the business pull. The notion that "we have to put the business people through IT so they can understand it" is good, with some success, but it only addresses one side of the business-IT equation. It is also fraught with risk to innovation as a whole, and to the technology leadership specifically, because it implies that IT people are relegated to a supporting role—unable to innovate directly and only there to serve the business innovators. Rather than address the problem of business-IT alignment, a "business pull" approach applied in isolation actually exacerbates the problem that has caused the rift between technology and business leaders and stifled innovation.

Certainly, it is important to encourage business people to take advantage of technology and work with them to actualize their ideas. But it is not enough to be an order-taker to the business, to merely ask them as customers what they want from technology. As the great innovator Henry Ford reputedly said after creating the model T and revolutionizing manufacturing *and* transportation, "If I'd asked my customers what they wanted, they'd have said a faster horse."

The other side of the innovation equation is to encourage passionate and innovative technologists to help drive the business, and enable these technologists to understand the business strategy, goals, and requirements. This approach will give them the knowledge and tools they need to work with business leaders on their terms, and will allow them to form a vision for what technology can do to advance the business.

This ability for IT to proactively push ideas out to the business can be a very powerful approach, as it encourages informed technology people to generate new technology innovation, but within the critical context of business outcomes.

Such an approach empowers IT leaders as trusted advisors to the business, bringing as deep an understanding of technology to the business as sales leaders bring regarding markets and customers, or as finance leaders bring regarding accounting, taxation, and investment strategies.

As a technology leader, you should absolutely look to deliver on your responsibility to "push" innovation into the business, through centralized technology evaluation, adoption, and distribution, just as other business leaders "push" new ideas and innovations in their own areas of specialization. Rather than wait for orders, choose to be proactive in experimenting with and learning about new technology so that you can offer it to your business peers to drive innovation.

That is what many great IT leaders have been doing for some time, and so have successful business people. Frequently they are one and the same. Amazon founder and CEO Jeff Bezos is reportedly a very hands-on business leader who pays enormous attention to the technology that his business is built on. Similarly, the co-founder and CEO of Kiva, Matt Flannery, is a very technology-oriented business leader, who started this innovative non-profit while working as a programmer for another innovator, TiVo.[11] We are constantly meeting with innovative CIOs who work in collaboration with their C-level peers to introduce new technology ideas and brainstorm about how they can help deliver business goals.

The innovative CIO has a new role to play, guiding an IT department that is an equal with "the business"—that is in theory and reality a full-fledged part of "the business." Technology leaders can and should be real partners in formulating business strategy and driving business success. They should be just as important as other areas of "the business" such as sales, marketing, production, finance, human resources, or operations.

Unfortunately, many business leaders are not thinking the same way. In fact, only 14% of executives see IT as a leading instigator of innovation; almost one-fifth see IT as the single greatest roadblock to innovation; but almost one-third see IT as no more than an enabler of innovation.[12] They are still seeing the "old school" of IT—where the CIO (or more likely a VP of IT, rather than a full C-level peer) can make suggestions and enable business, but ultimately ends up just taking orders. A subservient CIO who acts as a butler to the business is not enough to bring IT into the new millennium, where numerous third-party technology options are also available to order.

[11] The Kiva Team, Kiva, 2012, www.kiva.org/about/team, retrieved on October 2012.
[12] CA Technologies, *Why IT needs to lead now: the innovation imperative*, September 2012, http://www.ca.com/us/collateral/white-papers/na/Why-It-Needs-To-Lead-Now-The-Innovation-Imperative.aspx, retrieved on September 2012.

After all, if IT leaders never step outside their own domain to talk with their business peers, to learn more about the business, and to communicate new technology capabilities (and limitations), then the business is going to find their own technology solutions—and not always the best ones.

The same principle works the other way around. If the only reason that the business communicates with IT is to ask what it means when the printer says "PC LOAD LETTER," then IT will never learn how to help the business with its strategic goals, using the right new technologies.

Helping the business to pull innovation is important, but it is not the only approach. IT can clearly make a significant difference by innovating directly and by leading innovation, rather than just showing business leaders how technology works and then sitting back in the hope they take up the responsibility for innovation.

For example, a large telecommunication provider was about to release a new version of a wildly popular service. Business leaders were expecting activations to triple for this new service—a far larger uptake than their systems could actually handle. The business asked IT to spend millions on new hardware to accommodate this massive load. The technology leaders, however, decided to use the following new technologies instead:

- With modeling and simulation software, they determined the actual capacity requirements for best, worst, and likely case scenarios, instead of just guessing.

- With virtualization tools, they consolidated existing workloads to free up additional capacity internally.

- Alongside business owners, they evaluated and redefined the existing service portfolio to reduce capacity allocated to non-core applications (or eliminate them entirely).

- By utilizing cloud services, they were able to accommodate peak loads and any overrun not handled by the existing systems.

As a result, the company had an incredibly successful product launch and not only avoided massive spending on new hardware and facilities, but actually saved costs on existing capacity while maintaining a differentiated customer service across their product portfolio.

In another organization, a communications service provider CIO was talking with the head of his company's sales team about how his salespeople had to endure a very lengthy sales cycle. This was negatively affecting business results—reducing productivity, extending time to cash, reducing customer satisfaction, and reducing their ability to compete with established providers.

At this company, sales reps needed to consult with new customers several times to present their service offerings, explain different packages and bundles, assure service availability in their area and their office, and create and communicate pricing and contractual details before they could sign a contract. Even then, provisioning was slow too because sales needed to take their signed orders and input them into the provisioning systems. The sales cycle therefore ran over several months, not only because of this level of involvement, but also because the sales reps needed to negotiate multiple meetings with senior customer representatives—always a difficult and protracted activity—simply to collect and convey all this information.

With an understanding of the business needs, and a deep involvement in new technologies, the CIO set his team to develop a mobile app for the sales force to address the problem. This new tablet app included these features:

- The latest brochure and sales information (maintained in a central repository to ensure currency) for the meeting introduction

- Real-time, geo-specific service availability information (using tablet GPS and a Google Maps mashup) to ensure the service can be delivered

- Contract generation using a cloud-based CRM application with pre-approved terms and conditions to provide proposals instantly

- Electronic contract execution with an e-signature that allows the sales rep and customer to electronically sign a contract on the spot

- Integration with central fulfillment systems so that the signed contract triggers immediate service provisioning

As a result, sales staff could maximize the value of those precious customer meetings by ensuring their salespeople could prove value quickly, while recognizing the value of their customers' time. The more they could do in a single meeting, the better for both the salesperson and the customer.

Sometimes the best innovation comes from simply unleashing the tools, techniques, and possibilities on your business peers in sales, marketing, operations, finance, and other business units, thereby giving them every opportunity to shine.

However, sometimes the best innovation actually comes from technology (or other discipline-specific) experts applying their own unique thinking, based on their deep and career-long learning. It is therefore important for the innovative CIO to look at both sides of the innovation equation:

- To "pull" innovation from business leaders by educating and enabling them, providing a sounding board, an active partner, and an implementation resource.

- To "push" innovation by contributing new ideas based on a unique understanding of technology, as a trusted advisor to, and as part of, the strategic leadership.

The Third Way

It is clearly important to "pull" innovative technology ideas from the business and to "push" innovation from the technology perspective too.

However, we would encourage a third approach that is neither solely pull nor push, but rather both working together.

Combining the deep investment in business goals and the strategy needed to get there with the expertise of a technologist and practitioner, an innovative and assertive CIO can truly earn the right to sit with the rest of the C-team and make business decisions together—including ones regarding technology innovation. In an ideal world, this results in an organization where IT has educated the business on technology opportunities, the business has educated IT on the business goals and drivers, and both connect to drive innovation together.

Of course, this change may require new organizational constructs, such as forming cross-functional teams or working groups with people from different backgrounds, bringing their experience together. It may also require you to embrace rogue teams in your organization in pursuit of opportunity, and perhaps intentionally create them (even as a spinoff). These issues will be discussed later in Chapter 9.

It also requires you, as a technology leader, to get outside your domain once in a while and learn about outside topics. Study up on green energy or astrophysics; read new books or online articles about core business rather than just IT; spend a couple of hours every week talking with non-IT teams. This combined approach requires the innovative CIO to gain a new and informed perspective on the business, and on technology, and to recognize new opportunities of how to combine the two.

However, taking on a more educated and involved business focus does not mean always delivering exactly what the business wants. That is not the point of a collaboration at all. As a shaggy philosopher once observed, "You can't always get what you want." While being a service-focused CIO that is eager to deliver business requirements can be a strength, it can also become a weakness. As a technology leader *and* a trusted advisor, you will often need to look deeper than the request. Rather than look to deliver the request, you may instead need to look past the request *per se*, to figure out how to solve the problem, rather than just fill the order.

If the business is asking for tools, you need to investigate the need and figure out how to say "yes." Of course, you do not want to say "no" straightaway, but consider not saying "yes" immediately either, at least until you understand what they are trying to achieve. Rather than enabling them to solve their need their way, engage in a conversation with your business peers to find out what they are trying to accomplish, and look for the best way to solve their problem. Due to politics, organization structures, and even strategic focus, not every CIO can have such a conversation. Moreover, maintaining positive and persuasive input to these sourcing decisions will need constant reinforcement. It goes beyond merely having a business relationship manager—it needs a constant commitment to the business, from the CIO down.

For example, the business may ask to use social networks from their work computers, or to connect their tablet computers to the internal network and applications like e-mail. Business users may (or may not) have many valid reasons for these requests, especially considering the rapid consumerization of IT (which we will discuss in Chapter 7). Yet without engaging the business, it is easy for IT to see iPads as a gaming platform rather than a business tool or Twitter or Facebook as a place to chat about last night's escapades with friends and families, rather than a customer support tool. Inadvertently, IT can stifle the business by refusing these requests without really understanding them (as explained by "Chief and Chuck" in Figure 5-3).

Figure 5-3. Chief and Chuck explore consumer-driven IT.[13]

IT should instead try to understand better the business needs that are driving the demands for new technologies. IT may see business users buying unauthorized devices; signing up for rogue cloud services; or wasting bandwidth on social media. Meanwhile, the business simply needs to deliver corporate content in real time in a casual setting; issue electronic contracts and accept electronic payments from on the road; or chat online with customers about new products and services and to resolve customer service issues.

Understanding these underlying business needs can give you insightful new ideas about how to solve business problems, sometimes how the business wanted but other times in completely different ways. For example, many organizations block Internet chat applications like Skype to prevent external chat sessions from leaking information against regulations or even laws. If the

---

[13] CA Technologies' CHIEF & CHUCK is licensed under a Creative Commons Attribution-NoDerivs 3.0 Unported License. Based on a 2012 work at www.ca.com/cdit by Dave Blazek, retrieved August 2012.

business wants to get an exception pushed through the firewall to allow Skype use internally, perhaps a similar internal application would solve the problem without opening up compliance issues. Maybe certain tablet applications pose legitimate compliance risks but instead of rejecting the entire tablet, you can just block those applications—as IBM did with Apple's iPhone helper app, Siri.[14]

With this approach, you do need to be careful to hold back on the technology details, lest you fall back into being a technology component provider rather than a business service broker, or a parts machine for the business innovators rather than a trusted technology advisor. IT all too often will talk to the business about IT capabilities, not business solutions—explaining how the watch works, rather than just telling the time.

When IT leaders talk technology in too much depth, this effectively "trains" users to ask for clock parts, rather than asking for the time. They end up coming to you for servers, not services. In the process, they commoditize what you do, and draw far less value than you can provide.

This is especially true when the business does not really know what IT can do. Indeed, business leaders may have a set (and profoundly misinformed) idea of what IT can and cannot do, so they may go ahead and source solutions themselves (i.e., cloud SaaS). They may think that this allows them to save money and get better service, but if they do not really know what capability IT already has, they cannot be sure of either. In fact, they are more likely than not to drastically underestimate what IT can do.

However, if you look to provide solutions to the problem, rather than technology widgets and gizmos that someone can use to solve the problem, then the business is more likely to come to you for advice, and for service.

This third way puts to bed the notion of "business-IT alignment." Indeed, the notions of IT pull vs. business push are really just a symptom of a lack of alignment. If both IT and business work together to drive and enable innovation, then the alignment is not only obvious, but becomes second nature.

Ultimately, pull and push should bring IT and business together, rather than allowing them to run separately. The combination of these two forces creates a shared experience that can make magic happen. It is not IT vs. business anymore, but rather the whole becomes more than the sum of its parts—the classic M&A objective where 1+1 = 3.

---

[14] Chloe Albanesius, "IBM Blocks Employee Access to Apple's Siri," *PC Magazine*, May 2012, www.pcmag.com/article2/0,2817,2404786,00.asp, retrieved on May 2012.

6

Opportunities to Innovate Today

We have mentioned before that you do not need to invent new technology to innovate in your organization, industry, market, or geography. Innovators do not have to be inventors.

You may find many opportunities to innovate today by putting existing technology to use in new ways, whether universally new (something no one else is doing at all) or just new to you (something your organization has not done before). This approach to innovation can even be better, faster, and cheaper than new inventions, as you reduce the costs of R&D, failure, and invention while still providing new opportunities for your business.

Finding these existing sources of innovation is not difficult. Scour the Web for ideas, check out what your competitors and partners are doing, discover what technologies you already have that others are exploiting in new and different ways, or ask your users and customers what experiences they have found and valued elsewhere. Perhaps more importantly, determine what your competitors and partners are *not* doing and what experiences your customers and users are *not* finding.

An innovative CIO can help their business to drive value from any number of existing technologies. Our experience with innovative IT organizations shows they are exploiting a range of current and emerging technologies today, to drive business innovation. Technologies like virtualization, automation, cloud computing, and data analytics are continually at the top of CIO priorities; while emerging areas like near field communications, personalization, the Internet of things, and gamification are just starting to revolutionize the business of technology. In the rest of this chapter, we will explore these technologies, explain how they are being used by innovative businesses today, and show how they can help you drive innovation for your business too.

Virtualization

Perhaps the most apparent application of old technology to new innovative use cases is virtualization. After all, virtualization is not new but harkens back to the mainframes of the 1960s. However, that does not mean virtualization cannot be innovative. With new use cases and technologies for x86 servers, storage networks, desktops, and applications, virtualization has gained new life for the modern CIO as an enabler of innovation.

Multiple definitions of virtualization can be found, but we like the definition first published in 2006 by one of our authors, which subsequently has been reused and republished very broadly:

> *Virtualization is . . . a technique for hiding the physical characteristics of computing resources from the way in which other systems, applications, or end users interact with those resources.*
>
> *This includes making a single physical resource (such as a server, an operating system, an application, or storage device) appear to function as multiple logical resources; or it can include making multiple physical resources (such as storage devices or servers) appear as a single logical resource.*[1]

However, agreeing on the definition is of secondary importance. The key is what virtualization can do for you, primarily by enabling fast, efficient, and detached use of compute resources to deliver business outcomes.

The most obvious outcome is consolidation—of servers, storage, data centers, and so on. Without doubt, consolidation is an attractive use case which deliver measurably significant benefits in hardware efficiency, but it is not highly innovative. Similarly, virtualization can help to reduce costs, by requiring fewer servers and administrators as well as less power and floor space. This is also very positive for the day-to-day operational and budgetary impact of IT, but again not highly innovative.

However, when virtualization is fully exploited as an enabler of automated, dynamic computing, the benefits shift from simple workload efficiency to business innovation.

---

[1] Andi Mann, *Virtualization 101: Technologies, Benefits, and Challenges* (Enterprise Management Associates, August 2006).

The innovational opportunity of virtualization is better understood when viewing the evolution of virtualization maturity from consolidation to the "cloud-like" state of dynamic IT, as seen in Figure 6-1.

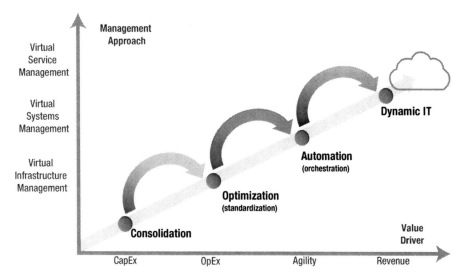

Figure 6-1. The virtualization maturity curve has four phases: consolidation, optimization, automation, and dynamic IT.

Across the four phases of virtualization maturity—consolidation, optimization, automation, and dynamic IT—the derived value of virtualization increases significantly and moves from IT-centric to business-centric.

In early stages, the value of virtualization accrues mainly inside the data center. Consolidation results in fewer servers and facilities, reducing hardware, software, power, and lease costs. Optimization brings incremental improvements to IT administrator efficiency by helping to lower resource costs. However, in both phases all the business sees is a lower number on the annual budget.

As virtualization matures, it starts to deliver higher values that accrue to the business. Automation of compute resources delivers greater agility so that IT can respond faster to business demands. The business then starts to see more rapid time-to-market for new products and services.

Then dynamic computing raises the value again, as IT can support rapid and innovative approaches to opening new markets, leveraging new alliances, and adding new sales channels. The business then starts to see IT helping to deliver new revenue streams.

In addition, some of virtualization's biggest contributions to innovation are not from consolidation and optimization, but from the rapid mobility of workloads and the acceleration of dev/test cycle times, allowing for rapid deployment of new business-focused capabilities with lower costs and minimal user disruption. Moreover, as virtualization reduces the time and money devoted to keeping the lights on, you can spend that time and money on innovating and driving business value instead.

You are almost definitely using virtualization in some way already, probably with server virtualization at least (some studies show over 90% adoption for this technology). To drive additional innovation, find ways to move up the maturity curve. Freeing up resources by gaining efficiency is good, but moving up the value chain—from cutting data center costs to delivering new business revenue—is far better.

Even if you have a fully matured server virtualization deployment, challenge yourself to leverage other virtualization technologies that you have not fully exploited, such as virtual desktops, application streaming, storage and networking virtualization, and grid or cluster technologies. Each brings unique opportunities to redefine how you view location, resources, ownership, scalability, mobility, and more. Go beyond simply freeing up your server farms and saving IT time and resources. Instead, focus on what you could do if you freed up end users from their physical locations with desktop virtualization, from their physical devices with application virtualization, or even from their applications with user virtualization.

Virtualization means you can abstract these services from how they are delivered and used. By contrast with physical infrastructures, virtualization means you are no longer locked into a platform, architecture, location, or even a specific application in order to deliver a business service.

When fully exploited to support innovation, virtualization unlocks the power of mobile and agile individuals to rapidly iterate new ideas and apply them everywhere on demand.

Cloud Computing

Virtualization naturally leads us to cloud computing. While the two concepts are not identical, they may leverage each other, and virtualization definitely provides an evolutionary path to cloud computing.

While many people may (legitimately) see cloud as any Internet-connected service, there is some consensus around this NIST definition of cloud computing:

A model for enabling ubiquitous, convenient, on-demand network access to a shared pool of configurable computing resources (e.g., networks, servers, storage, applications, and services) that can be rapidly provisioned and released with minimal management effort or service provider interaction.[2]

The NIST definition goes on to define five essential characteristics:

- On-demand self-service
- Broad network access
- Resource pooling
- Rapid elasticity
- Measured service

. . . three service models:

- Infrastructure as a Service (IaaS)
- Platform as a Service (PaaS)
- Software as a Service (SaaS)

. . . and four deployment models:

- Private cloud
- Community cloud
- Public cloud
- Hybrid cloud

That said, there is no need to be dogmatic—sometimes "almost cloud" is good enough. The key is to take the essential characteristics of cloud and apply some or all of them to your business-focused technology initiatives.

When looking to drive innovation from cloud computing, it is important to understand the different levels of "cloud conversation." For most traditional

---

[2] Peter Mell and Timothy Grance, *The NIST Definition of Cloud Computing: Recommendations of the National Institute of Standards and Technologies* (National Institute of Standards and Technologies, US Department of Commerce, September 2011), http://csrc.nist.gov/publications/nistpubs/800-145/SP800-145.pdf, retrieved on March 2012.

IT leaders, the conversation is mostly about "feeds and speeds," focused on how to shave marginal costs (much like the early opportunities in virtualization).

However, as with virtualization, there is a breakpoint between internally focused IT benefits and externally focused business benefits. Reducing administrator ratios with cloud servers is important to the CIO—moving costs from CapEx to OpEx by leasing cloud infrastructure is important to the CFO. However, aspects of cloud like faster product delivery, global mobility, access to new customers, and instant response to market changes is important to the business as a whole. Virtualization can also free up time and resources to devote to other in-house innovation in order to drive competitive differentiation.

Unfortunately not every IT leader can or will have this top-line discussion. Most traditional IT leaders are focused on the bottom-line cost benefit. But to be a truly innovative CIO, you must focus on cloud computing as an enabler for other business-focused initiatives, rather than as an efficient end in itself.

Examples of successful cloud computing initiatives are everywhere. Several years ago, software and services provider CA Technologies implemented a new "Labs on Demand" capability to provide internal developers a private cloud to self-provision server platforms in order to create and test code for new products and releases. With automated server provisioning, system builds, and reservation processing, CA Technologies saved more than 33 years of developer time in FY10, which amounted to approximately $4 million worth of savings through improved productivity. The company also estimated a further $12 million of savings over the course of just 2 years solely from real estate reduction of lab/data center space.[3]

Cost savings were not the only—or even primary—benefit. Among the most important outcomes was the ability to get new product releases out the door faster and with higher quality, because this new cloud approach allowed much faster and more thorough development, testing, and quality assurance. The financial benefits were important, but cloud also set the stage for more critical business improvements.

The simplest way to adopt cloud computing is by using public SaaS for nondifferentiating services, such as backup and recovery, customer relationship management (CRM), sales force automation (SFA), collaboration, ac-

---

[3] CA Technologies, "CA Saves $16 Million and More Than 25 Years of Developers' Time by Automating Provisioning for Labs on Demand Service," 2010, www.ca.com/~/media/Files/SuccessStories/ca-lod-tb-110510-wm_232246.pdf, retrieved on March 2012.

counting, or web marketing. Any service that does not make you a better business is a signal opportunity to leverage cloud.

Consider adding or replacing services that your business needs but you do not or cannot do as well, as quickly, or as efficiently as an "on-demand" service provider. Be honest with yourself and your teams, thoroughly examine your service portfolio, and identify ways to take on cloud.

It is easy to cherry-pick this low-hanging fruit; it is harder to evaluate your entire portfolio for what should go to the cloud. Organizational tools and techniques such as portfolio management software or other published evaluation models (as shown in Figures 6-2 and 6-3) will help.

For example, in Figure 6-2, we can see a basic methodology for balancing the different capabilities and requirements of enterprise applications, taking into account the differences in differentiation and performance requirements, and mapping each candidate to specific types of cloud environments.

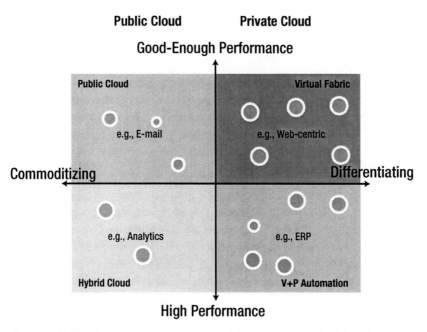

Figure 6-2. This figure depicts a generic portfolio evaluation methodology for cloud adoption with four types of environments.

In Figure 6-3, we can see a different methodology (taken from the popular handbook, *Visible Ops Private Cloud: From Virtualization to Private Cloud in 4 Practical Steps*) that is more prescriptive. This approach emphasizes balancing requirements like cost, agility, service quality, and environmental footprint to separate each different type of cloud or virtual environment, according to which has better relative characteristics for each workload.

	Physical	Virtual	Private Cloud	Public or Hybrid Cloud
Unit cost	$$$	$$	$	$ or $$
Agility	-	--	---	??
Service quality	*	**	***	??
Footprint	%	%%	%%%	%

Figure 6-3. The Visible Ops Private Cloud approach to portfolio evaluation stresses balancing requirements like unit cost, agility, service quality, and footprint.[4]

By using objective insight based on best practice tools and methodologies, most organizations will find opportunities to adopt better cloud options.

Another alternative is to use internal resource pools to deliver on-demand, scalable, elastic, and measured business services—also known as a "private cloud"—cheaper, faster, and better than available public offerings. Multiple studies by McKinsey, Forrester, 451 Group, and Gartner (to name a few) have found that over time the cost of a public cloud service often exceeds the cost for delivering the same service internally.

Start small to establish skills and encourage open minds with on-premise IaaS—a logical evolution of virtualization. Try to get to PaaS or SaaS quickly by standardizing and replicating "known good" platforms and services, packaging them into reusable "virtual services" and making them accessible on-demand. Again, start with low-hanging fruit before migrating mission-critical services, and make intentional decisions with an informed portfolio analysis.

While the benefits from these "cloud-migrant" services can be significant, cloud really comes into its own for new "cloud-native" services, where you can treat cloud as an opportunity to do new things in new ways.

Cloud enables you to develop and deliver new business capabilities that did not exist before—online services that are immensely scalable yet still inexpensive even at small scale, new social and mobile services available to any

---

[4] Andi Mann, Kurt Milne, and Jeanne Moraine, *Visible Ops Private Cloud: From Virtualization to Private Cloud in 4 Practical Steps* (IT Process Institute, 2010).

consumer anywhere, and instant access to global markets for suppliers and customers. You can also incorporate third-party cloud services into your business services, which is a gateway to even more significant innovation because it creates the ability for your business to do new things in new ways that it simply could not do before.

Most importantly, do not see cloud computing as an admission of failure. Business users often see cloud as the answer to IT leaders who cannot respond to business demand. However, an innovative CIO can use cloud proactively to respond positively to business demand. Leveraging available technologies to enable your business to try things it otherwise cannot—because of the cost, scale, time, or effort—is an opportunity, not a failure. By being critical and honest about where you should use cloud computing to replace or augment your internal technology services or to build and deliver new ones, you can be an authoritative technology expert and a trusted advisor to the business.

Personalization

Most online systems and services can use a number of indicators to identify unique individuals to varying degrees of certainty. These indicators include explicit usernames or login details, IP addresses or address ranges, cookies set by previous visits, cookies set by third parties (e.g., via ad placement), specific logins, traceable URLs and URL referrals, or GPS and other location data.

Even anonymous users can be identified easily enough. Research conducted by the Electronic Frontier Foundation has shown that up to 84% of browser configurations are "unique and identifiable," while browsers with Adobe Flash or Java plug-ins raised this percentage to 94% that are "unique and trackable."[5] In a TED speech in 2011, Eli Pariser (senior fellow at the Roosevelt Institute and author of the book *The Filter Bubble*) noted that Google looks at "57 signals . . . everything from what kind of computer you are on, what kind of browser you are using, to where you are located, that it uses to personally tailor your query results."[6]

With this capability comes the ability to provide a specific and personal service to each visitor. This can be as simple as welcoming web site visitors from Twitter or Facebook by suggesting they follow your corporate Twitter handle

[5] Electronic Frontier Foundation, "Web Browsers Leave 'Fingerprints' Behind As You Surf the Net," May 2010, www.eff.org/press/archives/2010/05/13, retrieved on March 2012.

[6] TED Conferences, "Eli Pariser: Beware Online 'Filter Bubbles'," 2011, www.ted.com/talks/lang/en/eli_pariser_beware_online_filter_bubbles.html, retrieved on March 2012.

or like your Facebook page. It can also be much more complex, such as recommending or even discounting specific items a visitor to your web store may have looked at previously but not purchased.

We see the effects of personalization in action every day. Google serves advertising tailored to each visitor's interests, based on login details or the 57 "signals" mentioned earlier. Amazon welcomes return visitors by name, recommending items based on previous purchases. News sites identify a visitor's location based on geo-IP location services to promote local news and advertise local services.

Personalization provides opportunities to drive business value with innovative improvements to your online services, such as the following:

- Provide special offers to promote higher spend, conversion, and attachment.

- Provide discounted registration fees to return visitors to capture loyalty.

- Customize content to increase appeal for different demographics.

- Emphasize specific links or actions that are relevant to each visitor.

- Display ads or articles with higher click-through rates for similar visitors.

- Change navigation options to promote certain actions for specific visitors.

- Promote specific partners to people in markets and geographies you do not operate.

- Promote a local store or branch based on geographic location.

- Correlate location with local demographic data to target promotions.

Be aware though that personalization also raises significant privacy and compliance issues. For example, some regulations prohibit the use of personal content information for anything other than the specific purpose it was provided. For example, you can send newsletters to customers by e-mail if they subscribed to it, but you cannot use their e-mail addresses for direct marketing. In some circumstances, it may even be illegal to use certain information (sex, race, religion, etc.) in a discriminatory way, even if it provides an arguably better service. Even absent regulation, be careful not to overreach into someone's personal information. Your personalized service may appear to be more "creepy" than "helpful"!

Automation

Automation is barely a new invention—to some degree it has been around since computing has been mainstream—but it can still help you innovate in your business. Being able to make simple tasks or complex processes happen independently of any human activity or intervention helps in numerous ways:

- Drives down the cost of IT by reducing the costs of labor, training, licenses, hardware, downtime, recovery, and more.

- Reduces human errors by ensuring "known good" processes are followed every time, even for the most complex activities.

- Improves security by creating functional isolation between IT staff and their activity.

- Improves audit control by tracking activity from end-to-end of any automated process.

- Accelerates service delivery by performing activity at computer speed, not human speed, and eliminating human stoppages.

- Improves service delivery by detecting, triaging, and fixing service problems and faults faster and more effectively.

- Attracts and retains quality staff by ensuring activities use valuable talents and skills, rather than being mundane and unsatisfying.

Automation also frees up the "innovation surplus," releasing time and resources for new development rather than wasting them on repeatable processes. It also allows fast, cost-effective dev/test cycles so developers can try new ideas, fail fast where they need to, and deploy good services to market faster.

Starting a new automation program is reasonably simple. Any repetitive task that your staff performs regularly is a strong candidate for automation. If your people are manually running batch jobs, managing backups, creating reports, e-mailing status updates, reviewing log files for exceptions, logging errors, performing data extract/transform/load operations, fixing recurring errors, allocating licenses, building servers (or virtual machines), installing software, onboarding and offboarding staff, reconciling data, or any number of other tasks—you could (or should) be automating.

Look at your staff's manual activities and figure out if they can be standardized and made repeatable. This is your starting point for automation. You may already have these manual activities and procedures documented in existing run books.

By automating just a single operational task, you can deliver measurable benefits. By stringing tasks together, you can automate entire processes. By stringing processes together and connecting software components, you can orchestrate entire services. And at every extension, you will exponentially expand the benefits of automation.

Despite the clear benefits, a new automation program is not necessarily without input costs. You may need to purchase additional software, pay for training, and engage some process re-engineering, for example. However, you can achieve some of these results even with built-in system tools, such as Windows Task Scheduler, UNIX/Linux "cron" jobs, or DOS "AT."

E-commerce

Electronic commerce a.k.a. e-commerce is again not new—organizations have long been using online web environments to drive and process commercial transactions. Nevertheless, from the billions in revenue for sites such as Amazon or eBay to the incremental revenues from online table bookings for a local restaurant, Internet-based transactions (or increasing existing capabilities) drive revenue, productivity, customer loyalty, cost reduction, staffing efficiency, market reach, and much more.

Setting up a web portal for customers to peruse your catalog and purchase goods and services is simple. Several software providers offer out-of-the-box e-commerce capabilities, including open source systems like Magento or PrestaShop or large enterprise software from powerhouses like Oracle, IBM, or SAP. You can even start immediately with small-scale trials leveraging existing third-party e-commerce sites like Amazon and eBay.

If you are already leveraging e-commerce, consider how you can extend the benefit beyond Internet sales. For example, you could use sales information to feed more granular and effective marketing or improve inventory and stock control. You could expand operations into new markets, new geographies, and new products, replacing or augmenting traditional storefront redesign, branch office expansion, and new product development.

Review your competitors' e-commerce activities and see what they are doing, how you can replicate, and even more how you can improve on their online experience. Research adjacent markets and see what e-commerce innovations they are trying and determine if you can benefit from similar approaches. Consider mainstream and edge cases—from your industry and others—to determine what is at the leading edge and what can help you drive new innovation from existing concepts. Whether simply starting to offer products and services through an eBay store or building your own portal, e-commerce offers a huge innovation opportunity.

Big Data and Analytics

The ability to take massive data sets—larger than traditional content and data management systems (e.g., databases) can manage—and analyze that data for patterns, correlations, and other useful insights is creating a sea change in how businesses use information technology.

For example, by analyzing and correlating records for stock control, inventory, purchasing, customer demographics, shelf space, aisle traffic, and staff levels, a retail organization could better understand inventory requirements to reduce stock-on-hand, rearrange products on shelves and in aisles to promote and sell more higher-margin items, and manage the location of adjacent goods to improve attachment rates.

Walmart is an impressive real-world example of turning big data and analytics into real business value. The retail giant's attention to detail of shelf and stockroom inventory, restocking times and processes, supplier transportation and logistics, and more "big data" have allowed it to squeeze immense value out of its supply chain and drive competitive advantage. Web sites like Google, Facebook, eBay, and Amazon also track hundreds of millions of data items every day—page clicks, product purchases (and rejections), search terms, books read, page times, bids made, and much more—in order to analyze behaviors and preferences and better target advertising and other sales and marketing activity.

Big data and analytics may be difficult to start immediately, as they do require specialized resources. From new equipment (especially high-volume, direct-access storage) to unique new skills (analytics engineers, statistical scientists), big data analysis is a new capability you may not be prepared for.

However, you can start relatively small and/or use data you already possess in new ways. Consider these examples:

- Connecting client data, demographics, transaction histories, problem histories, and other service and product information can provide insight into triggers and patterns for service requests or product purchases to inform sales, marketing, and service provisioning.

- Connecting inventory, production, facilities, staff levels, product movement, and energy costs can help determine better, faster, and cheaper ways of running a factory floor.

- Connecting information about patients, symptoms, equipment, consumables, and staffing can help bring down treatment costs, form better responses to particular conditions, or better predict, prepare for, manage, or eliminate infections, transmissions, and outbreaks.

- Collecting and analyzing social media and networking data like Twitter or Facebook comments and correlating with customer, product, and demographic information can encourage deeper understanding and better reactions to customer service issues, demand fluctuation, or competitive campaigns.

- Even inside the data center, analyzing and correlating data about service requests, provisioning requests, staffing levels, and response times can improve the speed, cost, and security of delivering IT services.

One word of warning: be careful about what you learn from this new aspect of data analytics. Any business from travel to retail to medical and more could potentially run into significant privacy issues once data is correlated and used for sales and marketing activity.

For example, retail giant Target analyzed purchase data and found a correlation between a certain combination of products and pregnant customers. This analysis allowed them to target direct mailings to customers whom the company believed were pregnant with relevant maternity products. However, Target did not anticipate that these mailers might reveal private personal information to others who had no previous knowledge of the pregnancy, such as cohabitants or, as happened in one case, to a teenage girl's father.[7]

Similar privacy issues may occur in many different industries. For example, a hotel chain, travel agency, credit card bureau, jeweler, etc. can probably de-

---

[7] Kashmir Hill, "How Target Figured Out a Teen Girl Was Pregnant Before Her Father Did," *Forbes*, February 2012, www.forbes.com/sites/kashmirhill/2012/02/16/how-target-figured-out-a-teen-girl-was-pregnant-before-her-father-did/, retrieved on March 2012.

termine through large data set analysis whether customers are cheating on their spouses. An insurance company, health care provider, or pharmacy can probably determine if someone has a specific condition based on an analysis of symptoms, visits, medications, demographics, etc. An e-commerce web site can potentially analyze purchase histories and reveal personal interests, hobbies, "surprise" gifts, and more. Big data analyses can expose customer secrets, and using that data can damage your brand, cost revenue, and even lead to fines and other punishments for privacy or discrimination breaches.

Remember that just because you *can* correlate large volumes of data to determine certain information, does not necessarily mean you *should* correlate that data or use the resultant information.

"The Internet of Things"

The "Internet of Things" is a phrase coined by Massachusetts Institute of Technology technologist Kevin Ashton in 1999 to talk about what would be possible if every and any device in the world was connected to the Internet.

In execution, this concept opens up a massive range of opportunities. Imagine what could be possible in your business if you could actively communicate with every patient monitor in a hospital, every heat exchanger in a factory, every Point of Sale (POS) terminal in a shopping mall, all via the Internet.

Many of the devices in your organization may be providing or generating useful data already—if only you could access it. Figuring out how to access that data via physical or wireless connection could create new insight into your business and enable a wealth of innovation.

For example, researchers at the US National Center for Atmospheric Research are experimenting with data from automobiles including onboard sensor and computer data (temperature, speed, RPM, distance, time, etc.), headlight state, windscreen wiper activation, and antilock brake engagement. This data allows them to infer real-time information about the environment, weather, road conditions, hazards, traffic levels, and more.[8]

Similarly, a national railroad operator connects sensors on its tracks, stations, crossings, switches, and gates over a private IP network. By analyzing data from these devices, the operator can optimize operations to increase the rate and speed of railway car movements. With such a complex network, where

---

[8] Laura Snider, "NCAR Scientists Work to Glean Weather Data from Cars: Project Aims to Make Roads Safer," Boulder Daily Camera, 2011, www.dailycamera.com/boulder-county-news/ci_19413818, retrieved on March 2012.

rolling stock is making money and anything sitting still is losing it, even a one-minute improvement can turn cost into profit.

Insurance companies use telemetry devices in your car to detect and attract good drivers and reduce their risk. Logistics companies use GPS and location data to improve their fleet and dispatch operations. Cell phone operators use tower locations to triangulate location even without GPS data.

Leveraging the "Internet of *Your* Things" may be easier than you think. Many items in your organization may already be connectable, such as physical access systems, environmental controls, inventory systems, sales terminals, in-vehicle GPS, cash drawers, factory equipment, patient monitors, staff IDs, and cell phones. Others may be relatively easy to connect to the Internet, even as simple as just adding a radio-frequency identification (RFID) tag.

Find those devices that can be Internet-enabled, understand what type of data those devices might be able to produce and communicate, and determine what could be inferred if you could correlate that data. Perhaps you can reduce the cost of transport, increase sales opportunities, reduce spare inventories, provide faster patient care, improve attach rates, or increase production speed.

Gamification

Broadly speaking, gamification is the application of gaming principles to stimulate competition and engagement in a way that drives business outcomes. The idea is to promote desired business interactions by making them fun and accessible by turning them into games and competitions.

The goal is to make interactions faster, more frequent, more "sticky," so you attract and retain more customers, increase satisfaction, create evangelists, promote purchases, and drive revenue. It helps customers (and staff) to enjoy doing business and even encourages them to promote you to their friends.

Gamification has been a staple in print and other traditional media for many years, with games like crosswords and "fill-in-the-blanks" competitions being used to attract newspaper readers since at least the 19th century. However, the current wave is very different, as technology now enables much different interactions that are instant, global, online, and social. For example, your customers can now play online games that lead directly to a purchase on your website, something that is impossible with an old-school mail-in requiring customers to "fill in the blanks" to enter a competition.

FourSquare is an incredibly popular modern example of innovating with gamification. By encouraging people to compete with each other for most visits to a location, this company offers customers prizes (even if they are just virtual pins, badges, points, or levels), discounts, special offers, and exclusive services and products. Becoming the "mayor" of a diner may give you a permanent 10% discount or a 2-for-1 bonus on meals, getting the first check-in at a new retailer may let you buy select merchandise, and a designated number of visits may qualify you for a loyalty club card with exclusive benefits.[9]

Similarly, Vail Resorts' "EpicMix" is providing customers with an engaging and competitive game where visitors compete with themselves and each other to earn badges (and bragging rights!) for more vertical feet, combinations of lifts, sequences of runs, multiple resort visits, and more. This implementation of gamification encourages customers to return more often, purchase more products and services, and tell their social networks about their great experiences at the Vail Resorts ski fields.[10]

You probably already have some gamification in your own business, perhaps in your own department. Competitions among staff for sales results, improvement suggestions, customer satisfaction, turnaround on complaints, finishing projects ahead of target, etc. are all types of gamification, whether based in technology or otherwise.

As a CIO, you can start by bringing a technology footing to those competitions to establish the capability, experience, and acceptance of a gamification approach to more activities, both internal and external. Track sales competitions online and globally by automating and connecting sales results with sales competitions on an intranet web site. Gamify your own innovation by mounting an online "suggestion board" and crowdsource the best ideas. Within IT, you can track support calls, closed tickets, customer satisfaction, and other metrics and offer prizes for higher achievements.

When it comes to gamification externally (with customers, partners, etc.), how you proceed will depend on your key goals. You may want to increase engagement, drive direct sales, improve customer satisfaction, drive competitive advantage, or turn customers into evangelists. Different goals will drive different approaches and different games.

Offer something of value for winning or even just playing. Even virtual prizes (online pins, badges, or points) can be successful in promoting your objectives. It can be surprising what people will say or do for you, even for an icon or sticker! Consider how participants track their progress, and perhaps compare their progress to others, whether in their own network or globally, to increase competition and engagement. Plan a full and ongoing experience

---

[9] For more information, see http://foursquare.com.

[10] For more information, see www.epicmix.com.

with clear objectives linked to specific goals for both competitors and your business. Include social components like the ability to brag on Facebook to help competitors promote the game and/or your brand to their networks. Add mobile support to connect with your gamers wherever they are, and use location and personal information to connect to local stores, branches, and locations.

Again, be mindful of privacy issues. Make sure to protect critical data and tightly control access especially to personally identifiable information.

Near Field Communications

Near Field Communications (NFC) refers to the ability of mobile devices to communicate with each other (and with static devices) simply by being near to them—typically no further than a few centimeters.

There are many different standards for NFC, but most applications utilize RFID standards. Bar codes, QR codes, Bluetooth, and even WiFi can provide similar capabilities, but unlike these technologies NFC does not need pairing or an explicit connection or scanning process—data exchange is initiated simply by proximity—and can involve a two-way data transfer. This makes NFC less complex to use, more interactive, and especially practical for casual use cases.

NFC enables an easy and automatic way to track movement of devices, inventory, people, and more. For example, you can track inventory through a production line, track shopping carts through a supermarket, or track the movement of corporate assets into and out of a secure building.

It also allows more complex two-way interactions, such as triggering a digital interactive display (e.g., on a billboard, tablet, kiosk), initiating a data exchange (e.g., swap contact information, copy a file, deliver a coupon), or establishing a secure connection (e.g., WiFi login or Bluetooth pairing).

Perhaps most interesting, NFC allows a smartphone to act as a so-called "digital wallet," making real-time payments at the POS as simple as waving the phone past a contactless reader. This new payment method has the potential to rival or even overtake credit cards for payment processing.

For example, the Museum of London uses NFC to deliver vouchers for their shop and cafés, information about exhibits, downloadable music, and offers to join the Museum's Friends program. For them, it provides additional "stickiness" to a customer visit and drives additional contact and revenue opportunities, while promoting repeat engagements.[11]

In Sydney, Australia, radio station Nova teamed with JCDecaux to use NFC for outdoor marketing, allowing casual consumers with NFC-capable devices to start listening to the station by touching their phones to advertisements mounted on bus stops, train stations, etc.[12]

Start adopting practices and processes to exploit NFC by initially leveraging existing RFID tags on plant, equipment, inventory, access cards, etc. Consider what (or who) moves within your organization that requires tracking. How can you track them, and what information will that give you? How could this knowledge and insight improve speed, efficiency, or security?

Also research how you might benefit from exchanging data with customers, whether casually in a neutral location (shopping mall, information kiosk, or billboard) or in a more controlled environment (POS, waiting room, or front desk). This exchange can include sending promotions to customers such as advertisements or coupons to providing static information such as brochures or web links.

Combined with other technologies such as mobile, social, gamification, or geolocation, you can connect your customers with each other to establish communities, run games, promote evangelists, and drive brand loyalty. You can also use NFC to establish secure connections with customers in order to transfer, update, or report customer or account information.

Implementing a mobile payment capability is another option, but be aware of how many of your customers have NFC-enabled devices. This may well be a gating factor for widespread digital wallet use cases in the short term.

NFC has numerous use cases with staff, suppliers, agents, and other business partners too. Unlike Business-to-Consumer (B2C) applications, you can know (and even control) which users have compatible devices. Use cases include, for example, checking suppliers' payment credentials before exchanging order details, checking customer details and exchanging product information with sales agents, connecting with inventory systems to access up-to-date stock reports, or exchanging client, production, system, or patient status updates during a roster handover.

---

[11] Museum of London, "NFC at the Museum of London," 2012, www.museumoflondon.org. uk/Explore-online/mobile-apps/NFC.htm, retrieved on March 2012.

[12] Chris Griffith, "Touch-Screen Bus-Stop Ads," The Australian, September 2011, www. dailytelegraph.com.au/touch-screen-ads-to-enliven-a-bus-stop-wait/story-fn6b3v4f-1226141410370, retrieved on March 2012.

NFC can also take the place of fobs and ID cards for security—both physical and network—and in many cases are compatible with existing systems.

One key limitation of NFC is the need to accommodate your user (and customer) base. While support is broad—including MasterCard, Visa, Sony, Microsoft, Nokia, Samsung, Intel, NTT Docomo, and Broadcom—NFC-capable smartphones are not common. You should also be aware of potential and perceived privacy issues. Smartphones are the repository of much personal information, so be cautious when working with customer smartphone information.

Agile Development

Agile development is an approach to software engineering that promotes a rapid, iterative, and collaborative development process. As much a philosophy as a methodology, *The Agile Manifesto* outlines the core values of agile development as follows[13]:

> *Manifesto for Agile Software Development*
>
> *We are uncovering better ways of developing software by doing it and helping others do it.*
>
> *Through this work we have come to value:*
>
> *Individuals and interactions over processes and tools*
>
> *Working software over comprehensive documentation*
>
> *Customer collaboration over contract negotiation*
>
> *Responding to change over following a plan*
>
> *That is, while there is value in the items on the right, we value the items on the left more.*

The aim of agile development is to develop fewer, smaller, and lighter capabilities, but do this more often—as opposed to traditional methods that deliver more capabilities but over longer release schedules. This contrasts with traditional methods (e.g., waterfall) that tend to follow slow, linear, and segmented processes, as illustrated in Figure 6-4.

---

[13] Kent Beck et al, *Manifesto for Agile Software Development*, http://agilemanifesto.org/, retrieved on March 2012.

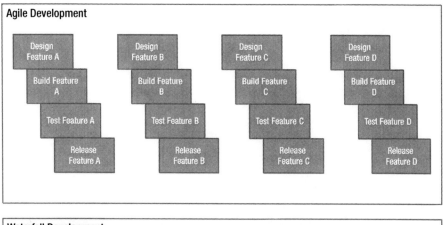

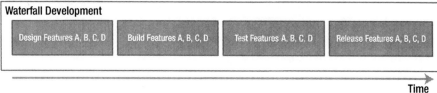

Figure 6-4. The top of the figure shows the iterative cycle of agile development. The bottom shows the linear cycle of waterfall development.

Through iterative development, features can be tested more easily, delivery times radically reduced, and feedback acted on much faster. While agile development is much more complex in practice—and as much a cultural transformation as a coding project management methodology—it is one way to deliver better service features, faster and more frequently.

Key to this outcome is agile development's flexible approach to feature prioritization during development. Customer or business requests can be delivered much sooner, as the development cycles iterates much faster. Agile development brings you closer to your customers, to their needs, to their demands, and to their feedback.

Agile development also helps to innovate faster. You can create new code, see if it works, fix any problems, evaluate success, and recycle. You can try out many small innovations, easier and faster. These smaller innovations can add up to some big innovation too, as we discussed in Chapter 2.

For example, you can use agile development to implement more effective A-B testing on web applications, to maintain better utilization of creative team resources, or to drive continuous enhancements into existing services. Freeing up your people from the typical 6–12 month (or more) software development life cycle also means you can adapt more rapidly to changing circumstances, be more reactive to innovative ideas, and react faster to changing market needs, demands, and business pressures.

Because the development phase is rarely in the public eye, it is hard to see the impact of agile development. However, some companies promote agile as a differentiator.

UK telecom giant BT, for example, introduced an agile development methodology in 2005. As a result, the company reduced development work in some cases from over 2 years down to 90-day and even 30-day delivery cycles. They also used agile to encourage programmers to close the gap with their end users, and the gap between requirements-gathering and product delivery. With agile development, BT was not only able to deliver new capabilities faster, including new mobile support, but to improve end-user satisfaction and change perception of development from a cost center to a revenue generator.[14]

Other organizations have been able to reduce their feature delivery times even more radically. US-based hosted service and cloud provider Rackspace, for example, set its full release cycle to just one week.[15]

In order to get started, look for new, manageable development projects where fast delivery of a limited feature set will be advantageous to your business goals. This is not always the case—such as with the launch of a large "big bang" product—but in many cases innovation is more successful when you focus on providing new capabilities quickly, rather than completely.

Of course, it will be important to provide your developers the correct training up front—and perhaps to hire new ones. Agile requires a significantly different project approach, with significantly different skills throughout the software engineering team. Do not underestimate the cultural change that agile entails either.

Conclusion

These opportunities to innovate with current technology are far from exhaustive. Indeed, this topic alone could cover an entire book! However, in this

---

[14] Thomas Hoffman, "BT: A Case Study in Agile Programming," InfoWorld, 2008, www.infoworld.com/d/developer-world/bt-case-study-in-agile-programming-112, retrieved on March 2012.

[15] Jack Vaughn, "Case Study: Agile Development Moves at Rackspace," TechTarget, 2008, http://searchsoftwarequality.techtarget.com/news/1297491/Case-study-Agile-development-moves-at-Rackspace, retrieved on March 2012.

chapter, we hope that we have provided at least some food for thought, whether it is in areas you can improve on your existing technology use to enable further innovation, or where you can take the initiative to innovate today by adopting existing technologies and approaches.

One point to remember—if you combine these technologies in new ways, then you can enable brand-new innovations and really start to differentiate your business and boost your own strategic value and that of your department. For example, even if you are already using social media, consider how much more valuable those efforts could be if you combine them with cloud or gamification. If you are already using virtualization, imagine how much more effective that could be when combined with automation and cloud. If you are already using big data, examine how you can add value by combining it with gamification and e-commerce.

With so many opportunities and so many combinations, even these few examples ensure that you have a wealth of opportunities to innovate today. When you add these to other old technologies in your organization—and in the next chapter we will discuss even more new opportunities—then look at how they can be combined to deliver innovation: the sky's the limit.

Remember, you do not have to be an inventor to be an innovator. You just need to do new things in new ways, even if that is simply reusing existing technologies.

Innovating with Consumer-Driven IT

Consumerization of IT is about the growing trend for consumers to adopt technologies well before the companies they work for, and subsequently to bring them to work. Typically, this refers to the increasing use of personal devices at work, such as smartphones and tablets (commonly referred to as "bring your own device" or BYOD), and the use of cloud and social services (Gmail, Dropbox, etc.) by employees at work.

Consumer-*driven* IT is an extension of the consume*rization* of IT to institutionalize usage of new (formerly designated "consumer") technologies by the business itself, not just individually by its employees. More than just a passive acceptance of workers choosing, buying, using, and bringing their own devices and services, consumer-driven IT is where the IT department is compelled to become active in choosing, buying, using, and supporting new consumer-style approaches.

In the rest of this chapter, we will examine the opportunities for innovation that are created by consumer-driven IT.

Understanding Consumer-Driven IT?

Driven by the growing demands of increasingly tech-savvy customers and staff, consumer-driven IT incorporates social, mobile, BYOD, cloud, and other consumer-oriented technologies. As the CIO, your customers (internal and external) are no longer just "IT users"—working with whatever IT supplies or allows. They are "IT consumers"—mobile, aware, enabled, and demanding. Some key changes between these states are illustrated in Figure 7-1.

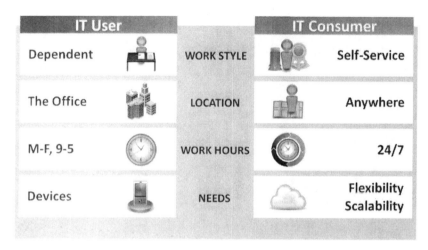

IT User		WORK STYLE	IT Consumer	
Dependent		WORK STYLE		Self-Service
The Office		LOCATION		Anywhere
M-F, 9-5		WORK HOURS		24/7
Devices		NEEDS		Flexibility Scalability

Figure 7-1. IT users have matured to become IT consumers.

These changes present a fundamentally new opportunity for innovation, and a critical one in the life of the CIO.

Consider the rise of consumerization of IT and the technology that encouraged it, including cell phones, Personal Digital Assistants (PDAs), smartphones, cloud services, and tablets. During this consumerization era, many (if not most) traditional CIOs were at best absent from, and at worst actively resistant to, this change. In this new era of innovation, CIOs need to do more than accepting or enabling consumerization—they need to be driving it, suggesting it to the business, and showing ways to adopt these technologies institutionally to drive new opportunities and new business-focused technology initiatives.

You can immediately look for opportunities to adopt and encourage new consumer technologies institutionally, such as these examples:

- Would your sales force benefit from having lightweight and easily accessible technology to deliver presentations to clients, find and transfer inventory, and allocate production to new customers? Perhaps you can officially adopt tablet devices and develop custom applications that deliver what your sales teams need in a compact, instantly accessible app.

- Would you be able to attract new customers and maintain higher loyalty from existing ones if your staff could communicate with customers instantly and not only acquire but spread positive endorsements and references? Perhaps you can develop new social media programs that take advantage of popular social networking platforms.

- Would your product designers and engineers be able to bring new products to market faster if they could collaborate simultaneously across multiple labs and multiple regions to model, simulate, and test new ideas together? Perhaps you can leverage global cloud services to create an internal collaboration platform based on wikis, instant messaging, blogs, and shared capabilities to bring these groups together more efficiently.

The possibilities are, almost literally, endless. In the rest of this chapter, we will consider some more opportunities to bring innovation to your business through the adoption of consumer-driven technologies.

Bring Your Own Device (BYOD)

BYOD is the practice of end users using their own personal computing devices for work. You may also see it referred to with many variations, including "Bring Your Own PC" (BYOPC), "Bring Your Own Computer" (BYOC), or—somewhat pejoratively—"Bring Your Own Toys" (BYOT). These devices can include smartphones, PDAs, laptops, personal computers, tablets, and other consumer technology devices—even personal desktops at home. BYOD is driven by and is a subset of the consumerization of IT.

BYOD is an important evolution of the IT device cycle. Since the widespread adoption of computers in the 1960s, IT has undergone a series of iterative epicycles in response to ongoing demands from end users for greater ownership (both figuratively and literally) and control of their computing experience. From mainframe to distributed, from distributed to desktop, from desktop to smartphone and tablet, each iteration has added to the previous one.

The adoption of distributed systems was driven by a reaction against the rigid controls, high cost, and difficult access to centralized mainframe systems. The adoption of desktop and personal computing was a similar reaction against the costs, unfriendliness, and inflexibility of the (by then) IT-owned distributed systems. Similarly, BYOD is a reaction against the rigidity, slow innovation, and lack of corporate options for users in an age of increasing penetration of portable computing devices.

Each reiteration of this cycle has freed up end users from the constrictions of the IT department as it existed at those times, and allowed users to boost their productivity, explore new opportunities, and drive fundamental change. The evolution to BYOD is just the latest iteration of this phenomenon.

These evolutions do not happen because users want to buy, own, and manage their own technology *per se*. They happen because users want freedom and choice in how and when they acquire and use new technology, even if it is not blessed by the IT department. Therefore, support for BYOD can free up your people to be faster and more productive. It also gives them the confidence, budget, permission, capability, understanding, and engagement to try out new capabilities and services.

When staff are not limited by IT standards, they are free to experiment with smartphone and tablet applications only available on otherwise nonstandard environments (e.g. OS X, iOS, Android, Linux). Being outside the firewall and away from administrator and policy restrictions, they are also released to use cloud applications and overcome the constraints of policy. Because they are no longer prevented from buying what they want, staff are also able to experiment with new routes to productivity without having to clear them first with finance, procurement, contracts, legal, and, of course, IT.

This freedom from IT control is potentially both good and bad, but it is also inevitable. Users *will* use their own devices—and arguably always have—so your choice is how to enable, guide, and benefit from this new iteration of the IT device cycle, not how or whether to shut it down. If innovation is about saying "yes" to good new ideas, then you need to be the department of "yes," not the department of "no." Embrace BYOD, while still maintaining essential security, control, and audit. Manage the risk that comes with these new business opportunities; do not simply try to ignore or reject it.

By embracing BYOD, you may be able to reduce costs, but don't count on it. Hardware and software acquisition is unlikely to be cheaper. Individuals have no economies of scale or buying power to drive down device prices. Centralized system costs may increase too if you need to provide additional capabilities for remote access, virtual desktop infrastructure, streaming applications, or application (re)development. Ongoing OpEx can be lower, depending on how you structure your support policies, but it can also rise due to the need to increase skills and resources to support a new diversity of enterprise devices. Be aware that cost reduction is not always a key driver for BYOD programs.

However, BYOD does come with many other benefits. While not definitive, there is a growing body of research[1] that suggests the freedom to choose their own devices is an important factor in attracting and retaining skilled workers. Research has even found that up to 45% of employees, and 40% of college students, would rather accept a lower paying job with a choice of device than a higher paying job with less flexibility.[2]

Similarly, research shows that BYOD is especially appealing to a coveted pool of skilled, college-educated younger workers.[3] This includes so-called "millennials" (a.k.a. "Generation Y," "Generation Next," the "Net Generation," or "Echo Boomers") who entered the workforce around the new millennium, and other so-called "digital natives" who have grown up using (and choosing) these personal technologies. These younger workers contrast to earlier generations (including their parents) who typically had their desktops, laptops, PDAs, and smartphones assigned to them by their employers.

This freedom to use your own device also enables highly effective, distributed, and low-cost business continuity, because it enables individuals to work from home or from other remote locations on their own devices in case of emergency or disaster. Moreover, BYOD supports yet another unavoidable and related trend, the rapid adoption of telecommuting, which is forecast to nearly double, reaching as much as 43% of US workers, by 2016.[4]

BYOD also allows the business to rapidly change the makeup of its workforce—from rapidly onboarding new, temp, casual or permanent staff to sourcing staff from global resource pools or to rapidly expanding resources on demand. As long as they bring their own devices, employees can work anytime, anywhere.

Embracing BYOD can be passive or active. Passive support is to include nonstandard (i.e., noncorporate) devices in your IT policy—making sure applications, VPNs, provisioning tools, remote desktops, security systems,

---

[1] Three examples: a) Cisco, "Cisco Connected World Technology Report 2011," www.cisco.com/en/US/netsol/ns1120/index.html, retrieved on September 2012; b) pwc, "Millennials at Work: Reshaping the Workplace," 2011, www.pwc.com/gx/en/managing-tomorrows-people/future-of-work, retrieved on September 2012; c) Accenture, "Global Research on Millennials' Use of Technology," 2010, www.accenture.com/us-en/Pages/insight-millennials-jumping-boundaries-corporate-it-summary.aspx, retrieved on September 2012.

[2] Fiona Graham, "BYOD: Bring Your Own Device Could Spell End for Work PC," BBC, February 2012, www.bbc.co.uk/news/business-17017570, retrieved on March 2012.

[3] Ibid.

[4] Ted Schadler, "Telecommuting Will Rise to Include 43% of US Workers by 2016," ZDNet, March 2009, www.zdnet.com/blog/forrester/telecommuting-will-rise-to-include-43-of-us-workers-by-2016/165, retrieved on September 2012.

and other IT capabilities support these devices. Active support goes further, such as providing reimbursement or a stipend for device purchases or setting up specific systems for multidevice access.

In either case, some important supporting technologies you will need to consider include the following:

- *Secure web applications*: integrated security to allow users to access web-based applications from any browser on any platform

- *SaaS*: enabling any user on any browser to access the same functionality, and in many cases with specific support for different devices and form factors

- *Virtualization*: including remote desktop (VDI or terminal services), application virtualization, virtual desktops, and application streaming

- *Custom app development*: building specific tablet and smartphone compatible applications to enable mobility

Also, make sure to match IT policy updates with HR and legal policy updates. BYOD is as much an operational change as it is a technological one. While form factor, network access, application support, and other technological challenges are important, many of the most significant challenges will be related to responsibility and accountability for acceptable use, data security, system support, purchasing, etc.

Mobile Computing

Mobility—not only using mobile devices like smartphones and tablets, but also enabling a mobile workforce and growing an "always-local" business—is a major driver in business innovation and growth. However, given that your business is dependent on technology and computing, your business mobility is absolutely dependent on mobile computing. This includes using mobile devices internally so your staff can take advantage of the opportunities that workforce mobility provides. It also includes leveraging the widespread adoption of mobile devices externally amongst your customers, partners, channels and suppliers, to help achieve your business goals.

Leveraging Mobility Internally

Adopting mobile computing does not necessarily mean buying 40,000 iPads for your internal staff, as the CIO of SAP reportedly did[5]—although it certainly can. Adopting mobile computing internally does mean giving both IT and line of business staff the ability to work whenever, wherever, and however they work best.

For many people, mobile computing means the ability to work on the road—consider the prototypical road warrior, visiting the office maybe once a week (or once a month) just to do expenses and report to local management. For these employees, mobility means doing business anywhere, anytime. They can see a client at their home or work, late at night or early in the morning, on a weekday or a weekend. They can provide a service or close a deal on the spot, sign a contract or agreement on their tablet, and even take payments (scan a check, swipe a credit card, or enter purchase order details) instantly. Mobility allows these employees to bring in new revenue faster, expand addressable market opportunities, and open up entirely new sales channels and capabilities.

For others, mobility means being able to work from home, whether part-time or full-time, and maintain a work/life balance. For these employees, mobility means they can take the kids to school in the morning, pick them up in the afternoon, watch their baseball game in the evening, and still get a full day's work done. They can take care of sick dependents, or manage their complex lives without having to take time off from the office 9-5. Moreover, these employees do not need dedicated office space and associated resources. All of these benefits flow through to the business in better staff retention, lower on-costs, the ability to leverage part-time and casual workers, increased leverage of global sourcing, and better business continuity in case of a disaster (i.e., office fire, hurricane, flood).

Still for others it means being able to work from anywhere inside the organization's campus—whether on the factory floor, in the showroom, at a branch office, on the job site, in the stockroom—or even on-site at a partner's or supplier's location. The ability to see a production fault and instantly communicate a recall to the sales channels while arranging to fix the fault will save time, money, and reputation. Being able to identify low production inventory and reorder input stock is a critical first step to reducing inventory and better managing stock-on-hand. Seeing firsthand as progress slips or accelerates on a new construction project means being immediately able to realign resources and schedules to avoid costly scheduling issues. Mobility

---

[5] Dave Rosenberg, "Consumerization of IT Is More Than Using an iPad at Work," C|Net, January 2012, http://news.cnet.com/8301-13846_3-57360376-62/consumerization-of-it-is-more-than-using-an-ipad-at-work, retrieved on June 2012.

means your business will be better equipped to respond cheaper, faster, and better to all these situations.

In order to deliver these and other business opportunities arising from mobility, you will need to consider multiple solutions. Your success will depend not only on traditional mobile devices like laptops, but also on many other technologies.

You should start by enabling appropriate workforces with smartphones and tablets. Connect these devices to and utilize enterprise applications, whether through web-based services, published APIs, or installed (off-the-shelf or custom) applications. Typical use cases here include connecting to corporate mail over the Internet using technologies like ActiveSync, securely connecting to internal network resources over VPN or two-factor authentication, or using corporate credentials to access cloud applications directly over the Internet.

However, be prepared to be more committed to mobile innovation too, with specific support for mobile devices and workers. You can develop new applications that assist staff in the ways they work today, streamlining their work by leveraging existing investments in technology and process. You can also work with strategic business peers to exploit mobile technology to enable new ways of working, and free your line of business staff from location and other constraints.

Virtual desktops and virtual applications will also play a part, as they abstract the business service for the mobile user away from the location where they need to use that service. For example, virtualization allows you to provide secure remote access to confidential business data even from a potentially insecure location or device, and allows you to provide "instant-on" access to critical applications for a new or temporary support worker in a far-flung location, on a wide range of devices and operating systems.

Cloud computing will be an important foundation for a mobility program. Cloud provides on-demand applications, always-accessible storage, and scalable compute resources that are accessible over the Internet from almost anywhere on the planet, and on almost any mobile device. You may look to incorporate GPS with cloud-connected mobile devices to enable location tracking, satellite phones to ensure an always-connected workforce even in the remotest of locations, or content delivery networks (CDNs) to handle the bandwidth requirements for high-volume remote content delivery.

However, while supporting mobile devices and other new technologies is an important part of delivering this larger mobility story, you should consider many other technologies to support mobile computing. At a minimum:

- Connect these devices to private and/or public networks that ensure security and compliance.

- Protect and secure data at rest and in transit to mitigate the possibility of accidental data loss or malicious data theft.

- Modify existing systems and applications to support new devices and locations whatever and wherever they are.

- Provide delivery channels that can support the new traffic volumes caused by mobility, such as by video conferencing or content delivery.

You also need to accommodate the nontechnology aspects of mobility, such as procedures, policies, and best practices.

Leveraging Mobility Externally

Your customers, clients, constituents, patients, partners, channels, and other stakeholders are all adopting mobile computing. According to Nielson, for example, 43% of adults in the US now own a smartphone.[6] Whether it is a simple cell phone, a smartphone, or a tablet, more consumers are adopting mobile technology and more searches and purchases are being done on mobile devices. As an innovative CIO, you have the opportunity to help lead your business in responding to that adoption.

Your stakeholders' mobile devices open up an opportunity to adopt new and innovative mobile commerce (also commonly referred to as "m-commerce") applications. One outstanding early example of mobile commerce is Starbucks for iPhone and Android.[7] These applications, championed by the company's award-winning CIO Stephen Gillett, allow customers to find their nearest Starbucks location, manage their stored value card, add to the balance on their card, track their loyalty program, and even pay for their purchases with their phone.

In addition to providing convenience for customers, while driving loyalty and brand reputation, the Starbucks applications also significantly impacted spending decisions. In fact, according to Forbes, in 2011, the Starbucks mobile

---

[6] The Nielson Company, "Beyond Clicks and Impressions: Examining the Relationship Between Online Advertising and Brand Building," 2011, http://nielson.com/content/dam/corporate/us/en/reports-downloads/2011-Reports/Nielsen-Beyond%20Clicks%20and%20Impressions.pdf, retrieved on March 2012.

[7] Starbucks, "Starbucks at Your Fingertips, No Matter Where You Are," www.starbucks.com/coffeehouse/mobile-apps/mystarbucks, retrieved on March 2012.

applications accounted for 26 million transactions and $110 million in card reloads.[8]

Probably the fastest and easiest way to leverage mobile adoption in order to drive mobile commerce is to participate in a third-party program, such as a social location network service like Foursquare. You can even create your own program leveraging existing social networks, such as Facebook, LinkedIn, or Twitter. Increased attachment through increased mobile interaction can help drive additional business—and revenue—to your physical locations through a combination of mobile and social.

Once customers are already at your location, you can take advantage of their mobile connectivity to provide easy interaction and drive additional or incremental transactions via bar code, localized SMS, QR codes, NFC, Bluetooth, or WiFi. For example, you can deliver (or exchange links to) coupons, brochures, promotions, special offers, and other content directly to their mobile device. This can be good for immediate use, or can be used to encourage return visits and additional business (2-for-1, valid-next-visit, etc.). Or you can provide forms, instructions, information, or assistance to reduce queues and make customer visits faster and more satisfactory while requiring less employee time for each customer.

A very affordable investment in mobility is developing a specific mobile application for your business. This is a great opportunity for attracting and retaining customers, and for driving marginal up-sell and net-new revenues. You do not have to start with a full-fledged mobile app either. With mobile commerce especially, you can quickly enter a relatively early-stage opportunity with minimal functionality. Perhaps start by developing a loyalty app, using an existing third-party app, or publishing a simple informational app. Work with customers to crowdsource enhancements, target additional platforms, and quickly push out additional functionality incrementally.

As an aside, mobile applications are especially well-suited to agile development—with mobile developers working directly with customers, understanding what they want, and building a great mobile app with small, fast new feature increments.

Then if you connect mobile and social with cloud and gamification, you can drive anytime, anywhere access to high-value services from any customer device. Leveraging multiple consumer-driven technologies at once provides an attractive opportunity to promote customer contact, gather customer

---

[8] Darcy Travlos, "Apple: More Than the New iPad," Forbes, March 2012, www.forbes.com/sites/darcytravlos/2012/03/08/apple-more-than-the-new-ipad, retrieved on March 2012.

intelligence, improve sales and attachment, drive higher satisfaction, strengthen customer loyalty, and reinforce your brand.

Social Networking

Social networking is a rising phenomenon that is rapidly permeating every online consumer's life. The ability for multiple people to all share some commonality by connecting together online in a broad interconnection is changing the way people relate to each other. As consumer-driven IT becomes the norm rather than the exception, social networking is changing the way people do business too. Some examples of social networking sites, applications, and services include Facebook, Twitter, LinkedIn, YouTube, WordPress, and Wikipedia.

Online social networking is merely a logical progression from the real life practices of social networking—getting people together to connect in social groups both big and small to exchange contacts, ideas, or opportunities. In the modern context, it has simply morphed to refer to online interactions in general. As such, many of the outcomes are fundamentally similar, but they can occur at much larger scale and across broader geographies. Online social networks also are able to leverage new "social" media like blog content, online video, interactive chat, and more.

Social networks can be very simple, localized, and specialized—for example, the subscribers to your corporate blog or the customers connected to your support team's Twitter account. They can also be massive and global in scale—such as the million-plus followers for Coca-Cola on Facebook.

While some may think social networking is synonymous with Facebook, in reality it is much more than a way for you to know when your son or daughter is "in a relationship." As Coca-Cola's online presence shows, social networking is also a way for your business and its employees to connect directly with customers, partners, agents, suppliers, and each other. It fosters closer relationships internally and opens up new (often more convenient) lines of communication and especially collaboration. It also builds connections externally by engaging with customers, partners, suppliers, influencers, and others in more personal ways.

Social media clearly delivers measurable business benefits too. According to Nielsen, advertising in social media generates a 55% greater lift in ad recall than nonsocial ads, with a 4x improvement on click-through rates when friends endorsed products and services online compared with standard online advertising.[9] Moreover, adults who are active on social media are more likely to purchase a range of goods and services, from gym memberships and music to clothing, shoes, and accessories.[10,]

Expanding these connections makes your business better informed and more able to react to even the most subtle and nascent of market forces. Even if what you hear is 90% noise, you can still identify many new ideas and digest useful new information from customers, suppliers, academics, researchers, journalists, pundits, and competitors. Social networking also opens up two-way communications beyond just the usual suspects to a wider range of views, which you can find instantly, as long as you can filter out the extraneous detail. It can even help you to find, attract, and retain talented and connected employees.

A positive adoption of new social networking technologies can drive improvements in outbound reputation, additional sales and marketing opportunities; expanded connections with new partners, agents, and suppliers; and increased loyalty from existing customers. Social networking also provides you with new opportunities to interact, learn, share ideas, and perhaps even become recognized by your peers and others as an expert in your area.

Moreover, your competitors may already be using social media—connecting with your customers, your suppliers, your partners, your advisors. If you are not using social networking, then *you* are out of the game, and potentially losing business and missing ideas.

Yet perhaps the most compelling driver is that your customers are already using social media. For example, imagine the rapidly increasing group of online consumers, who would primarily interact with your organization via social media, but cannot. Ask yourself the following questions:

- If they cannot tweet you with questions about your product— or even worse, their tweets are never answered—but your competitor tweets back with answers, guess which company they will buy from?

- If they cannot "like" your business or product on Facebook, "+1" you on Google+, hashtag or "@" mention you on

[9] The Nielsen Company, "Ads with Friends: Analyzing the Benefits of Social Ads," 2011, http://blog.nielsen.com/nielsenwire/online_mobile/ads-with-friends-analyzing-the-benefits-of-social-ads/, retrieved on March 2012.

[10] The Nielsen Company, "State of the Media: The Social Media Report Q3 2011," September 2011, www.nielsen.com/content/dam/corporate/us/en/reports-downloads/2011-Reports/nielsen-social-media-report.pdf, retrieved on March 2012.

Twitter, then they will not be able to tell their expanded social networks about you.

- If they cannot get a discount from you on Groupon or a special deal on Foursquare, but they can get one from your rival instead, they will probably visit your competitor's store, not yours.

- If they are on the go when they need your service, but your web site does not support their smartphones, then they will probably log in to your competitor's mobile site instead.

- If they cannot buy from you online by clicking through from your social network homepage or profile, then they probably will not buy from you at all.

Conversely, of course, if your competitors are not using social networking, you have a chance to put *them* out of the game.

To make a start with social networking today, begin by making it easy for all the stakeholders (staff, customers, partners, yourself) to contribute, to join a conversation. If it is difficult, high-effort, or high-risk, or if there is no real incentive to do so, then inertia will outweigh action. Remove the firewall blocks, at least on selected social networks that are directed more at business (LinkedIn, Twitter, or Quora) than personal use (Facebook, Google+, or Foursquare). Remember, however, the premise of consumer-driven IT. Even consumer-oriented technologies can be turned to business use—indeed Facebook (perhaps the quintessential personal social network) is now driving massive volumes of corporate connection through company pages and the like (pun intended).

Start to promote the use of social networking technologies internally in IT and across the business to help communicate, document, and collaborate with each other. For example, you can start to crowdsource your institutional knowledge using enterprise social networking technologies like instant messaging, blogs, wikis, social media, etc. These private social networking solutions can be installed on your infrastructure or acquired as a service from a cloud provider, but are accessible only to authorized users (e.g. employees, contractors, agents, suppliers). Unlike publicly crowdsourced data (Wikipedia) or a cacophony of voices speaking at once on an infinite number of topics (Twitter), using social networking technology internally allows you to take greater control. Where you need to, you can limit access to the right stakeholders, and ensure information is verified (or at least note where it is not), while laying a foundation for adoption of external social networking

It can be a great boost for you as the CIO to blog professionally. Not only does this set an example for your business leaders, but it will give you more insight into your customers, better understanding of your markets, and an authoritative and connected reputation to bring to the C-level meetings. You can even use this as a springboard to help your C-level peers to start connecting on social media too by helping them to blog, connect on LinkedIn and Twitter, and more. You may need to involve your professional communications teams (i.e., public relations, corporate communications, marketing) to help engage your C-level peers in social media, but at least you will be communicating a controlled and immediate message out to your market, and hearing their feedback unfiltered and instantly.

Find ways to connect with your partners, agents, and other third parties too. Connecting with resellers, agents, suppliers, and others online via Twitter, FaceBook, or LinkedIn for example, will give you the ability to use a broad and allied social network to promote your own capabilities and messages, while sourcing better partners and resources. Connecting with trade and financial journalists, analysts, thought leaders, bloggers, and other influencers can help you drive awareness, brand recognition, and even demand.

You should be careful to avoid treating social networking as a megaphone or as a channel for your personal voice alone. Most social networks are definitely better for two-way conversations than for broadcasting, and you need to decide how to balance your personal brand and opinions with those of your organization. However, if you are fair and even-handed in promoting and supporting your allies (and sometimes even your competitors) on social networks ("liking" their pages, "plussing" their posts, "+K'ing" their advice, "RT'ing" their tweets, and "reblogging" their blogs), they may well do the same for you, increasing the value to both brands.

Talk to your Chief Marketing Officer about the wealth of marketing opportunities available through external use of social networking too. Consider these examples for your business:

- Hosting an online chat with experts for (or with) your customers and prospects

- Using external messaging for customer support or soliciting references and testimonials via social networks

- Running customer acquisition or satisfaction promotions through Facebook or Twitter

- Promoting a new product or service with Internet videos or other nontraditional (and maybe viral!) media

- Running a syndication program for your ads and downloads through LinkedIn

- Promoting an ongoing conversation by sharing information through your blog posts

All of these opportunities are new ways to use new social networking technologies to drive new and innovative marketing opportunities and build relationships.

However, a word of caution—social networking can also have a negative impact. Consider the post on Twitter from Qantas Airways, in the middle of a highly publicized and inconvenient industrial dispute, asking for bouquets about customers' "dream luxury inflight experience."[11]

This tweet received instead mainly critical (and very public) brickbats from a highly dissatisfied and highly vocal segment of its customer base.[12]

No matter how you approach social networking, you will need to adopt new policies, monitor their adoption (or transgression), and enforce remediation where necessary, to make sure you avoid potential nightmares like this one.

Consumer Cloud

We have already discussed the opportunities for innovation by adopting *business*-oriented cloud services (see Chapter 6). However, there are many options for individuals to access *consumer*-oriented cloud services too—and many legitimate business reasons for them to do so:

- Creative workers may use YouSendIt to exchange large media files with coworkers, partners, or even customers to bypass unworkable file-size limitations that are typical on many corporate e-mail servers.

- Knowledge workers may adopt online productivity applications like Prezi, Zoho, or Google Apps to access new features and capabilities that existing corporate-owned software cannot or does not deliver.

---

[11] Qantas Airways on Twitter, http://twitter.com/#!/qantasairways/status/138777262895009792, retrieved on March 2012.

[12] Alicia Wood, "Qantas Makes Hash of Tweet Campaign," *Sydney Morning Herald*, November 22, 2011, www.smh.com.au/travel/travel-news/qantas-makes-hash-of-tweet-campaign-20111122-1nsa4.html#ixzz1pWTp7YxU, retrieved on March 2012.

- Partner or supply chain managers may use iCloud or Dropbox to share workgroup content with partners or suppliers if it is too difficult (or simply impossible) to get a shared environment from IT.

- Marketers may use YouTube, Vimeo, HootSuite, Facebook, and other consumer cloud services to deliver content through new media, in new locations, and to new customers where central IT cannot.

- Sales reps may use Skype, FaceTime, or Google Chat to have sales meetings or management reviews while they are on the road, avoiding corporate VPNs and other "hassles" that keep them from selling.

- Mobile and multidevice workers may use iCloud, so they can work with the same content whether they are at their desk or outside the office or at home on their personal computer or iPad.

- Programmers may use Google Mail or bitTorrent to exchange files that are prohibited from e-mail by corporate policies, such as zip, exe, jar, iso, or other potentially malicious file types.

Of course, each of these consumer cloud services poses challenges to the traditional IT department. To address these issues, as CIO you could try to shut down all but the centrally approved systems. You could apply network and firewall policies, conduct domain filtering, use deep packet inspection, etc. You could attempt to identify and prevent use of these "rogue" cloud services. However, realistically it is too easy to work around even the most capable technology barriers. For example, workers can simply use these same cloud services, but on personal devices and networks instead (including smartphones, tablets, and mobile device tethering). They can quickly find and switch to alternative services and alternative domains. The more tech-savvy can use proxies and other deceptions to bypass the controls. Your business faces the same outcome.

A better (and more realistic) approach starts by understanding and officially accepting the need for consumer cloud and sustaining corporate interests through policies and guidelines, not by (at best partially-effective) technology barriers. Rather than try to block them, instead assist and guide users in their selection and operation of consumer cloud services.

After all, it will probably happen anyway. But if you get ahead of consumer cloud adoption, you can make sure it goes well for the business as a whole, not just easy/cheap/fast/available/etc. With IT taking the lead, you can enable the innovative use of consumer-grade cloud services while maintaining important policies that balance individual enablement and corporate protection. With IT stepping up to proactively offer (and even pay for) cloud services that address user requirements, it reduces the incentive for those users to go around IT and use rogue cloud services.

Consider these steps as you open up safe and responsible opportunities to adopt consumer cloud:

- *Discover what is in use*: look for existing cloud services in use and catalog them and their common users.

- *Look for new options*: Honestly review internal systems to see where existing consumer cloud services could do better.

- *Determine the requirements*: Look for the common users, and ask why they did or would adopt consumer cloud services.

- *Discover the business value*: Understand what value cloud services could add to the business, including cost, speed, ease, etc.

- *Consider the risk*: Determine the possible impacts that each cloud service poses, including cost, compliance, reputation, etc.

- *Investigate alternatives*: Look for more options that may be cheaper, safer, more scalable, more reliable, etc.

- *Consult with business leaders*: Join your peers in an informed decision on whether or how to support consumer cloud services.

- *Communicate expectations broadly*: Explain and justify your policies and limitations clearly and then enforce them appropriately.

Of course, approval and acceptance of consumer cloud services—whether tacit or explicit, accidental or intentional—does not mean just opening up the spigot and allowing any user to adopt any cloud service for work purposes. Not all services are equal, and there will still be a time to say "no," and to do it with business support.

Nor can you simply stop at the adoption of consumer cloud services. It will also be incumbent on corporate IT to provide management and security— some "adult supervision" —for the consumer cloud. When cloud services are being used by just a handful of workers, you may opt to just monitor them.

But when services are being adopted *en masse* by entire departments, business units, or divisions, then the business as a whole will need to apply more intentional and scalable management and security systems.

For example, at any significant scale, even (or especially) the consumer cloud will need at least some basic management and security, such as the following:

- Discovery and inventory management to detect, catalog, and secure any "rogue" cloud activities—not to shut them down (though sometimes that may be necessary) but to be ready to support them while maintaining security, governance, and compliance

- SaaS-enabled security systems to protect corporate data and knowledge in the consumer cloud—such as Single Sign-On, identity and access federation, social media login integration, data loss and intrusion prevention, etc.

- Cloud-oriented financial management, such as asset management, ERP integration, budget control, procurement, contract management, etc., to ensure both IT and the business operate with fiscal responsibility, mindful of corporate assets and expenditures

Who better than the innovative CIO to lead an informed, secure, and profitable adoption of the consumer cloud?

In the end, you may not be able to discover, monitor, and support every one of the seemingly limitless array of consumer cloud services your employees have adopted or will adopt in the future. Indeed, you may not want to, unless or until it becomes a business issue. But you should get at least some visibility, if not always control, of the "rogue" consumer cloud services, so you can at least make informed business decisions about them.

Other Consumer Technologies Driving Business Change

This is by no means intended as an exhaustive inventory of consumer-driven technologies that are entering the business world. Multiple other consumer technologies are having substantial impact. Some examples of these technologies are:

- *GPS*: From military to business to consumer . . . and then back to driving business, GPS is resurgent. It is no longer restricted to expensive, specialty devices, but has become commonplace on smartphones and tablets. Cloud-based cycling application Strava, which uses GPS to track and compare riders' times and achievements, was *Velo* magazine's "Technical Innovation of the Year" in 2011. The location check-in mobile application Foursquare relies on GPS too, and its developer is working on a reported billion-dollar valuation.[13]

- *Camera phones:* Cell phone cameras are also incredibly widespread. In mid-2012, for example, the iPhone camera was the leading source device on photosharing site Flickr by a significant margin.[14] Of course, not every business can leverage camera phones into a $1 billion sale like Instagram, or drive hundreds of thousands of positive impressions like Vail Resorts' "EpicMix." But many businesses can and do leverage the ubiquity of camera phones to create and expand customer engagement, intimacy, spend, share of wallet, feedback, loyalty, retention, and more.

- *Set-top boxes:* The rise of the set-top box (including dedicated boxes like Roku or Apple TV, as well as multifunction gaming and media devices like the Sony PlayStation 3 or the Microsoft Xbox 360) is rapidly taking share away from traditional TV audiences as they become more legitimate alternatives to broadcast, cable, and satellite TV. Especially as they add more streaming media, interactive applications, and integration with traditional PCs and applications like XFINITY, Netflix, Hulu, and iTunes, set-top boxes have the potential to transform many businesses, not just media and gaming companies.

- *Personal Area Networks (PANs):* PANs have moved on from the difficult-to-navigate Bluetooth connections of old to the plug-and-play simplicity of personal WiFi and 3G/4G hotspots that are connected by simply tapping an NFC-enabled device. These can be a great boon to productivity and innovation, allowing immediate collaboration—anywhere, anytime, across the table, or across the world. However, if used injudiciously, they can become a burden as they open up a new, unauthorized,

---

[13] Michael Arrington, "Square Raising New Round, Joining Billion Dollar Valuation Club," TechCrunch, June 2011, http://techcrunch.com/2011/06/07/square-raising-new-round-joining-billion-dollar-valuation-club, retrieved on June 2012.

[14] Flickr, "Explore/Camera Finder," www.flickr.com/cameras, retrieved on June 2012.

unmanaged, and likely unsecured penetration vector for malicious entry directly into your corporate data and network.

- *Unified communications*: Few of today's technology consumers would accept having different devices and/or networks for voice calls, video chat, social networking, e-mail, and text messaging. These are all just core capabilities of a single device—the smartphone—with many of these capabilities already tightly integrated in applications like Skype, Visual Voicemail, or Google Chat. Businesses are also unifying communications, whether through corporate adoption of consumer smartphone technologies and applications, or more sophisticated enterprise capabilities, driving outcomes from cost reduction to productivity and more.

As we have noted, this list is not designed to be exhaustive. Look around you, and especially at the devices and technologies that are exciting your younger workers (or family members). They may just open your eyes to the next big technology change that you need to exploit.

Combinations of technologies add multiple dimensions too. In combination, there are almost limitless opportunities for consumer-driven IT to enable and increase business innovation.

Conclusion

Even with this relatively cursory exploration, we can see that the rise in power of the consumers of information and other technology is truly changing the way businesses and governments adopt, adapt, and leverage new technologies for business innovation.

This trend will only grow more powerful over time, as millennials and other digital natives continue to enter—and subsequently lead—the workforce. This new wave of workers will bring with them an ever-increasing demand to attach to new technologies, bring them into the workplace, and drive new ways of doing business.

As we explore in upcoming chapters the ability to innovate tomorrow, and the need to make innovation intentional, you will see that your success as an innovative CIO to change the way you do business will substantially depend on your ability to identify and exploit these new technologies, and empower your new workforces to do the same.

8

Opportunities to Innovate Tomorrow

Rescuing Your Company with Future Innovations

Over the years, many once-successful companies have vanished. The move from household name to has-been is sometimes swift. A look back over the IT industry can point to a number of sizeable organizations that have ceased to be or that have morphed into a new form. You may remember companies like Prime and Wang in their heyday. These were major players in the computer industry and their names only exist today as part of other organizations, but in the early days both were large successful companies. At its peak, Wang had revenue of $3 billion and a staff in excess of 30,000. What caused the demise of these large organizations? Sales slumps, economic depression, poor service, poor financial management, and unrealistic pricing are certainly some of the reasons for failure. Other organizations from this time survived and thrived. It was not that long ago that Apple was considered a basket case. How did other organizations survive all of the management and financial turmoil? In our view, one part of the reason that some companies fail and others grow is based on the failing company's lack of foresight and innovation. Innovation in this context needs to be the right kind of innovation. Foresight needs to account for trends that were obvious in hindsight but were obscured or not even considered as important. I can remember being told a few months after the first IBM PC launch, "Don't worry about the IBM PC: memory and storage are well below business requirements—it's just a toy."

Controlled Innovation Can Save . . . Uncontrolled Innovation Can Destroy

Vision and strategy are elements that are important in the continuing success of any organization and can sometimes save a company. IT strategy does not always map to business strategy, as we have remarked earlier in the book. Some IT leaders have said that they don't have an IT strategy—they only have a business strategy that IT supports. We believe that this is the right mindset: business-focused IT.

Innovation can definitely reinvigorate a company. For example, until the advent of the first Motorola flip or clamshell phone, the Motorola handset range was no more distinguished than the competition. Before the advent of the iPhone, the flip phone generated great interest in their handsets and was the highest-placed phone in the PC World's "Greatest Gadgets of the Past 50 Years.'" Company failure is sometimes attributed to a failure to innovate. There are many reasons for a company to stagnate and fail. Jim Collins has discussed these reasons in several books, including *Built to Last* and *How the Mighty Fall*. It would be wrong to suggest that failure to innovate is a major factor in company failure. Indeed, Collins notes, in a *Time Magazine* article, that businesses are often innovating extensively up to the time of their demise[2]. This could be seen as a natural, knee-jerk reaction. You can almost hear the directive from the CEO to product development:

> *The company is not performing well. Sales are down. We need some new products to reinvigorate our catalogue. Go out and get me some new products—something innovative that will deliver the growth that we need.*

In our view, this demand for innovation—taking resources and focus away from the immediate problems—is too little too late. Collins makes the point that uncontrolled innovation and risk-taking are prevalent up to the final failure of a company. Controlled innovation, as part of the company culture and ethos, is a way of ensuring that the product lines stay vital and build growth. Using innovations as the basis of a corporate strategy will maintain

---

[1] Dan Tynan, "The 50 Greatest Gadgets of the Past 50 Years," PC World, December 24, 2005, www.pcworld.com/article/123950/the_50_greatest_gadgets_of_the_past_50_years. html, accessed on October 2012.

[2] Randy James, "Jim Collins: How Mighty Companies fall," Time Magazine, June 10, 2009, www.time.com/time/business/article/0,8599,1903713,00.html, accessed on May 2012.

and grow the organization. Innovations that are panic measures or "the only way out" are doomed to fail and bring the company down with them. Uncontrolled innovation may not save a failing company. It can have a disastrous effect on a healthy company.

Some years ago, I was in a board meeting of a company I worked for. The chairman outlined an innovation to the business model that would enable the company to grow into new locations. He asked us all, one by one, for our opinion. We unanimously endorsed the plan, providing there was some caution. We suggested that we use this to consolidate locations where we had a small operation, grow into new locations that were likely to yield further growth, but stay away from locations where the costs, infrastructure, and customers were more risky. We were told that this was timid thinking—the company would exploit all areas and the rest of the business can support weaker locations. We all left the meeting with a sense of foreboding, and we were right. The company started failing in only 18 months and failed completely after 2 years. This can be directly attributed to the decision taken by the chairman.

The negative effect of too much uncontrolled innovation is supported by comments from Thorsten Heins, the CEO of Research In Motion (RIM). He stated in an article in *CIO* magazine that the staff at RIM got so excited about innovation that they inserted the innovations in the product lines causing delays and quality problems. Delays and quality issues plagued RIM in 2011 and early 2012.

Using innovation as sticking plaster to heal a broken company is not a long-term plan. Using innovation to prevent a company needing sticking plaster is a better strategy. Innovation should be part of a growth strategy, of business transformation not business salvation. We are not suggesting that innovation is the best way to get your organization back on track, but lack of innovation will certainly be more likely to prevent the organization from growing. In the economic climate prevailing since 2007, growth is important.

Innovation may be essential, but it would have little value if it were not in line with the corporate vision and strategy. In Chapter 4, we have already mentioned the link between IT, innovation, and the corporate strategy. We recommended that CIOs review the corporate strategy and become more involved in the strategic decision-making. This is possible if you have access to the corporate strategy or the people developing the strategy. Evidence from a recent survey, however, shows that only 16% of CIOs questioned were always included in corporate business strategy discussions.[3]

---

[3] CA Technologies, "The Future Role of the CIO," October 2011, www.ca.com/us/collateral/white-papers/na/The-Future-Role-of-the-CIO-Becoming-the-Boss.aspx, accessed on May 2012.

If you, the CIO, are not an integral part of setting the corporate business strategy, you may feel that there is little that you can do while you wait for words of wisdom from on high. This feeling of being an "order taker" for business IT demands is magnified if you do not have a direct reporting line to the CEO. In this case, you may have to be politically savvy and look for allies outside the CEO's department. In most dynamic sales-focused organizations, the Chief Marketing Officer and the head of sales are influential and may be able to see the potential for innovation in their areas more easily. This is more of a political strategy and outside the scope of this book. Nonetheless, business-savvy CIOs should make themselves visible even if they are not yet seen as the trusted IT partner for the CEO. A business innovation led by IT would raise visibility where mere cost-saving would not. High praise is unlikely for merely doing your job.

A Look Ahead

In the remaining sections of this chapter, we will look at how you can develop a "nose" for innovation, enabling you to recognize the potential benefits of innovations early. Recognizing that an innovation will have little or no return for the organization is as important as recognizing an innovation that will generate millions. We will also consider where you can generate information that will help your crystal-ball gazing into the future. For instance, can you use mergers and acquisitions as a way to drive innovation and what are the pitfalls of this approach? We end the chapter with a few of the far-horizon innovations that would be interesting to put on your watch list.

Recognizing That You Are at a "VisiCalc or iPad Moment"

When it comes to innovation, many business managers anticipate an innovation that will make headlines. Searchers for the "VisiCalc" moment or the "iPad moment" may be overlooking significant innovations that will deliver business improvements. These improvements can often be made without the need to qualify as a world-changing innovation. Both VisiCalc and the iPad had a long gestation, and both had to wait for technology to catch up with requirements.

So what is a "VisiCalc moment"? VisiCalc was waiting for an affordable personal computer—step forward the early Apple II. This enabled an affordable alternative to the manual balance sheets or expensive computer bureau time available. Dan Bricklin, the inspiration behind VisiCalc, needed to write a spreadsheet for a report during his MBA studies at Harvard, and he had either to write it by hand or develop a program to give a visual representation of the spreadsheet. This program was improved and compressed to run on a microcomputer, and the VisiCalc moment had arrived. Was this a big-bang, world-changing innovation, or an incremental innovation? Pen and paper spreadsheets had been use for years but involved a lot of rewriting and correction. There were clumsy time-sharing programs available, but they were expensive and cumbersome. I would suggest that the best measure of the impact of VisiCalc was the gasp of surprise from a room full of accountants when I demonstrated VisiCalc recalculating a complex business spreadsheet in seconds. Their surprise turned to excitement when we explained the cost and other uses. At that moment, I knew how a magician feels when his best trick stuns his audience. Yes, this was a big-bang innovation, but it was the culmination of several smaller innovations:

- Using a microcomputer rather than a mainframe or departmental mini-computer

- Delivering an on-screen grid as the user interface

- Allowing the sheet to be recalculated when a value was changed

Demonstrating VisiCalc, I could tell that this was a winner, but how do you know when your innovation will strike gold? How do you decide to continue investments in an innovation that has not delivered on its promise? This is the most difficult part of innovation and one that most organizations struggle to master. The balancing act between patience to see an innovation through to a successful conclusion and the ending of an unproductive project is difficult to manage.

Spotting a Winner

There is an old adage that you should not look for needs to fulfill but create a need that only you can fulfill. This is easier said than done, but there are examples of this throughout history. Some of the more recent have been the sticky note and our earlier examples. How do you spot the winning idea? There is a popular innovation myth, quoted by Scott Berkun in his book *The Myths of Innovation*, that good ideas are hard to find.[4] He states that creativity has been sidelined in the current world because it is easy just to reuse someone else's ideas. Look at all the people in your organization. Are they lacking in creativity? Are they bereft of ideas? Most people have ideas, but they don't know what to do with them, as we discussed in Chapter 4. Finding the good idea or the great idea is more difficult because there are so many

---

[4] Scott Berkun, *The Myths of Innovation*, O'Reilly Media, 2010.

ideas. Innovations are ideas that are acted on, so in this section we will consider the terms as identical.

If you consider that ideas don't leap fully formed from the research lab but are often incomplete, untidy, and needing some development, then it is clear that you need to filter the ideas that are generated. The trick is to make sure that your filter is not set to exclude everything, just the ideas that are waiting for technology to catch up or are not likely to meet a business priority.

The filter for ideas should be set so that ideas can be categorized by the following:

- *Cost*: how much an idea will cost to develop and implement. If you ask futurists what future they want, most of them will have major transportation improvements as a wish. This is not likely to happen in the short term because of the high cost of infrastructure developments.

- *Scope*: the breadth of vision for the idea. If you were in the domestic water heating business, you would not want to invest in an ocean boiler, unless it is relevant to your business plan.

- *Impact*: how will it change things? Will it create new value or efficiencies? Will it have a negative impact on some or all of your business in the future?

- *Relevance*: a category this is often the sticking point. When people are asked to think "out of the box," many of the ideas may not be relevant to your business or your part of the world. This could lead to their rejection unless one of the parameters of the idea creation is that your organization is looking for new lines of business or adjacent lines of business that the idea can fit in to.

Once ideas have been categorized, they can be reviewed, and in many organizations a committee of the great and good does this. These folks will have to evaluate the ideas and decide which ones are worth progressing. I am not sure that a committee would have given the iPad approval, based on the high cost of development. Here is one of the dilemmas of innovation. Often the best person to deliver the world-changing innovation is the inventor or visionary. That is not to say that a committee has no place, just that it is more likely to have organizational, political, or even social reasons to abandon something difficult with high potential. Innovators may have to argue well and fight hard to get their ideas acted on.

Times of economic crisis will generate innovations. Innovation has a value to the organization. Many organizations are keen on protecting the value of their innovations, and this can have a negative effect. There are few ideas that cannot be improved by discussion. Discussion is one area that innovators are wary of. A private inventor may not want to disclose his idea before it has some kind of protection, such as a patent. Corporate inventors may want to keep the innovation quiet so that others in the hierarchy do not claim it as their own. There are rules about prior disclosure of ideas if they are part of a patent application. Your coworkers' discussion of ideas can be a valuable exercise and result in a stronger more valuable innovation, unless you are paranoid.

Collaboration and Communication

The reputation of the IT department as a source of understanding and delivery of innovative ideas can be enhanced. Innovative CIOs should review their communications both internally and externally. In particular, CIOs should continually review the information delivery and control systems that they are managing. You should ask some searching questions about your use of the information that you have at hand as a CIO. One source of information for dissemination is the technology futures information that you have probably gathered over time.

A more significant future development that is gaining traction in the industry relates directly to the fact that the CIO has access to most of the data the corporation owns. This access is through internal applications, databases, e-mail systems, and web sites. Having ultimate control of this data can lead to some serious innovation. A problem in virtually any organization is that this massive amount of data will continue to grow. It needs to be analyzed and the CIO is in the best position to organize this. Having control of the data, CIOs can develop analysis tools that will help them understand the complex business world that the company operates in. This understanding can lead to innovative opportunities.

The growth of social networking tools and the ability to use them to increase collaboration may also generate an "iPad moment." In the past, collaborators had to be co-located with their team to be able to generate momentum and ideas. There were naive attempts to use distributed teams with conference calls and e-mails. In many organizations, these are still the staples of a distributed team. It has been clear for some time that not all the best-qualified thinkers in an organization will live near or travel to a central location on a frequent basis. Social networking and imaginative use of telepresence and collaboration tools are overcoming this problem. It is interesting to note that the birth of the World Wide Web would not have been possible if Tim Berners-Lee had no access to hypertext developers around the world. The Web would have stayed in CERN and probably not made it outside his department.

Real-time collaboration is in its infancy. I am someone who experimented with Google Wave and I can tell you that being able to read what someone miles away is typing, in real time, makes for clearer conversations. More importantly, online brainstorming can become a reality and idea development does not have to wait for complete sentences. I also found that if colleagues were not fluent English speakers, they were happier to collaborate in real time through text, even though they seldom spoke on a conference call. Other new developments in online collaboration are discussed later in the chapter.

Is Innovation Insight or Luck?

Innovation has often been associated with an idea that has just popped into your head—a lucky thought, in fact. Ideas don't just happen. If you consider the creativity of a small child compared with a middle-aged employee, the child has many more ideas. We have discussed creativity in previous chapters, but it is worth mentioning here because luck, creativity, and serendipity are closely related. Serendipity can be thought of as a happy accident. Steven Johnson in his book *Where Good Ideas Come From* has a whole chapter on it.[5] The important point he makes in this chapter is that the association between ideas is one strength of serendipity. The happy part of a happy accident is due to the significance of the accident to you. Social media and collaboration encourage serendipity. Serendipity is reduced by secrecy. As we mentioned earlier in this chapter, secrecy is often the stock-in-trade of the inventor. One way to decide if serendipity plays a part in your organization is to think back to all those corridor conversations over the coffee pot. Quite often an idea will develop because of the different backgrounds and objectives of the coffee drinkers. It is not just the stimulant effect of the coffee, but the sparking of new trains of thought generated by discussing ideas and chance meetings. We will discuss the personal network effects in a later part of this chapter.

Creating the Crystal Ball

Whenever I hear the words "predicting the future," I have this image of a shawl-covered lady sitting in front of a crystal ball and delivering pronouncements to the hushed audience. It is interesting to contemplate that

---

[5] Steven Johnson, *Where Good Ideas Come From*, Riverhead Press, 2011.

the businessman needs some of the skills of the crystal-ball gazer. I am referring to research, understanding of the impact of small changes, observation, analysis, and deduction that can create a credible prediction.

To predict the future you need to be able to look at the world in which you and your company operates. Social, political, and economic macro trends can have an influence on corporate strategy and have an impact on IT. A luxury goods supplier would be a good example of a company who would use these trends to help them develop a strategy to expand out of their own country. They would consider trends that indicate the capability to pay for the goods and the societal changes to the population to be more status-conscious. Once the company has created a strategy based on an analysis of the trends, there may be a direct effect on the IT department—for example, by localizing applications. Identifying opportunities to innovate in the future will depend on some understanding of that future.

Can You Predict the Future?

Predicting the future is not easy—so many factors influence the way the world changes. One of the most difficult problems is to account for the major factors that may have an influence and develop a contingency plan if things change. There are no simple cause-and-effect relationships in world trade. If there was a simple cause-and-effect relationship in business, the process could look like the following:

1. Our company has a product that consumers like.
2. There are a growing number of consumers in China.
3. We should open an office in China.
4. Sales will increase due to the extra units we sell in China.

While this may be simplistic, there are times when this type of logic has led to a decision that has unpredictable results. There are ways that some of the guesswork can be taken out of the decision-making process and companies often have a team of people who are tasked with building the knowledge to transfer the guesswork just mentioned into an educated guess. There are a number of recognized theories that can be brought into play. They all have to start with some basic knowledge about what is going on in the world.

There is a lot of emphasis on world conditions in this chapter. The simple reason is that these conditions can affect the markets in which you are selling your goods. If you are restricting sales to one country, no matter how large, world conditions such as the current economic crisis will affect that country.

Prediction of the future is based on three layers of knowledge and understanding:

- Knowledge of world political, social, and economic factors and trends that may affect the market you are interested in

- Knowledge of the market and competition that you are interested in

- Knowledge of new developments that may influence the market you are interested in. These are often disruptive developments that you need to understand. In IT terms, this is where knowledge of new and emerging technologies is valuable.

Gathering this information for the first time is a daunting task and can take many, many months. Once the knowledge is gained, it only requires frequent periodic review and amendment. This exercise is not the corporate strategy. It develops the knowledge base on which a strategy can be built. Even if you are not involved in developing the corporate strategy, this information will be valuable as it can help you understand and possibly contribute to corporate strategy. You may also find that other parts of the organization have not taken a comprehensive and organized approach to knowledge gathering.

Predicting the future is not based on guesswork but on experience and knowledge of external trends and factors that will influence technology direction. Don't be like the guy who bought a room full of CPM-based minicomputers the week before IBM announced the IBM PC, making his investment obsolete in a matter of weeks. CIOs need to plan for the future and ensure that they are always aware of changing conditions in the business and wider world before making a plan. Gathering information is the first part of becoming knowledgeable enough to predict future innovations.

Gathering Relevant Information

A knowledge base can be constructed from a large number of information sources. You should check with the marketing and PR departments for any specialist sources they may have access to. The finance department is also a good source of economic data. You may also find some closet politicians and economists within your own department who may be interested in taking part in this exercise. Table 8-1 lists some sources of information in the three layers just mentioned.

Table 8-1. Sources of Information

Layer	Source	Information Type
World	News media	Macro trends that may affect you: war, economic slumps, major oil finds, energy shortages, raw materials trends
World	OECD and World Economic Forum reports	Macro trends but often with a less sensationalist approach compared with the news media
Market	Business and market analysts	Understanding of the market for your company's products and services. These will have a view of the impact of world trends and enable you to create a better understanding of the relationship between market and world.
Market	IT industry analysts	Although these are specialists in IT, they often have a view of world and business trends. They may also help you to understand emerging technology trends.
Emerging and Disruptive Technologies	IT industry analysts	There is value in the emerging trends that analysts can identify; however, these are often looking further into the future than is necessary for day-to-day operations. But looking into the future is where you will discover opportunities for future innovation.
Emerging and Disruptive Technologies	IT staff	You should not neglect the knowledge and interests of the staff in your department. Some members of staff are enthusiastic and knowledgeable about the technology they work with and can provide valuable insight based on experience as well as wide reading.

One additional area of information that you may find useful is from the research labs of universities and research institutes. These organizations often produce regular reports that can be scanned for interesting information. Gather as much information as you can, as long as this does not impact the next stage of understanding future trends and opportunities. You may find that it is difficult to stop the information gathering since there is always something new on the horizon.

Information and Knowledge Can Help with Predictions

Eventually you will need to make a decision. This can sometimes be hindered by an obsessive information-gathering exercise. No answer is perfect; just good enough will do for most decision-making. The next stage is the analysis of the information and the synthesis of a strategy based on that knowledge. Business innovation is generally searching for new ways to grow the business. Less frequently it is focused on cost reduction, but the most influential innovations tend to be growth-oriented. Growth is often associated with entering a new product market in your own geography or opening a new office to increase existing product sales. While the CEO or head of sales typically initiates this type of innovation, the need for IT support will often mean that the CIO is involved during the decision process.

As an example of the use of this knowledge, we can look at a company planning to open an office in a different geographical region. There are many logistical problems needing a solution. In IT, there are a number of related questions to be asked that may highlight further problems to be solved:

- Will you need local IT staff? This will be partly determined by the size of the new operation, the resilience of the local infrastructure, Internet, etc.

- Do your existing suppliers operate in this region? What are the delivery conditions and costs?

- Will you need to partner with other organizations locally?

- Who will be in charge of outfitting and equipping the new office?

Added to these IT considerations, the prudent CIO will need to be familiar with the new region, its customs, and local regulations. It may be that the new region has unique privacy laws or laws restricting information that noncitizens can hold. A knowledge base to answer these questions would be of value in discussing the broader IT impact of working in this region. The innovative CIO can also use this as an opportunity to create an atmosphere of trust by demonstrating an understanding of the geo-socio-political realities of this region in meetings with senior management. This may be part of a shared knowledge base should the CIO be a part of the decision-making team. In the likely case that the CIO has been informed, much further down the decision timeline this data may reinforce or add caution to a decision. It is too late for the CIO to suggest restrictions on delivery of Internet access when the office lease has been signed. Having a good knowledge base that will become trusted in your company will help prevent IT from being considered as an afterthought.

The information that you would gather for such a knowledge base can be allied to a review of the innovation potential of a new market. Are there technologies that will work better in that region? Mobile phones are the computing device of choice in sub-Saharan Africa. The landline infrastructure is weak or nonexistent. Planning an expansion into this area may call for repurposing of your internal IT applications to a mobile platform. The expansion into a new geographic area can be used as a test bed or pilot for increasing the mobility of the whole workforce. The logistics of recruiting local staff in the new location may generate a review of IT management and recruitment across the entire company. It may be prudent that investing in remote management and one central IT function rather than duplicate functions in many locations will bring benefits to the whole of IT, not just the new location. The innovative CIO will be looking for these opportunities in any major business innovation.

Networking Is a Future Opportunity

As we have mentioned in other parts of this chapter, social networking and collaboration are having an impact on innovation. In this section, we will explore two meanings of network. The first meaning is one more familiar to technologists: the physical network that runs the business. The second meaning is that of the social network of friends, colleagues, and other personal contacts. Improving networks in both senses can yield dividends.

Physical Networks: Faster, Further, Cheaper

The most obvious effect of network improvements is in the increasing numbers of remote and distributed workers. This change is delivering benefits such as reduced travel time and more motivated employees. Increasing broadband performance is also allowing Voice over IP and video conferencing. Soon there will be enough network capacity for high-quality telepresence and virtual reality interaction. These areas may enable better communications between the company, suppliers, partners, and customers. This is not to suggest that face-to-face communications have no place. People still buy from people for high-value items, but there are increasing numbers of alternatives for commodity items.

Future innovation will depend on how technology fits together—how it communicates and relates to other technologies and users. Cloud computing is offering a partial solution to this problem. Part of the value of cloud computing is that connecting to a service requires no knowledge of the underlying technology supplying that service. Cloud computing in itself is not likely to cause many problems to end users. After all, anyone who uses Gmail or Hotmail is already an experienced cloud user.

The challenge being faced is in the physical network. At the enterprise level, companies can afford to have networking experts who will resolve issues quickly. The increased consumerization of IT, moving the IT capability out to the users, has generated a group who have little understanding or interest in solving the networking problems that may exist. Anyone who has had a problem on their home broadband will empathize with the complexity and large number of points of failure on this physical network.

The proliferation of technology in the last 20 years has generated complex networks both at home and in the office. Many complexity challenges have been solved, but some remain before the full potential of the network can be realized. Internet users are vulnerable to the impact of additional complexity and traffic. There is a potential for further congestion from the explosive capacity of Internet Protocol version 6 (IPv6). If your home broadband is already at capacity with streaming videos and other Internet traffic, the additional load of noncomputing devices using the network could expose undiscovered network vulnerabilities that cannot be hidden behind cloud computing.

"Internet of Things": Getting Your Fridge and TV Chatting

Retail and logistics companies are leading the implementation of Internet of Things (IoT) applications today. We have already discussed the innovation opportunities generated by IoT in Chapter 6 "Opportunities to Innovate Today". Some of the experiments in healthcare and transport applications of this technology are also described in Chapter 6. Logistics and retail companies are leading the field in implementations at the moment. Although there are concrete plans in the IoT space now, IoT is also something to consider for the future.

Many analysts and commentators talk about instrumenting the world and see a greater potential for IoT in the future. There is recognition that the application of IoT technology will be a long time arriving in some business domains. Analysts have suggested that 75% of companies in the energy, automotive, utility and aerospace world will adopt IoT in the 5 to 8 year timeframe. Opportunities for innovation in IoT are both current and in the future.

One big issue drives this dual potential of IoT; there is currently no "killer app" for IoT. This issue is acknowledged widely in the IoT field and is a constant discussion point at conferences and in analyst reports. The lack of a compelling business reason for the whole of IoT is not preventing the experiments and trials. There is a feeling in the IoT world that we should just instrument things and eventually the nuggets of gold will emerge. Our instincts tell us that there is something valuable about IoT but at the moment we are not sure what that is. IoT is an area that should be kept on a watch list for future innovation as well as being considered in your current innovation plans.

Let your imagination run a little wild thinking about what you could do in your business if everything in your business world could be instrumented and capable of communicating. Consider waste disposal as a problem: if all your household or business waste was instrumented it would be possible for you or your company to take better decisions about where and how your waste can be handled. There will be the inevitable protests about "town hall snoops" checking you are disposing of your garbage properly, but these may be silenced with decent security and privacy measures. The potential advantage is the focus on the disposal chain, aiming to deliver similar efficiencies to the supply chain. An efficient disposal chain could, potentially, generate major cost savings on taxes and disposal fees. This example illustrates both the potential of IoT and some barriers to its adoption. It is already possible to instrument a lot of the disposal chain with RFID tags on goods and garbage handling. There are no compelling financial reasons to do so currently, other than avoiding fines for putting the wrong garbage in a recycling bin. Efficiencies in disposal would need a re-think of attitudes to garbage and a government plan to create an incentive for greater efficiency.

We feel that the potential of the Internet of Things will be greater in the future once there is an understanding of the wider benefits of being able to link to most parts of the physical world to the Internet. When the killer app comes it would be remiss of you to have missed it.

Smartphones Are the Computing Platform of Choice

In the developing world, smartphones are the computing platform of choice, for many of the millennials and even older generations are becoming more phone-centric. In many parts of the emerging economies, the mobile phone has the same appeal. Broadband capacity is increasing and in particular mobile broadband is increasing in capacity. This will have an impact on both the scope of the mobile network and its capabilities. As the spread of mobile broadband increases and the cost decreases, more individuals will use the smartphone.

This will push the mobile capability further and further out to the edge of the network. It will bring a whole new customer base into contact for goods and services for the first time. Mobile phones are already being used in ways we never would have thought of even four years ago. In parts of Africa, users can send an SMS with the drug batch number to a pharmacy phone number and get a return SMS telling them if the drug is counterfeit or safe to use. Will the mobile phone enable more intimate conversations with customers? Are your internal applications ready for the request for mobile enablement? It may be a good time to start looking at the potential for your company and the customer requirements to decide to invest in a mobility strategy.

One area to consider beyond mobile is the potential for augmented reality via the increased capacity mobile network. We will discuss this later in the chapter.

Expanding the network and improving the network is one of the topics that really appeal to the technologist. IPv6, wireless, pervasive computing—all are comfort words and resonate with the technologists. Don't get caught in the trap of explaining how these things work; look for the business potential.

Networking for Pleasure and Profit

As we mentioned earlier, another meaning of networking is the interaction between individuals and groups of people. Sales and marketing executives regard networking as a critical skill, leading to ideas, opportunities and friendships. The innovative CIO needs to embrace this style of networking as much if not more than the physical networking. The CIO can enable increased networking of the company, customers, and suppliers by the use of social networking tools. The IT department should accept the challenge of managing social networking for the company to ensure that the users are successful and protected.

More organizations (including your own), customers, and suppliers' organizations, are networked and becoming increasingly porous. Porous is used here to describe how suppliers and customers may use your organizational tools. If you have a help desk service that customers can enter trouble tickets in to, that is a porous application. This is a growing trend, with some organizations giving suppliers access to stock levels so that the suppliers become responsible for maintaining stock rather than the retailer. All of this is part of a more networked world of business. This is frequently used as a way of cutting costs.

Social networks are being used increasingly as a communication medium. Companies are increasingly putting instructional or advertising videos on YouTube. Contact and newsworthy information is posted on Facebook and

LinkedIn and executives, and thought leaders often use Twitter to disseminate information and links to relevant information. All of these are ways of increasing the level of networking that can add value to your organization. It does not matter if LinkedIn is where you reach out to customers or if Facebook is where your marketing material is located, social networking is here to stay. The old-style data center was a tightly controlled world of tried and tested applications that had been in place for a long time. Most IT managers and some CIOs still prefer it that way and have locked the company systems away from social networking. I was at a large bank recently and was told by staff that they cannot even look at their own company pages on Facebook from within the office network. This style of IT management has a negative effect on the perception of IT. Social networking should be encouraged with only small amounts of company data secured: financial information, planning and customer information, and of course, anything that is covered under the various regulations and privacy laws.

One area that social networking is enabling is collaborative working. E-mails are good communication media, but they are still stuck in the memo school of business. Social networking is allowing more interaction. A post on a social network can attract ideas and discussion that has the potential to gather more views and opinions. This can help make ideas better, help the company avoid bad decisions, and help in creating an innovative atmosphere that is open rather than closed.

Open Innovation: Enlarging Your Network

"Open innovation" is a term that was originally coined by Dr. Henry Chesbrough at Haas Business School in UC Berkeley.[6] It has been well-promoted and is an initiative that is gaining some traction. The basic premise is to use a group of people to make an innovation better by collaborating. Companies should use external and internal resources to create innovations, develop products, and go to market. This model changes the emphasis from commodities that are sold to services that are supplied. In this world, IP is truly in the service delivery rather than the product being implemented. This may be counterintuitive to many existing IT organizations, but a case can be made that an open source/open innovation approach can work if the internal resources are not available to maintain a nonstrategic product line. This would require significant buy-in from the management team and in particular the finance department, but it may apply in some future cases and can be considered in future product retirement plans.

---

[6] Henry Chesbrough, "Program in Open Innovation," University of California Berkeley, 2003, http://openinnovation.berkeley.edu/index.html, accessed on May 2012.

Business Expansion Using Future IT Innovations

Opportunities to innovate in the future are likely to be focused on technologies that may be emerging today or the synergies in technology that will come from future developments. Business expansion is the most important function of the IT innovator. Leading the field with an innovation will gain visibility and drive growth. While it may not be long before other organizations catch up to you, they will always be in second place. And as long as focus and execution are in step, you will always be able to keep one step ahead—if you are first. You don't always need to be the best.

Expansion through New Ways of Working

One of the important trends we noted in the discussion on network expansion is the growth of the network both in capacity and reach. It was only in the very early years of the 21st century that broadband technologies became commonplace in the office, then the home. Initially the Internet was accessed through dial-up modems, and then early broadband cable modems started the move to inexpensive connectivity in the developing world. Broadband capabilities in the developed world are becoming more prevalent with a small number of rural communities still to be connected. In the developed world, this has led to process and facilities innovations such as remote or home working. The spread of wireless hotspots, tablet computing, and mobile applications have meant the workforce can participate from many locations. While there are implications for social and economic developments, the tethering of employees to a location is no longer necessary. Organizations can recruit the people best able to carry out work rather than the people who can get to an office. The innovative CIO has to become more aware of the requirements for this style of working and the configuration, management, and security problems of remote working. Adapting to this new way of working will be mandatory in the future, but since it is driven by IT capabilities you have to be integral to the decision process but not seen as a negative influence. Using emerging technology such as ambient telepresence and enhanced reality will also generate new ways of communicating and delivering information.

Mobility Generates Further Expansion

While the developed world is well served by wired broadband and an increase in the number of WiFi hotspots, the developing world is relying more on mobile broadband. Predictions have been made that mobile broadband is the next growth area in networking. What are the implications for your organization? Will mobile broadband, phone tethering, and tablet computing deliver the same location independence? What advantages will that bring to your organization? How can you, as an IT leader, ensure that your company is ready to take advantage of this trend before the competitors? You should consider how a growth in mobile broadband will enable you to tap into new locations for markets and the staff to service those markets. Once the mobile broadband revolution has arrived, markets in Africa, South America, and other more remote locations will become open to your organization with a faster, cheaper start-up cost. Most importantly, employees and customers in those areas will have the same quality of service that they would have in the developed world. This may be worth considering as you plan for expansion into new locations in new geographic regions.

Increasing Your Global Reach

The global drive to expansion of the physical network capacity can also generate new markets. For example, in the health care world some communications and diagnostic tools require a network to be able to function.

The reach of other technologies can help expand your business. It will not be long before you can connect to a 3D printer, print some components on the other side of the world, and have lower-cost labor assemble the components into a finished product.

The amount of data that you have can drive better analysis of customers outside your own region. Most marketing organizations are aware of the different meaning associated with the color red in different cultures. Using red as a color for an emergency device would work in the West. In China, it may be assumed that this device is a lucky device. These broad cultural differences are well-documented. It would be a crass sales or marketing employee who ignored them when considering an expansion into a new geographic area. As data is gathered, more subtle differences will emerge, and this will enable the personalized marketing that will ensure that each customer is treated as an individual and that individuals have offerings especially for them.

New Lines of Business from Old Data

"Big data" is a phrase that is becoming a little overhyped, but describes an interesting condition. Now most organizations are focused on getting more value from their data. These organizations are being swamped by data coming from existing enterprise IT systems. Supermarkets are looking at highly personalized shopping experiences based on complex analytics. They hope to be able to upsell items based on an intimate knowledge of the customer's individual buying pattern. A quick analysis of my buying patterns at a supermarket would indicate that I buy different wine and cheese at different times. I tend to buy lighter flavored varieties of both in the summer, heavier flavors in the winter. Marketing targeted on my seasonal preferences can result in an increased sale even with such scant analysis. Retail analysts have already delved far deeper than this into the behaviors and buying patterns of their customers. Until the current aggregation of enormous amounts of data, finer-grained data analysis has been difficult. In some strategic conversations, we have been told that the amount of data stored in an organization is a problem and costing too much. This attitude is starting to change with the realization that this data can be a gold mine of new information. New techniques and technology are starting to make new knowledge available from this amount of data.

Expanding Your Business and Market with Innovative IT

Innovative IT can deliver new lines of business to an organization. One of the more recent examples, as we mentioned in Chapter 4, is Amazon moving into the provision of cloud services. Amazon executives have recognized that the computing power they use for supporting the business could be used to provide a different service to their customers. Amazon has reused their existing resources to expand into a new line of business. They have entered a new market that is not related to their main line of business. Organizations can exploit some of their expertise and resources to deliver these opportunities. You should take a fresh look at your company's resources to look for new opportunities.

Identifying adjacent markets can also develop new lines of business. An adjacent line of business would be expanding into the sale of magazines if you already sold books.

Innovation Delivers Growth Through Mergers and Acquisition

As an organization develops, there are several opportunities that present different options for growth. Most startups have an innovative idea that develops into a growing organization and other innovations fuel that growth. Organic innovation of this type can generate large corporations, although frequently there is a mix of merger and acquisition (M&A) activity in parallel.

Some companies start small and fuel their growth by acquiring customers, products, and market share by acquisition and have little or no organic growth beyond the start-up phase. In both these styles of growth, there will be some merger and acquisition activity. There are some common acquisition pitfalls in this approach. In regard to mergers or partnerships, the problems are slightly different.

In an acquisition, one company acquires another with a view to using their resources to grow. The acquired company may be left as a totally separate business unit, or even a separate "wholly owned" company. This separation removes some pitfalls but also may remove some of the economies of scale in property, administration, and all-supporting activities. Many acquired companies are merged into the owner's company at least at the administrative level to drive economies in both companies. It is assumed that the acquisition would be due to some synergy between the organizations and if they are left as separate entities then there is no advantage to ownership. In IT terms, one of the most common economies of scale is the merging of internal systems. There should be no need for two accounting, human resources, or enterprise resource planning (ERP) systems as a start. This would also simplify the company regulatory compliance requirements by bringing all the systems into one central organization.

In a merger, there is a less clear "who owns what" demarcation. There may be an attempt to discuss the use of separate internal systems and management. Most importantly, the IT systems that are more flexible and standards-driven in a merger are likely to be the ones that win out. This is because the flexible systems can absorb other IT processes easier than more rigid or difficult-to-modify systems.

In a partnership, both organizations have to have some synergy and the partnership may be to enable expansion into new markets or locations or to have a cross-selling opportunity. In this case, the security and privacy of both organizations have to allow some porosity of the companies' internal systems.

IT innovation can reduce the impact of merger and acquisition. The innovative CIO will be preparing for M&A by looking for ways to overcome some of the pitfalls.

Pitfalls of M&A

In any M&A activity, the business decision-makers tend to ignore most of the IT implications of that activity. Two banks planning to merge would not specifically discuss the internal IT systems to ensure compatibility or ease of integration; they would be concerned with other areas of the business. The integration of IT would be important but not a gating factor for the deal. Merging two separate corporate IT systems can be a long and difficult exercise, particularly if the IT systems have not been designed with flexibility in mind.

Greater consideration should be given to customer needs if the customer-facing applications are to change. Merging several applications is an opportunity to make innovative changes to the user interface and processes that these applications support.

In a partnership, there is a different requirement. A partner probably would not want to use the same customer-focused user interface to order goods. A partner would expect more information than a customer would normally expect. A partner may require supply chain information, shipping information, or marketing collateral. All of this information would need to be available to enable the partner to maximize their potential. Corporate IT systems are often locked down to such an extent that this information is difficult to achieve. If you also consider there may be incompatible IT systems, then a straight daily data dump may not be possible. This is also an issue if you and your partner have different processes to link goods and services with customers. What if your partner runs a "just-in-time" supply chain and your supply chain is based on batch behavior? IT should not be a limiting factor for mergers, acquisitions, and partnerships, but an enabler and better still an innovative factor in future success.

Innovation of Products and Services

The innovative CIO needs to develop a strategy that will allow an easy integration and exploitation of joint intellectual property (IP). Often a merger or acquisition is planned to fill a shortfall in an offering by acquiring new technology or capabilities.

One clear advantage of a merger or acquisition is the possibility of increasing your intellectual property portfolio. While there are obvious advantages to this strategy, it also enables additional innovations based on the acquired IP. In some cases, this can open up adjacent markets, as we have already mentioned, and grow the business by developing new products.

A strategy based on delivering IT as a service will increase the capability of the IT department and has the potential to create new innovative uses by aggregating the best services from both organizations in a single service. A single interface can then be developed to be the common interface to the underlying systems without requiring massive rewrites and redevelopment of those systems.

One area that can yield value is the increased understanding from access to the joint data set. Analysis of both data sets in a merger or acquisition can deliver more customer insight identifying cross-selling or up-selling potential. Developing and improving the current capabilities for handling the increasingly large amounts of data within the current organizational structure is a good way to ensure that data sets from M&A activities can deliver value quickly.

Innovation of Business Processes

We have mentioned in several chapters that the concept of IT innovating IT is not likely to win executive backing. Mergers and acquisitions are one of the few activities where IT innovating IT may be justified, as long as the discussion is on the why and business benefits level, not the how-we-plan-to-use-all-this-cool-new-technology. Modification of internal systems by taking a service-oriented approach will enable flexibility and the ability to integrate existing systems quickly. Moving from proprietary, in-house, and legacy systems to a more generally accepted standard-based system will ensure that when the decision is taken to merge two organizations, the IT department is in an open and flexible architecture.

As an M&A process is underway, there will be a change to business processes requiring an underlying change to the IT applications that support them. Delivering an 18-month plan for completing all the work may mean that you are never going to complete any task, since there may be another merger or acquisition in the next 6 months. You may want a Rolls-Royce solution to "fix this for once and all," but you may not get this luxury. Plan for fast and near-enough right. Plan to be flexible and service-oriented, but plan to be aggressive in support of the massive business process changes that M&A will bring.

Delivering a flexible, easily integrated system to the business will create confidence in the executives that any merger, acquisition, or partnership can be viewed in purely business terms with IT enabling and smoothing out technology problems. In this way, the business remains focused on the business, and the CIO will be regarded as a trusted advisor rather than an obstacle.

Crystal Ball on Standby: The Future Is Nearer Than You Think

In this chapter, we have talked about the opportunities for future innovation. We have suggested how the future can be predicted based on a solid knowledge base and some of the areas that will influence your thinking on innovating for the future. In this section, we will talk more about the technologies that can have an influence and where they may be of value. We have mentioned a number of technologies in earlier chapters. Here we will discuss a few emerging technologies that are on the radar but are not considered a near-term option. These can be grouped into three broad areas:

- Collaboration and communication
- New user interfaces
- Smarter devices and environments

We will discuss these areas in the context of innovation for the future.

Collaboration and Communication

Social networking is an important feature that has allowed more collaboration between distributed groups of people but still tends to be a send/respond model of communication, although we have mentioned real-time collaboration earlier in this chapter. One of the things lacking in conference calls, or even video conferences, is the type of serendipitous encounter that is frequently talked about as a "water cooler" event. This is based on chance meetings away from the desk at a common area like a refreshment station. These chance meetings can spark ideas, remind participants of things to discuss, or even just remind you that next time you have a challenge with something there is someone you can talk to. A frequent cry from distributed groups is for a meeting in a single location because the informal interaction is so valuable. This is the one major loss in the drive for a more distributed team.

"Ambient telepresence" is a term that refers to mobility of a telepresence terminal. The technology ranges from simple laptop, microphone, speakers, and camera to a remote control robot containing all of these things in a single, vaguely human, casing. The portability of the device is important. This is not about opening a video conference window on your own laptop; it is about allowing a device to become a personal avatar for a team member. It is a one-to-one relationship. Microsoft Research has published research in this area, referring to it as "Embedded Social Proxies[7]." The concept is simple. If a device can represent one person, the device can be taken with the team to meetings, used for one-on-one sessions, and even taken to lunch. Microsoft Research uses a cart that is moved manually but there are other self-drive alternatives. The self-drive alternatives allow a person who is logged in as the user to drive these more expensive integrated units from place to place. Otherwise the device has to be carried or wheeled by a friendly person in that location.

---

[7] Rob Knies, "Remote Meetings – Thinking Inside the Box," June 2009, Microsoft Research, research.microsoft.com/en-us/news/features/esp-061009.aspx, accessed on October 2012.

There are many undiscovered challenges with this technology. For example, there is little proof that a wireless connection is fast enough to build a relationship with an avatar as a team member. Another intriguing question is how you "drive" yourself in the avatar robot down two flights of stairs and through a security pass–coded door. The challenges are real, but the technology shows promise, particularly in solving the team-building aspects of a remote or distributed team. As an innovative CIO investigating this technology, you may find a supporter in the CFO. In any international organization, the travel budget is always a major operating expense, so ways of improving productivity and teamwork that don't involve flights will find a ready audience in the finance department.

Mobile broadband is spreading, and fourth generation bandwidth is starting to emerge. This will have an effect on ambient telepresence but will also enable the use of augmented reality. Virtual reality is where a whole virtual representation is used to simulate some segment of reality. Overlaying additional data, information, enhanced skills, and effects on top of reality is augmented reality. Virtual reality has many existing applications in terms of simulation and virtual design. Augmented reality is emerging as a means of enhancing the views of reality. A good example would be a view of some real vegetables in a supermarket, and an overlay identifying the vegetables, recommending cooking methods and recipes that use the vegetables. Supermarkets and the retail industry are already investigating this technology. There are applications in most areas of business including customer relationship management, product support, and manufacturing. Although augmented reality is in its infancy, there have been some experiments that should be watched—for example, Google's Project Glass. Some of the planned capabilities that have been reported for this project are also in the user interface domain.

New User Interfaces

However much the display mechanisms are changing thanks to the huge uptake of tablets and touch screen technology, content production is still stuck in the screen, keyboard, pointing-device era of interface. There have been some commercial products that use voice interaction, such as Apple's SIRI and various dictation applications. All are having mixed success, but they will continue to develop aided by the increasing miniaturization, improved battery technology, and a need to create content for a content- hungry world. Some of your users and customers who are still having problems interfacing with IT may be ready to experiment with voice control and content creation. One consideration is the increasing number of millennials who are suffering from repetitive stress injuries from heavy use of text messages and social networking. There may be a need for an alternative to mobile device data interaction that does not require repetitive movement of fingers and thumbs. This may be an opportunity for innovation in mobile workforce interaction with IT devices and nontraditional devices.

A challenge going forward is the use of voice activation and dictation in a crowded area; privacy and nuisance issues may require subvocal voice activation, although this is a long way off. While this is a technology worth keeping under scrutiny, there are also social and psychological barriers that will become more evident as people interact more with devices. This interaction with devices is more obvious in the "Internet of Things" where devices get smarter and interact more with each other and with people.

Smarter Devices and Environments

The "Internet of Things" has already been referred to in this chapter. One of the research areas that are getting some investment is in the use of integrated command-and-control systems in Smart Cities. Smart Cities are cities that have a high degree of integration between the population, the services, and the people who supply services. Many visions start with citywide broadband, terminals for specific tasks, and transport systems that take a holistic view of the movement of people and goods across the city. As noncomputing devices get connected to the Internet, the possibility for more complex interaction increases. We are already seeing this with location-based services on mobile phones becoming more common. Sensors in clothing, books, streetlights, doors, vehicles, and drinks delivery systems can monitor and interact. This is developed to the extent that people are already creating believable scenarios. For example, a person is walking down the street, a garment is monitoring the person and recognizes a slight dehydration, and the garment then communicates with a street sign that recommends the person step into the next store where there is a water fountain. While much of this has a science fiction feel, a lot of the technology is available. Wearable sensors for monitoring an individual are being used more frequently in health care. Reactive street furniture is being experimented with in integrated command-and-control systems, and location-aware software is already on your mobile phone. The debate on the ethics of this direction is not for this book, but the innovative CIO should review all of these potentially disruptive uses for devices. Devices that are on the Internet and capable of both delivering data and interacting with each other are becoming more common. Is there an innovative business application for this technology in your organization?

CHAPTER

9

Making Innovation Intentional

Innovation Is a Butterfly: Where's My Net?

Opportunity is missed by most people because it is dressed in overalls and looks like work.

—Thomas A. Edison

We've all seen them—posters that proclaim that a company is an innovative company, that innovation comes from everywhere, and that it is everyone's duty to innovate. While these statements may be true, we also know that simply posting a slogan, even with noble intent and firm belief, will not make a company innovative. Nor will the absence of such things prevent innovation from occurring. While there is nothing wrong with promoting an innovative culture in these ways (they can help), organizations must take care not to believe that posters and screen savers will alone lead to innovation. Those that do so may limit their intentional initiatives to those campaigns and will miss innovative opportunities, or even discourage innovation as their messages may be seen as not matching their actions.

An organization that is suffering from one of the "innovation killers" discussed in Chapter 2, or possessing one or more of those innovation-killing personalities, could be in even worse shape if an internal PR campaign is their sole action. In most cases, no slogan or poster will cure those illnesses or change a destructive personality. Thus, deliberate action must be taken in order for your company to benefit from the innovation that occurs within.

The phrase "innovation that occurs within" is an important one to keep in mind. The most important aspect of making innovation intentional is not always related to doing things to help generate innovative ideas. It is often about doing things to capture those ideas and then, just as caterpillars must be nourished in order to become butterflies, caring for and feeding those ideas.

Fostering Innovation

So, where *does* innovation come from? Where does it happen? From whom do the ideas spring forth? At the risk of using an overused cliché, it has been our experience that innovation *does* come from everywhere and it *can* come from anyone. Therefore, we would have to agree that the slogan is correct. Our point is simply that the danger organizations face when using it is believing that simply saying or displaying it is the answer to all of their innovation problems.

There is also another key question we are often asked: "How can we encourage innovation? How can we become more innovative?" Our answer? You probably already have innovative people in your organization. Therefore, perhaps the questions should be rephrased: "How can we help our people to bring forth their innovations? How can we harness the innovative power of our people? How can we ensure we are gaining the most benefit from our innovations?" There are many techniques that may help. We will begin this chapter by discussing some of the approaches we have found to be effective.

Don't Think About It

Many times innovation and new ideas come when least expected by the innovator. To be clear, we are not referring to the type of innovation discussed in Chapter 2 as "fortunate innovation." Accidental innovations do occur, and when they do the experience is magical. Accidental innovations are gifts. Enjoy and appreciate them. What we are referring to here are cases when a team faced with a challenge or opportunity develops an innovative idea when they are not *consciously* thinking about the challenge or opportunity it addresses.

When this happens, it may appear to be unintentional innovation—something that just happened. We believe that quite often these things are much more intentional than one might believe. Some people think that when a person is unable to solve a problem and consciously moves on to something else, the subconscious mind can continue to work on the unresolved problems and challenges. Regardless of your opinion of the science behind this theory, our experience has been that not focusing on a problem can often result in its resolution.

Consider the following scenario and ask yourself whether it has ever happened to you. You had been working on a problem for an extended period, or perhaps at the end of an exhausting week, when you decide you are too tired to concentrate on it any longer. Fatigue has won the battle. Since you are exhausted, moving to another mentally challenging task is not a viable option. Perhaps you actually have that as a conscious thought, or perhaps you try something else challenging and soon realize it is not going to bear fruit.

So you move on to something a bit more mechanical. You fill out a form, take an online survey, or perhaps clean your work area. You may have even put some music on in the background to help you relax. Perhaps you clean your office for five or ten minutes. Perhaps for a half hour. Then, as if from nowhere, it hits you! You have the answer! You have a new idea! It is one of the best things you have ever thought of.

Certainly cleaning the office is one of the innovation techniques many of us use often—though the "office" in that phrase may really be your mind. Some of our most innovative ideas have come when we were not thinking about them. Before a person makes the connection between shifting focus away from a challenge and how that act can contribute to a resolution, the ideas can appear to come from nowhere.

A somewhat humorous incident caused me to personally recognize this pattern. Over a short period I had presented several creative ideas to a company's cofounder. On several of these occasions, when the cofounder had asked how I had come up with the idea, I started my explanation by saying, "I was in the shower and . . ." I had not made the connection until one day the cofounder ended a meeting by saying: "You need to take more showers." We shared a laugh about his observation, but unfortunately the people arriving for the subsequent meeting were highly confused.

While I cannot state with certainty whether that singular event was the turning point, I admit that once I realized the power of stepping away from a problem, I was able to harness it, at least somewhat. I also discovered that taking short breaks, even when not completely baffled by a problem, could help me get to a solution more rapidly. Incidentally, this works as well when applied to more routine tasks, such as working through a project plan as it does for creative ideas. Often a ten-minute walk can help bring forth a solution to something that may have presented a progress-delaying challenge for hours.

One key element to the success of this technique is not to focus on something else that is also mentally challenging. For example, initially during my ten-minute walks, I would listen to podcasts or books in order to learn something new while walking. At the end of those walks, it was often even more difficult for me to return to solving the problem I had stepped away from.

Once in a while I did get lucky and the podcast or book touched on something that resolved the issue. However, success came more often if I listened to music, or nothing at all, and let my mind wander. Sometimes I would fairly quickly come upon a solution or approach. Other times my mind would drift. Then, seemingly from nowhere, a stream of ideas would start to flow; so rapidly in many cases that I would have to stop and take notes.

And that is when I learned the value of the next tool: taking notes.

Before we address this next subject, it is worth noting that the "don't think about it" technique can also be applied in a group setting. In fact, consciously or unconsciously it is often in play. Group activities, such as dinners or sporting events, are often a part of team meetings. In addition, participants in team meetings are often given some time in between working sessions and the group activity during which to unwind – to explore the locale or visit a fitness center. These activities can provide down time that will enable each individual's ideas to ferment. Creating opportunities for people to "not think about it" in a group setting offers the added benefit of having others with whom to further develop ideas once they materialize.

Take Note

Ideas can come at any time and from any place. While not thinking about something can be a technique for making innovation intentional, it is not always intentionally employed. A walk to the grocery store, a bicycle ride with a child or friend—these are all opportunities for you to not think about your work. And then it hits us. Eureka! As you cycle down that beautiful path, you develop not only an idea but a complete solution—everything you need to develop, deploy, execute, and realize its benefits.

You arrive home or to your office fully energized. Perhaps you go straight to your desk to begin working on the problem. Perhaps (likely) you are distracted by someone or something, though eventually you get back to your new idea. Well, at least you thought you had an idea. Has this ever happened to you? Sure it has. Sometimes you can remember bits of the idea. Sometimes all you can remember is that you had an idea. It's even worse when the only thing you can remember is that the idea was outstanding.

Therefore, it is critical that you always have the capacity to stop and take note of any ideas you have. You can never be certain what might inspire you or where you will be when it happens. In fact, even in writing this book, there have been several times when I have stopped while on a walk or shopping . . . and written an idea, outline, or paragraph.

The good news is that today it is simpler than ever to be able to take notes anywhere and at any time. You can certainly carry a pen or pencil and paper. Smartphones can make note-taking simple, and tablets such as the iPad can enable the creation of professional-looking, ready-to-distribute documents while on the move. In fact, they can also enable the document's distribution. And there are various services that enable the storage of the notes or documents off the device (in the cloud) so that they are protected even if something happens to the device.

And "anywhere" means *anywhere*. I had an experience that was reminiscent of the fairy tale "The Shoemaker and the Elves." At that time, it was commonplace for programmers in my circle to work around the clock to deliver code. Often we would work to the point of exhaustion without realizing it. It was only when we were too tired to solve a problem that we would realize our exhaustion.

So completely tired, I would go to sleep. And then I would often dream of a solution. I would wake up in the middle of the night having solved the problem. Because I had solved the problem, I would then be completely relaxed and would fall back to sleep with a smile on my face. The next morning, I would wake up completely refreshed, with only a memory that I had solved the problem—but no memory of how.

I eventually learned to keep a pen and paper next to my bed. When I woke up in the middle of the night having solved a problem, I would write down the solution. In the morning, the solution would be there. Often I had no memory of writing the code or solution until I saw the sheet of paper. In homage to that fairy tale, I would refer to such code as having been created by the "Code Fairies."

Leverage Your Inexperience

Often organizations that are faced with a difficult challenge will respond by assigning their most experienced people to resolve it, and it's difficult to dispute the sound logic in that decision. Though we would not dispute that as an approach, we would like to suggest another approach be added to your arsenal: send in the new guy.

Newer employees are often able to find creative and innovative ways to solve problems or seize opportunities, even when those with more experience have not been able to do so. Why? One reason may be that confirmation bias is not a factor. New employees do not know that certain things will never work and that some things cannot be done.

Thus, for new employees, the impossible has not yet become impossible. A more experienced person may already possess the knowledge that a certain problem cannot be solved (or cannot be solved without certain constraints). More experienced employees may be encumbered by what they believe is possible and by what they know cannot be done.

The life experiences of new employees may also be different from those who arrived on the scene earlier. They may have grown up in a different locale or had atypical interests in their youth, at least for someone in their area of specialty. So, when faced with the problem, perhaps an employee who was a rock climber applies a rock-climbing principle to a business problem (maybe subconsciously), and in so doing solves a problem that had challenged others without even breaking a sweat.

Furthermore, new employees may have been exposed to tools and techniques throughout their formal and informal education that were not normally applied to the domain in which the problem exists. For example, today's graduates not only have a wealth of knowledge regarding social media tools, they also know how to get the most out of them. This might provide them with a vastly different view of a problem and solution space than someone from a different generation.

We must also consider passion. Youthful exuberance is a wonderful thing and, expressed properly, can be contagious to team members of all ages. The value of passion in innovation cannot be discounted. Passionate, young team members can also possess a remarkable level of diligence that can enable them to look at aspects of a challenge that may have been discounted by someone with more experience.

Are we suggesting you never again assign employees with experience to a problem or innovative challenge in their domain? That experienced people cannot be innovative? Of course not. Innovation *can* come from anyone, anywhere, at any time. We are simply stating that, in our experience, the value of inexperience should not be overlooked.

After all, Google founders Larry Page and Sergey Brin met when they were aged 22 and 21, respectively, made the initial version of Google available at approximately age 23, and officially founded Google at around age 25.

And diversity in a team's composition can often be the key to their success. This is not only the case in terms of differences in the age of the team's members, but also in terms of other attributes such as gender, work experience, and personal interests.

Listen to Your Customers

All right, we admit "listen to your customers" may appear to be a fairly common sense suggestion. Though our experience is that, in the context of innovation, this common sense may not be all that common. Even organizations that take very good care of their customers can miss an opportunity to leverage their customers' innovative ideas.

In some cases, customers are able to present an innovative idea in a form that is easily consumed. They may be able to articulate its benefits beautifully. They may even be able to propose sound methods for achieving it along with a detailed plan. In those cases, adoption of the idea may be a simple exercise. However, customers' ideas are not always expressed in terms this simple.

More likely, though a customer may have a great idea, it may not be evident at the outset. Because customers may not have certain skills needed to clearly articulate the idea they may not be able to effectively state its benefits to you, to other customers, or to themselves.

In other instances, you may be presented with a case of "solve the solution." In cases of solve the solution, customers do not communicate the problem they are trying to solve or the benefit they would like to receive. They believe they have arrived at a solution that will deliver that benefit, and that is what they present as the need. Members of internal IT departments are likely very familiar with this phenomenon, especially so if their constituents are technically savvy. The request arrives in a form such as, "I need three quad core servers (often a specific model is stated), a (specific model) router, some duct tape, and 50 meters of CAT 5." The specifications they present are very specific, and there is often no context at all with the request.

A request of this nature can be a defining opportunity for an IT (or any) organization. Here are three possible responses:

- *Do it*: Give the customers exactly what they asked for. On the surface that makes sense, though the risk is that the solution the customer proposes may not at all address their objectives. In other words, what they requested may not be what they truly need.

- *Say "no"*: This technique has a double "benefit". Customers do not get what they need. The respondent has perpetuated their team's reputation as an organization that exists to prevent things that they did not propose from happening. When responding to customer requests IT teams must keep in mind the common perception that they are not capable of innovating and that they are not of value in the context of innovation. The arrival of terms like "Office of the CI-No" or "CI-Slow" are evidence of this widespread belief.

- *Engage*: Work to understand the customer's objectives. Ask questions to determine what they are trying to accomplish. Learn how the solution they envision will make their lives or their services better. Understand how their workflows would change and improve following the implementation of the new solution.

The best choice is obvious. Whether the request be vague or solve-the-solution specific, it presents a tremendous opportunity for a team to engage with their customers and to learn more about their objectives and about the opportunities they envision. That does not mean saying "yes" to exactly what was requested, which may not help them. It does mean actively listening to them and having them explain their objectives, and the benefits they believe a solution will deliver. It means asking questions: "Help me understand how that would help your business?" "Describe how your business will function more effectively after we implement this?" "How would your workday or your work processes change after the solution is implemented?"

If you find yourself thinking, "But they don't know our technology . . . They don't know our constraints . . . Their solution will never work," you have fallen into a common trap. You have made the assumption that the skills required to build a solution within a domain are also required in order to have innovative ideas in that domain. Nothing could be further from the truth.

Carefully consider what your customers do. They use the products and solutions you acquire, implement, deploy, develop, and/or create to solve their business problems. Every day. It is likely the case that you (as a provider) may not. As such, it is highly likely that they understand the problem and opportunity spaces of the domain much more deeply than you. So it should be no surprise that they have ideas, although they may not have the ability to bring those ideas to life. That's where you come in. And the partnership is where the magic happens. Each partner can make the other's ideas better.

What do you have to lose by engaging your customers? At the very worst, you have a great conversation about ideas with them. Even if they do not bring forth ideas that can be leveraged, you have strengthened your relationship and partnership with them. And often the seeds of ideas that are planted in conversations such as those will bring value later on.

An added benefit is an increased level of trust between you and your customers. The benefit, and necessity, of trust between you and your customers cannot be overstated. Apart from the obvious, having your customers' trust can result in additional time being available to your team to work on innovative ideas (e.g., your customers may not need updates as frequently, or in as much detail).

Incidentally, the customer we are referring to could be someone who works within your company (an internal customer) or someone who buys products from your company (an external customer). In either case, the considerations are the same. In fact, it may even be more challenging to work with internal customers in this context.

Be a Socialite

The rise in popularity of social media presents organizations with never before seen opportunities to learn from their customers. In fact, it may be of even more value that services like Twitter and Facebook also present innovative organizations with opportunities to engage with people who are *not* their customers.

Without a doubt, a company's customers can, and do, have great ideas. Social media provides a direct connection to many customers with whom you might not otherwise be able to connect. Through social media, these customers can bring their ideas and suggestions to you. They can also use social media to expose problems they encounter while using your products and services. On the surface, this might appear to be a bad thing. It is not.

If there is a problem with your products or services, your customers are already telling everyone about it via social media and other means. We see it every day. It's there for you too. Each interaction of this nature presents a great opportunity for your company. Some companies do very well at responding to issues surfaced via social media—others, not as well.

Social media can make you aware of issues you would not otherwise have known about. These issues may lead to innovative solutions, or even new products or features. They also present a chance for you to show your current and potential customers what your company really stands for.

One of the most valuable aspects of social media is the connection you can make with people who are not yet your customers. Those people may also have ideas that will help your business. Since they are not already your customer, chances are that there is no other way in which you would have known about them. These potential customers could place groundbreaking, innovative ideas in your lap, and it won't cost you a cent. For example, a tweet like "Hey, @YourCompany. If your product had a home key I would buy 100 of them" might lead you to a breakthrough. In addition, they are not constrained by what they believe your company or products can already do. They will be focused on their actual needs.

Hug a Rogue

Rogue IT has been the topic of much discussion for quite some time, and it appears to be a growing phenomenon. Essentially the phrase refers to a group of non-IT personnel obtaining or creating a business solution (that would normally be within the domain of their IT team) without their IT team's involvement. Some think of it as a parallel IT organization. The common perception of rogue IT as a secret parallel organization, often conjoined with terminology related to clandestine operations—has caused it to be referred to by other names, such as the ominous "Shadow IT." This brings to mind visions of the director of Shadow IT sitting in a high wingback chair petting a cat. It's not usually that frightening, unless you a senior IT leader or CIO.

Rogue IT teams rarely have a fully staffed IT team, and they often consider themselves to be nontechnical. But there are exceptions. In fact, I was an "unintentional rogue," and worked in an environment where the parallel organization had enough of the attributes of a corporate IT team to be considered fully staffed. In contrast, rogue teams often acquire solutions that do not require an IT team's support. Or at least they believe that to be the case when they first acquire the solution.

Often rogue IT emerges in the context of the acquisition of a SaaS solution such as SalesForce.com. To be clear, I am not maligning SaaS companies. Rather, it is a testament to how those companies have created solutions that deliver compelling business value while removing the need for their customers to be concerned with some basic functions that are traditionally the domain of an IT team. Less often a rogue solution may be created (developed) by the shadow IT team itself.

Sometimes the rogue solution encompasses a customer's entire business service requirements. At times, the solutions only partially address their needs. Furthermore, customers may *believe* they are acquiring an end-to-end solution but later learn this is false. They may learn that they require additional functionality. As this phenomenon matures, consumers are realizing more that they may require integration between the new (rogue) solution and other services, which may include their own homegrown services or off-the-shelf, on-premise solutions.

Those who acquired a rogue solution may also come to realize that the solution requires more care and feeding than they had estimated. There may be a need to perform maintenance and operational activities, maintain relationships with vendors, provision new users, configure the system, ensure the system meets the required business continuity or disaster recovery standards, or manage contracts and agreements with the vendor. As a result, we are seeing the emergence of a phenomenon we call the service boomerang.

We use the term "service boomerang" to refer to what happens when someone who has acquired a rogue solution realizes that the IT team is good at performing functions (such as those just mentioned) and brings the rogue solution to the IT team with a request that the IT group take over management of the rogue solution. This presents IT teams with a golden opportunity to build relationships with their customers and to position themselves as more strategic partners. Improvements in relationship and trust may even result in the IT team being perceived as a more trusted advisor, which in turn may result in their obtaining a seat at the business team's innovation table.

Sadly, some IT teams do not want to catch the boomerang. Are you wondering why that matters? What does this have to do with innovation? If you don't have a seat at the table, if you are not a valued partner. If you are not a trusted advisor, you may never be given an *opportunity* to innovate. You may never become aware of opportunities or challenges that might lead your team to an innovative solution.

Therefore, the first step is to catch the boomerang. Though, unfortunately, some IT departments are unable to do so. I recall a conversation with someone who had gone rogue and subsequently brought their solution back to their IT team. This person's team had replaced an on-premise business system with a SaaS version of that same system from the same vendor. They did this because the IT team had not been able to make changes to the on-premise system quickly enough. As well as addressing their agility problem, the new, rogue, system had also saved their company a substantial amount of money.

During our conversation the person explained that the IT team wrapped the new, nimble system in processes and procedures that had not been designed with that type of solution in mind. In the words of a member of the rogue team, "[The IT department's] process is not built for nimble changes." The rogue team was forced to again go rogue. You are not likely to get a third chance, though your successor may. We have seen that happen.

However, that is the darker side of rogue IT. Rogue IT can be extremely positive in the context of innovation. As was mentioned previously, rogue IT happens on your company's frontiers. It is normally the result of the people who know the most about a specific aspect of a business taking action to meet a challenge or seize an opportunity they would not otherwise have been able to address. This is a good thing.

Sure, in a perfect world, it would be better for innovative IT leaders to be in tune with, and in front of, all of the needs of the business. Some are able to accomplish this feat. When this frontier innovation occurs, IT leaders are presented with a leadership opportunity. Does it really make sense not to accept an innovation that can benefit your company on principle or because you are upset? Of course it does not.

Presented with these opportunities, innovative IT leaders must embrace the rogues. If they do not, they will drive rogues further underground, limiting the value the IT team can bring to the organization. Such action will also prove that perceptions of IT being unable to innovate or even to support innovation are fact-based. Furthermore, when IT teams embrace rogues, they will be able to add value to the rogues' ideas, enhance them, and perhaps even deliver more related (or unrelated) innovation of their own.

Embrace Your Inner Rogue

Much can be learned from rogue IT, and it goes beyond the innovation delivered by these teams. IT leaders who take time to embrace rogue groups can also learn how the rogues operated, how they discovered their innovations, how they were able to bring their ideas to fruition, how they executed, and how they were able to overcome constraints that may have prevented others from creating their own innovative solutions.

As an innovative CIO, leverage these rogue techniques and recognize that the techniques (and the rogues) are not all that radical. You may even learn that you already posses some rogue qualities. You may also eventually adopt some rogue best practices, if not for everything, perhaps in situations where you are challenged to deliver a solution via your standard operating procedures.

Lower the Artillery

Have you ever heard a dumb idea . . . a really dumb idea? Everybody has.

Now, have you ever been in a situation where someone's idea—good or bad—was absolutely trampled by someone else? Perhaps it happened in a public setting like a team meeting. How did the person respond? How willing was this person to step up and offer an idea at the next opportunity? Chances are that next opportunity was not taken. Most people would remain silent, especially if the firing squad that attacked their previous suggestion was present.

On the other hand, have you ever been in a situation where a really *dumb* idea eventually morphed into a great idea? We have—many times. The critical point here is that not all good ideas appear to be good ideas when they are first proposed. It could be because the person who had the idea did not have sufficient time to articulate it well. In other cases, what starts as a truly silly idea can spark a sequence of creative thought that results in an amazing idea or innovation.

As a leader of a high-performance innovative team, you must create an environment where people feel free to exchange ideas. While we are not suggesting you let all of your meetings run wild with silliness, there are ways to handle a truly bad suggestion such that the person who made it does not feel like an idiot. Open nastiness cannot be tolerated. It really does not take much effort to create a culture where full frontal attacks on less than perfect ideas will be rare occurrences, at least within your span of control. Responding to truly bad ideas can, and must, be done with tact.

There are times to encourage a little bad idea generation. For example, during a brainstorming exercise you might encourage participants to share ideas whether they believe them to be good or bad. That is a fairly common technique. During such exercises, there is almost always a point, often early in the exercise, when the group cannot think of any more ideas to share. Or at least they cannot think of anything they are *willing* to share.

Take this opportunity to explicitly ask for a few bad ideas. It can be done in a lighthearted way, and can serve to return some energy to the room: "All right, does anyone have a really stupid idea?" or "I'll buy ice cream for the person who comes up with the dumbest idea in the next 60 seconds." Usually the ideas generated in this way are not of much use, but at other times the ideas are good. Sometimes they can even lead to the ultimate solution or innovation. But almost always, it restarts the brainstorming process, leading to more viable ideas for consideration.

Be Intolerant

In the previous section, we mentioned the "bad idea" firing squad and how an innovative leader must create an environment of trust and respect within their team. Intolerance of destructive, negative behavior and personalities must also be applied when some of the innovation-killing personalities discussed in Chapter 2 such as "The Protector", "The Perfectionist", or "The Innovative Authoritarian" are present.

The probability that an IT team will be innovative and productive is dramatically reduced by the presence of these destructive types of personalities. The negative impact a leader's tolerance of destructive personalities has on a team can be enormous. Even those who are not the targets of the negative personalities will be impacted.

To put it simply, when leaders tolerate this kind of behavior, they are responsible for it. Not just metaphorically. If permitted to persist, it is likely that the other team members will lose respect for the leader and will begin to interpret this inaction as an endorsement of it. What's worse, as a result others may also begin to display symptoms of those innovation illnesses. Like many illnesses, they can be contagious.

Make it clear from the outset that such behavior will not be tolerated within your team. Though that will not take care of everyone, it will constitute a strong beginning and send a message outside your team as well. Though you are not likely to cure the worst of the infected outside your team, positive culture can also be contagious—especially when it brings success.

One sure sign of success in dealing with this is having people from other teams want to work in your group. When that happens, be sure to ask the person who wants to join your group why they want to do so, even if you do not have a position for them. Sometimes the answer will be less than enlightening (e.g., "I wanted to work with virtualization"). Other times, you might be surprised by the insight the question will bring.

Take Time

These days it feels as if you cannot have a conversation about innovation without discussing what Yahoo! President and CEO Marissa Mayer referred to as "a license to pursue dreams" in 2006 while she was Vice-President of Search Product and User Experience at Google.[1] What we are referring to is Google's policy of permitting its employees to apply 20% of their time (one day per week) to pursue any project that might interest them. This process is often referred to colloquially as "Google's Innovation Time."

This topic usually generates a lot of discussion, excitement, passion, and even cynicism typified by phrases such as "OK, so if I had Google's money, I could throw away 20% of my staff budget and not worry about it too." or "Hey, we all have access to '20% innovation time.' As long as we schedule it before 9 a.m. and after 5 p.m. or on weekends." It is at this point that the discussions

---

[1] "License to Pursue Dreams," presentation by Marissa Mayer, recorded May 17, 2006, http://ecorner.stanford.edu/author/marissa_mayer, retrieved on March 2012.

become less than productive. But most people agree they would certainly appreciate having a similar program at their disposal.

There are some misconceptions regarding how Google's program works in practice that might change some people's opinions regarding its usefulness and practicality. During Mayer's presentation, she explained that the process was not exactly that regimented. Employees did not usually take a full day off every week to work on innovative things. It might be more common, for example, for someone to work on their core projects for a few months straight and then spend a few weeks pursuing their interests and dreams. (Google permits the accumulation of unused innovation time.) In addition, Google employees are also known to use the more ubiquitous approach of pursuing their interests after hours or on weekends.

Therefore, it appears that the program's success has at least as much to do with the people they hire and their corporate culture as it does with the program itself. But the approach cannot be dismissed as being only a gimmick. It has delivered quantifiable results. Mayer also mentioned that in the last half of 2005, 50% of the products and services Google launched started their life in the 20% time.

Will that work for you? Like any of the well-known, successful techniques, it depends on different factors, such as the business you are in, the people you hire, your corporate culture, etc.

However, there is a more universal lesson to be learned from this program, regardless of your opinion of it. Innovation does require a commitment of time. When organizations invest in programs like Google's, they are also sending a message to potential, and current, employees that innovation matters. They are making an explicit statement that, not only is innovation encouraged, it is expected. This can do wonders for a corporate culture and can be a tremendous recruiting tool.

To say that innovation, or almost anything, takes time is not that awe-inspiring. But managers and leaders need to be able to give their teams the time they need to pursue innovative ideas, especially if they show promise. This may be done through a formal program, or in the field where teams are allowed to pursue an avenue of exploration that may not have been part of a plan of record.

This concept is hardly new. For example, agile development methodologies often include a similar concept referred to as a "spike." In a spike, time can be allocated to pursue an avenue of research that was not part of the original plan. The outcome of that research might then be put into future development cycles (referred to as "sprints" in agile methodologies). Agile methodologies are well-suited to support the concept of pursuing an innovative hunch, although allocation of time for a person or team to pursue a possible avenue of innovation is not necessarily consistently practiced in agile or nonagile teams. It requires discipline and conviction.

This discipline is also relevant at a micro level. Even when teams have been given permission to pursue an innovative idea, they may not be given the right *kind* of time. Confused? You are not alone. At one point in my career, I was a manager in a role that required me to spend roughly half of my time managing and leading, and the other half creating and delivering solutions (innovating). I soon realized that it was becoming more and more difficult to complete creative tasks during the workday. I came across an article where Paul Graham pointed out that those who are creating things need large chunks of time to pursue their creative activities.[2] After much investigation and soul-searching, I realized the problem was that my daily calendar looked like a chessboard. It was filled with back-to-back meetings and meetings sandwiched between half-hour or hour-long breaks.

Further investigation led to the discovery that my schedule was dominated by meetings with senior managers. You have to take that time whenever you can get it, right? Wrong! Well, at least most of the time. I eventually learned to use my calendar as a strategic weapon.

I learned that often a meeting time suggestion is just that—a suggestion—and that alternate times were usually acceptable to even the most senior executives. Building a relationship with the administrative assistants who took care of the senior executives' schedules made that even simpler. And simply blocking two-hour or half-day chunks of time made sure there was ample time for working on creative tasks and other deliverables.

But I also learned something that was even more disturbing to me—I was doing this to my own team! I had been scheduling meetings with the members of my team, who were to spend most, or all, of their time on creative activities, solely based upon when I had openings in my calendar. I learned that scheduling a meeting at 10:30 a.m. can spoil a half day of productive, creative time. Scheduling a meeting at 1:30 p.m. or 2 p.m. can spoil an entire day.

I began to schedule meetings with my team members more strategically—first thing in the morning, last thing in the afternoon, or whatever made sense in the context of the meeting. Sometimes I would meet with the team or managers for lunch, which often had the added benefit of helping the team members to bond and increased their mutual trust and respect. In addition,

---

[2] Graham Paul, "Maker's Schedule, Manager's Schedule," July 2009, www.paulgraham.com/makersschedule.html, retrieved on March 2012.

meetings were only scheduled in midmorning or midafternoon when there were no alternatives.

The difference it made to the me, even early on, was amazing. As soon as I was convinced it made a difference, I met with the team leaders and discussed what I had learned. The team leaders had noticed a difference as well. Meetings had become less annoying. (OK, bad meetings were still bad meetings, though good meetings were less disruptive.)

The team made this practice a part of their culture. Sure, there were still times when they had to break the rules, but those became the exception more than the rule. This approach made a difference not only in the context of improving creative productivity, but team members also reported that it actually made them feel better and reduced stress both during meetings, and outside of them.

So whether your company adopts a formal innovation time program or not, managers and leaders must realize that creativity and innovation require time and focus. Their employees need time to pursue promising innovative ideas. Turning an innovative idea into a product, service, or process that is customer-ready requires investment.

Invest

Many theories exist about how companies can invest in innovation. Some organizations buy innovation by acquiring companies that have innovated, by investing in those companies, by embedding the innovations of others, or by licensing patents. Certainly those are viable strategies, but we would like to discuss an alternative to that type of investing in innovation – organic innovation.

Organic innovation, innovation that comes from within your company, requires investing in your existing employees. Even something as simple as an agile spike, as discussed in the previous section, requires the allocation of time and resources, which will impact your budget and expenses. It is not as simple as telling your team they can spend as much time as they like on innovation as long as they do it before 9 a.m. and after 5 p.m., or that they can spend as much time as they like on an idea as long as they do everything else they are scheduled to do and meet their existing deadlines.

We admit that we have seen this work, though we question the ethics of that approach. It also comes with a high price that includes a burned-out team, low morale, and destruction of employee trust and loyalty.

Obviously, there are times for teams to push hard. There are times when a person or team will become passionate and excited about something innovative and on their own decide to work on it day and night for an extended period. That is not what we are referring to.

In addition to budgeting for time and resources that are directly and obviously related to specific innovation initiatives, consider investing in your employees in other ways. This can be in the form of education, seminars, activities that inspire creativity, or even temporarily assigning them to another team, internal customer, or external customer. Working in a customer's shoes can make an amazing difference in the solutions that are later developed by an employee. It is also amazing how often something unrelated to a specific domain plays a significant role in the development of an innovative solution for that domain. Cross-pollination of personnel can create opportunities for that to occur.

Investments in innovation can, of course, also be more formal. For example, a specific portion of a department's budget can be set aside for innovative activities, though often any pool of funding set aside for innovation morphs to become the organization's emergency fund. Without careful management and governance, it can become a pool of funding that is used to address short-term needs that had not been planned for, which brings us to the next topic.

Take a Longer View

As was mentioned in the previous section, many organizations get caught up in short-term activities. They become driven by the day-to-day grind. This is similar in nature to the "Inbox" pressure mentioned in Chapter 3. A great deal of conviction and discipline is required in order to resist the urge to cannibalize an innovation fund in a time of need. It can be even more challenging when that fund is managed by the same person responsible for those shorter-term objectives. Companies that take only a short-term view can become irrelevant very quickly, or can be forced to take a less efficient or more expensive approach to maintaining their relevancy. They may never lead their markets.

One approach to funding innovation is to allocate a percentage of funding to different delivery horizons. For example, you might invest 85% of your research and development budget to near-term execution (up to a year ahead), 10% to the midterm (up to two or three years in advance), and 5% to things that may pay off in the longer term (e.g., two to five years), if at all. The bottom line is that there must be an acceptance by all that not every investment will bear fruit. This fact often leads to debate that then kills programs of this nature before they gain momentum, or even get off the ground. The discussion often goes something like the following:

Presenter: "So, not every one of these investments will lead to a successful product or service, though those that do should more than justify the overall investment. Any questions?"

Attendee: "So, suppose we commit an amount to a specific project, let's say $120,000 for each of the next two years. What if halfway through the first year we realize we are on the wrong path. The remaining $180,000 is given back to the operations budget, right? We can use it for whatever we need to use it for?"

Presenter: "No. That money stays in the innovation fund."

Attendee: "So, even though we know we are working on the wrong thing, we will continue to invest in it for another 18 months, throwing good money after bad. Ridiculous!"

This is where the meeting can turn into a slugfest, especially if there is already a great deal of political tension among the attendees. If the attendees continue to listen, if the team is mature and disciplined, they will learn about an aspect of successful innovation programs that is often lost on people, especially those with a short-term, operational focus. In a case such as the example just described, the remaining $180,000 would not be returned to operations. Neither would it be invested in the failing initiative. It would instead be invested in another long-term initiative that showed promise. The total amount invested in long-term innovation remains the same.

The key with these programs is to "fail fast." The more rapidly a team can recognize it is on the wrong path, the less investment there will be in the bad idea—and the more funding there will be for other innovative ideas that show promise.

The irony is that although organizations can benefit from a "fail fast" culture, innovation projects require decision makers to have a long attention span. New, innovative ideas rarely deliver huge returns in the short term. Unfortunately, management teams often measure them in the same ways they would an existing star product. Measurements such as the number of new customers per month, monthly revenue from the product, or combined annual growth rate are likely not as useful in the context of a product or service in its early life. Organizations that measure these new things in those (old) ways often abandon an initiative that *could* be a viable and profitable product because of their short-term view.

In some cases, organizational leaders who are not part of the innovation initiatives look for ways to kill them in order to obtain access to their funding. Use of those ("old") types of measures gives such people all the ammunition they need to kill a project. Therefore, leaders of innovative initiatives need to ensure those initiatives are measured in the right ways. Their measurements need to ensure the project is progressing and to provide insight into the longer-term viability of the initiative. At the same time, the measurements must help the initiative to fail fast if that is its ultimate fate.

The fate of innovation funds can be even worse if the discussion described earlier does not happen. In those cases, their funding is often moved to operations without discussion or forethought.

Spin Off: Do What the Rogues Do

Sometimes a business's standard best practices serve as huge barriers to innovation. A team may find that processes and procedures, that exist for normal projects, are slowing down the execution of an innovative idea they are trying to bring to life. Those processes may even prevent them from making any progress whatsoever, especially if the new innovation involves aspects that did not exist when those processes were put in place. Or the team may be subject to measurements that are not as useful in the context of their new mission (as was discussed previously).

In these cases, spinning the organization off and letting them do new things in new ways, using new tools might be a better approach. This approach may also enable such a group to take advantage of some of the other measures, such as innovation funding and new types of measurements.

To be clear, we are not suggesting teams not be held accountable for their work and objectives. We are simply suggesting that there are different methods that might be more effective at making them accountable in their new context.

Hire the Right People

This is likely the most critical element of making innovation intentional. Not only is it the case that innovation does not happen without people, it does not happen without the *right* people.

This is not simply a matter of skills. Sure, skills matter, but the presence of skills alone does not guarantee innovation will occur. As has been discussed throughout this book, there are many other things to consider, such as passion, personality, and whether the person is well-suited for the team's culture. One bad apple *can* spoil the barrel. One bad hire can damage a team beyond belief.

A team that values their culture and makes it a priority while recruiting can itself have a positive impact. It sends a message to potential team members that will not only help attract the right kinds of people to apply to join the team, it can also create benefits that far outlive the recruiting process. Team members who have passed muster will have a sense of team pride and *esprit de corps* from the minute they are accepted.

I recently had a conversation with someone who had been a member of such a team for approximately a year. The person was extremely passionate while describing how much he enjoyed working on the team. He specifically mentioned that during the interview process he had been asked a lot of questions that were aimed at determining whether he was a good cultural fit for the team. He thought his hiring manager's approach was outstanding, and it made his desire to become a member of the team stronger. Even a year later, this person was proud he had "passed the test." Clearly, a cultural fit was important in the hiring process.

Get It Out There

As discussed in Chapter 2, perfectionists are those who might never deliver a finished product because it would never be good enough to meet their standards. But even those who are *not* perfectionists can take too long to bring a product to the public and who can, in so doing, miss an opportunity.

This is a recurring theme in many of the innovation-related conversations and presentations by people who have worked at some of the most innovative companies that ever existed. For example, during a recent conference I attended, Guy Kawasaki, a well-known innovator and former Apple employee, summed it up by imploring the audience not to be afraid to ship <something before its time>.

There is more to this than you might imagine. It is not only about getting a solution to market so that your company can gain revenue from it sooner. It is also about listening to your customers.

In the previously mentioned presentation by Marissa Mayer, she gave an example from her own experience. She told of a deadlock between a team of engineers that could not be resolved. They could not agree which of two features to put into a specific product. Their solution to the deadlock was to release their product without either feature. They then waited for the customer feedback, which came in overwhelmingly in favor of one of the features.

So getting your innovation out there, even if a little early, can be a way to increase its value to your customers.

Active Techniques: "You! Go Be innovative!"

"So, you want to innovate, do you? Well, here's how . . ."

Sound familiar? There are many commonly used idea-generation techniques. Some are more successful than others, and certainly some fit specific cultures and challenges better than others might. Much has been written about many of these, so we will not spend too much time on them. We will, however, mention a few that we have used successfully for the sake of illustration.

Take a SWOT at It

SWOT analysis has been around for quite some time, and it has fallen out of favor with some. It is often used to provide an extremely high-level view of a competitive landscape or to add context to a plan. Under the right circumstances, it can be useful in the context of innovation.

At times, generating innovative ideas is more a function of asking good questions than it is about giving good answers, at least initially. It could also be argued that without a good question there will never be a good answer. Admittedly, sometimes it can be difficult to find those great questions, which is why SWOT analysis can be useful.

Sometimes you may find yourself in a position where you are thinking, "So, what now?" This may be when you are presented with an outright challenge to innovate. It may also be when you have just completed bringing an innovation to life. You might ask "what now" at a time when the innovation is in operation and all of the innovative ideas that were in your queue have been implemented.

Once a team has implemented all of the innovative ideas they had throughout the early life of a project there is a risk that the team will fall into an operational funk. That nothing new will be brought to the product or service—at least nothing innovative—and that it will begin to become irrelevant over time. The team's innovative spirit also becomes at risk.

At those times, a team event that includes a combination brainstorming-SWOT session can be helpful. These events normally consist of seven time-limited brainstorming exercises, one for each of the following: developing the team's "mission;" setting high-level "objectives;" enumerating "strengths, weaknesses, opportunities, and threats;" and a discussion of possible "actions." The exercises consist of a time-limited brainstorming session followed by a ranking of each of the ideas discussed during the session.

The output from a SWOT session is an updated mission statement; a statement of the high-level objectives (ways in which the mission will be accomplished); a prioritized list of the team's strengths, weaknesses, opportunities, and threats (the SWOT); and a prioritized list of possible innovative ideas that leverages the team's strengths, minimizes the impact of their weaknesses, take advantages of their opportunities, and addresses their threats. Ironically, the section teams often have the most difficulty with is the "strengths" exercise. That is where the facilitator is critical.

Like any other technique, this one is not a panacea, though it can help when a team needs to be revitalized and can serve as an effective team-building exercise. Often teams do not get many opportunities to spend a day (or a half day) working together toward the same objective. It can also serve as a vacation for the mind of each participant. It is worth noting again that a strong facilitator who can keep the exercise focused and moving, and who can maintain respect and trust among the participants, is key to the success of these sessions.

Idea Competitions

In an idea competition, employees—either all of them or those from specific organizations—are encouraged to submit ideas by a specific date. As with other types of competition, there are normally various prizes awarded. For example, we have seen these awards given: a (substantial) trophy for the highest number of accepted ideas (bragging rights are more powerful than you might imagine), a cash award for any idea that is submitted for patent (or receives a patent), and a guaranteed executive sponsorship for the ideas that show the most promise in terms of value to the business.

In order for these competitions to be successful, they must be well-defined. The objective or domain to be addressed the ideas must be clearly stated and understood by all. For example, I was the idea evaluator for a technology-related innovation challenge. One employee chose to submit a suggestion that a very specific type of fitness class be offered for free in the company cafeteria. The point is not that the idea was a bad one—it may have been a great idea—it simply would not help to achieve the objective of the challenge (innovation in a specific domain).

Why is that a problem? Whether or not ideas are relevant, the competition evaluators must read every one of them and include them in their deliberations. (You don't know an idea is not relevant to a domain until after you've evaluated it.) Even with a minimum amount of time dedicated to each of these suggestions, this task can consume an enormous amount of the evaluation team's time. Also, each must be responded to and, if appropriate, directed to the appropriate team in the company.

Popular competitions can generate hundreds of ideas, and processing that much detailed information can be mind-numbing. A large volume of irrelevant submissions can also create a risk that the evaluation team might overlook something with great potential (i.e., due to fatigue).

Competitions with more specific objectives can often deliver more spectacular results—with the added benefit of a lighter workload for the evaluation team.

If you decide an idea competition is right for your organization, set the potential participants' expectations for evaluation and follow-up so that you can meet those expectations. Otherwise, you risk sending the subliminal message that innovation does not *really* matter to you. It's just something you need to check off as having been accomplished.

It is also critical that the evaluation criteria be clearly set, even if that includes a statement that the beauty of an idea may be subjective. In one such competition, the rules clearly stated that a winner of the grand prize might not be chosen. This was because the prize was executive support and budget to bring the innovation to life: a substantial commitment. The team was not at all obligated to award even a single prize, and the entrants respected the sensibility and honesty of the no mandatory winner regulation. Ironically, in that case there was a tie for first, and two grand prizes were actually awarded.

Finally, you must recognize, even before you launch it, that an investment will be required. That investment will usually include a significant commitment of time from very senior people (to act as sponsors, mentors, and evaluators). It may also include funding for prizes, a system to collect the ideas, and even commitment to follow through on the ideas (or why collect them).

Follow-through on those commitments is critical. A competition of this nature represents a promise to the employees (or customers) who participate. Following through on the commitments you made at its outset will tell them a lot about your organization and its culture and integrity.

Be prepared to invest before, during, and after the competition.

Speed Rounds

In a speed round, each person or team with ideas are asked to present them to a group, one after another. Normally they are given only a brief period of time for their presentation, often five or ten minutes. The presentations are often followed by a brief period for questions (usually five minutes). Following all presentations, attendees (or specific attendees) are allocated one or more votes that they can award to one or more of the ideas. (If given more than one vote, they are usually permitted to allocate more than one vote to one or more of the ideas they might be strongly in favor of.) The idea with the most votes is the winner, and presumably will be pursued by the team. Often multiple ideas are selected for follow-up, and there is nothing to prevent someone from following up on an idea that did not win should they believe in it.

As with all types of competition, follow-up and commitment are critical. It is also important to reinforce throughout the entire exercise that the votes are to be cast for the idea with the most promise, not for the best presentation, funniest speaker, or person they liked the best.

Done right, this can also serve as a great team-building exercise. This type of exercise is also well-suited for all-hands meetings that many teams often host annually, or even more frequently.

In addition to its value in promoting innovation, a speed round competition can have the additional benefit of improving morale (e.g., as people are allowed to voice their ideas in a public forum). They can also serve as an opportunity for managers to help their team members grow professionally.

Prescreening ideas can help ensure the best, or most ready, presentations are brought to the competition. Coaching and mentoring the presenters will ensure those people obtain the best possible experience, as do the attendees.

Many Others

There are many, many other techniques that can be used to generate innovative ideas, such as trend unbundling, product deconstruction, and recombinant market analysis. There are even different styles of brainstorming. Though we could fill an entire book with a discussion of these, we will limit our discussion to those we have already covered and move on to something else as important. In fact it may even be more important.

Catching the Butterfly

A chrysalis is to a butterfly as an idea is to innovation. If not allowed to develop and grow, the idea never becomes an innovation, just as the chrysalis never becomes a butterfly. Once a butterfly exists, its beauty must be captured (on film, of course). Without proper care and feeding, the butterfly will not survive. Without proper care and feeding, innovations are simply flights of fancy people have spent their time on.

We have been witness to a large number of great ideas—creative innovations—that never delivered to their full potential. Many never really delivered any substantive benefit whatsoever, even though some had huge potential. In some cases, other companies went on to take the market space that these innovations would have addressed, even when the competitive solutions may have been inferior to those innovations. Why does that happen?

In many cases, this is due to one of the innovation killers that were discussed earlier. But for others, the reason was perhaps both simpler and more disappointing: those in possession of the innovative ideas did not know what to do with them. They could not execute. Or they simply got caught up in their day-to-day operations and eventually forgot about the innovative idea. These things are more common than you might believe. And they are far more common than they should be.

Own It

One of the most common ways in which we have seen innovations wither in their chrysalis is due to lack of clear ownership. In order for an innovation to have any chance of success, there must be clear ownership of the activities required to turn that idea into a product, component, or service. Some would say this is where the real work begins.

Bringing an innovation to life requires strong leadership and disciplined execution. These projects are not likely to be successful without the strong sponsorship of a senior executive. Preferably the sponsor should be willing to invest time coaching the project's leader if the leader is not a seasoned or more experienced executive. A passive sponsor may not be sufficient unless the appointed leader has a tremendous relationship with that sponsor and knows how to manage upward.

Co-sponsorship is something to be avoided if possible. Obtaining funding from many groups is fine, provided the funding is transferred at the outset; however, having more than one senior leader in the role of executive sponsor can create more problems than it solves. On one end of the spectrum, all leaders may possess plausible deniability as a result of shared ownership. This can mean nobody is truly accountable, and the project will receive no attention as a result. On the other end, all leaders may decide to become active, which can lead to conflicts in direction or even in simple things like reporting formats and measures. At the very least, this will consume an inordinate amount of the project leader's time. At worst, the project will fail because of it.

With a clear owner, there is no ambiguity with regard to who is accountable for project structure and execution, and for follow-up with the innovators.

In addition, without the proper investments in resources and personnel, the owner will have little chance at success. The sponsor must invest in the owner and in the project, which may require assigning some of their best and brightest people to the project. One would hope this would make obvious sense to sponsors, since they would not likely be sponsoring the project if they did not see its potential value to the business. However, someone suffering from one of the innovation illnesses may decide to lead or sponsor the initiative so they can ensure its demise. That does happen. We have witnessed it in action, and some are very good at hiding their intentions.

Don't Be *Too* Smart

It is often stated, "Sometimes less is more." That is certainly often the case in the context of delivering an innovative solution to others. It can be tempting to dump every feature and option possible into a new, innovative solution, but it is much better to keep things simple at the outset. Put the most valuable and compelling features in the solution, roll it out in a small scale, and shake down the processes required in order to deliver the benefits to a broader set of consumers.

The more complex the solution, the more room there will be for error. It will also be more challenging to deploy and more difficult for potential consumers to understand, especially when implementing a breakthrough idea that is dramatically different than things that have come before it.

Do you find it hard to believe that simple things can be difficult for people to understand when they are first introduced? Consider the introduction of the mouse. Today most of us take using a mouse for granted, and actions such as double-clicking are second nature to us. However, one of the most difficult challenges some of us faced in the 1990s was teaching mainframe technicians how to use a mouse to double-click: "Press the button on the left twice while your cursor is hovering over the icon. No faster. Not that fast. Why is the system slow? We just launched the program 27 times. We need to wait until it's finished." This may appear nonsensical now, and that is exactly the point. What is second nature to us today was not always so.

In addition, complex solutions will be potentially slower, and they may cost more to operate.

This topic reminds me of a lesson I learned as a child. On occasion, I would approach a simple problem in a work setting with what I believed to be a very elegant approach. At times, (usually) these solutions would require more effort, which I did not mind at all. However, the lesson I often learned was that the elegant solutions often did not deliver any more value to my customers or employer than a much simpler solution would have. In fact, the elegant solutions were sometimes less valuable. Furthermore, sometimes the additional effort required would put the timelines at risk. It was at those times my family would impart some small town wisdom: "Sometimes it's best not to be 'too smart.'" That is, it is possible to overthink and over deliver.

Finally, delivering simple solutions will bring forth the added benefit mentioned in the "Get It Out There" section earlier in this chapter. It will provide others with an opportunity to help you make your solution better and more relevant while you are still in a position to act upon their suggestions.

Get Out of the Way

There are many things that organizations do—either intentionally or unintentionally—to impede the delivery of innovative solutions. Two of the most common we encounter are inflexible, heavy process and overactive leadership.

Consider that an innovative idea by its very nature may be something that those who designed your corporate business practices might never have considered while developing those processes. For example, a development process built to manage 18-month projects may be so heavy that the developers working on a short-term innovation initiative are putting more actual effort into the maintenance of project artifacts and compulsory activities than they are into the project itself. We have seen that happen, in some cases over and over. This presents another leadership opportunity for the project owner.

It is the project owner's responsibility to be a resource to the team in this regard by tearing down walls, understanding the issues, and driving the necessary changes and exceptions into the business processes. Incidentally, many large organizations have one or more people who are exceptionally good at removing obstacles. They can rapidly break through to the most important issues—understand what can and must change, and understand what cannot and should not change. They also possess the networking skills required in order to overcome the obstacles any project team may encounter, and usually have a substantial personal network. One of these master networkers may not always be the leader of the project. If it is not, enlisting the assistance of such a person can have an enormous positive impact on a project's outcome, and it will allow the owner to focus on other things.

Another way in which leaders and managers can help teams during the execution phase is to leave them alone. This is not to suggest managers and leaders should not lead their teams. Rather we are suggesting they not do the work for them. While leaders, especially those higher in the organization structure, need to set direction and ensure their teams are progressing toward the achievement of their objectives, micromanaging their teams will most likely be more than counterproductive.

While working on a project with the members of another team, I asked them to show me one of the new projects they had been working on. They were, of course, proud to do so. During the demonstration, I asked whether a specific function was available or planned. The response was shocking.

The person demonstrating the solution completely lost his temper and went on an amazing rant. Why? The team had wanted to put that functionality into the product. They believed it addressed a key requirement and would make the solution compelling. They had not included the feature because their senior executive ordered them to leave it out.

That executive, a former developer with deep technical skills, reviewed their work regularly. When he encountered something he would have done differently, he made them change it. He made them do it his way. If you think this is bad, it gets worse.

This team was created from the most talented engineers in the company. They had been tasked with developing new, innovative solutions—to create break-through innovation. Every member of the team was at the peak of their craft, and they had a proven track record of innovations and patents to prove it.

Not only were the team members completely frustrated, the senior leader's ideas were often worse and sometimes outright wrong.

We have found that providing the right people with the right objectives and questions and letting them develop creative solutions on their own can deliver far better results. Give them some creative freedom and watch them amaze you, but remember, the phrase "the right people" is important in this context.

To be clear, we are not suggesting that teams not be managed. Nor are we suggesting that managers should let their teams wander off in a direction they know to be wrong. (Sometimes a team will misinterpret an objective.) We are simply proposing that there are often many ways to accomplish something, and that sometimes more than one of them are equally valid. To all leaders and managers, we also suggest that someone else's way may actually be better than yours.

Develop Good Habits

Sometimes little things can make a big difference. That is certainly the case in the context of innovation. Simple habits such as always having a way to record ideas wherever and whenever they occur to you and having the discipline to review those ideas regularly can make an amazing difference.

Even the existence of a regularly scheduled idea competition can be an impetus for people to capture their ideas. Sometimes a financial incentive or public recognition can result in the development of better habits throughout an organization. For example, many companies offer a financial reward to inventors whose ideas pass a review and are submitted for patent. In some cases when patents are granted, inventors receive another award or are recognized in other ways (e.g., on a plaque or trophy that is placed in a prominent, public area in their office). Though on the surface these gestures may appear to be small, they can go a long way to building good habits, and they have resulted in increases in idea capture and patent applications.

Taking action to develop good habits for capturing and sharing ideas can deliver amazing results.

Do Not Welcome Failure

Initially the title of this section was to be "Do Not Accept Failure." While I do feel that title appropriately communicates the sentiment of this section, I recognized it might give a false impression that I believe that one should never give up on an idea, no matter how bad it turns out to be. Or that one should never look at the brutal facts and admit when they were wrong about an idea. They should.

However, too often people are willing to give up on a good idea without so much as a whimper. That is, they give up without at least giving some consideration to a broader set of factors. For example, perhaps the innovation is being delivered to the wrong audience, applied to the wrong problem, or offered under the wrong business model. It may simply be that the idea is good and the execution is bad—all that is needed is a new approach to breathe new life into the innovation. This is yet another reason why listening to customers and not-yet-customers is critical. They will often provide the answer in those cases. Often what is not obvious to you will be obvious to them.

It may also be the case that the innovative offering is just too far ahead of the market, or at least the market to which you are presenting it.

Train the Coaches

Training your coaches may be the single most important thing you can do to increase the innovative output of your organization.

If you believe, as we do, that innovation can come from anyone, then you might also want to take note that there are usually a lot more "anyones" at the bottom of an organization's hierarchy than there are elsewhere. Great ideas often come from those people, so it is critical that all managers, even the most junior team lead, know what to do when that happens.

All managers must know how to capture and evaluate an idea. They need to know how to assess its value and applicability. They need to know where to take it when it addresses an opportunity outside their own domain. They need to know whom to contact if they are not sure about its value.

Though all managers and leaders must possess these skills, this type of coaching is extremely important for more junior managers. There are usually a lot more of them, and they are often the first to learn of new ideas. These managers must also know how to respond when presented with a truly silly idea. They must know how to funnel the creative spirit demonstrated by the employee in a direction more likely to result in a relevant innovation. Above all, they must know how to do so in a way that will not crush the innovative spirit of their colleague or employee. Their team must continue to feel comfortable to share creative ideas freely. (OK, they must also know how to ensure their team's time is not being wasted on too many obviously unproductive ideas.)

If you are not yet convinced of the importance of this, consider the television series *Undercover Boss*. In this series, senior executives of major corporations (often as senior as the CEO) put on a disguise and go to work on the front lines of their organization. They perform tasks ranging from manufacturing line jobs to customer service to custodial functions to telephone support to back office functions. Quite often what they discover delivers amazing value to their organizations. They are also often presented with high-value, innovative ideas from their front-line employees; ideas that these employees have had for a long time. In most cases, these employees had no idea what to do with their ideas, and they often felt that nobody would care about their ideas or even listen to them.

It is also critical to make it as simple as possible for employees to share ideas and to reduce the friction of creative sharing. Some of the techniques that have been discussed earlier in this chapter will help reduce that friction. In addition, classic approaches such as idea walls, which are places—usually online—where people can share their ideas and advice, and can encourage innovative ideas and aid in their metamorphosis. Each approach has its challenges, though we believe capturing an idea, even in a less than perfect way, is better than not capturing it at all.

Connecting IT Innovation with Business Value

You will be as much value to others as you have been to yourself.

—Marcus Tullius Cicero (January 3, 106 BC–December 7, 43 BC)

In this book, we have often said that an idea must be accompanied by action to turn it into an innovation. Action demands investment, and investment will only be made if there is a potential return. We have stated that IT innovations for the IT department that are not for cost-cutting purposes only have value if they are considered as investments that will grow the business. This may be the development of a more flexible and adaptive system for M&A activity. It may be to improve the speed of response on a critical part of the infrastructure. Innovation needs to be related back to business value to have credibility.

The business case is frequently the place for stating the value of a fresh innovative project. Establishing a value for an existing IT infrastructure is not easy. IT is an intangible and only really noticed if it is absent. This statement was illustrated clearly when a major UK bank failed to update customer accounts for several days. The failure made worldwide news. That an organization is functioning normally and there are no problems reported is not news unless you are a part of a very disorganized company. Ask a few executives in any organization, and they are likely to say that IT is vital to that organization. They will tell you that the organization cannot function without it. Despite this assertion, some organization's executives have a negative view of IT, colored by perceived problems like poor web site navigation or the failure of a document to print. I know of one organization where the CFO threatened to reduce the budget of the IT department because of this reason:

> We spend all these millions on IT, and I can't even print a simple document. Oh, and the copier is out of toner again.

In this chapter, we will explore the characteristic differences in attitude that CIOs, CEOs, and CFOs have toward innovation.

We will discuss reporting and measuring innovation and the typical pitfalls, barriers, and objections facing someone who is developing an innovation push. We will also talk about how these can be identified and addressed in the context of a real-world example. This chapter is all about how you persuade your organization to see the business value in your innovation project and to keep the project on track by communicating that value to the right person at the right time.

How to Align Efforts in Innovation with Broader Business Values

Aligning innovation with business values has similar challenges to aligning IT with business. Aligning IT with business implies alignment with business requirements. Aligning IT with business values implies a judgment call that the business requirements will add value. Much has been written about aligning IT with business through the years. In the halcyon days of business IT, when functionality moved from the geek-infested IT departments to be closer to the user, people were predicting that IT would change the world of work and play. Microcomputers became cheaper and large numbers of desktops were purchased, but underneath this seeming success was a frustration. IT did not seem to deliver what the business wanted. It was also said that IT couldn't deliver what business wanted because business could not define what they wanted well enough. This is one of the reasons for the rise of requirements engineering as a science. The disconnect was seen as an alignment problem, and it has been with us ever since.

Aligning innovation efforts with business values suffers from the same issues. An innovation may not have an immediate or obvious business value, yet have a complementary value to another innovation. The complementary innovations need to be evaluated together. There has been a lot of research into so-called complementarities in innovation. This research has been conducted mostly in the domain of resource-based views of strategy. Establishing the complementary nature of many innovations is not easy. Using an analysis of complementary innovations can deliver a better understanding of the value of the innovation portfolio. With each proposed innovation, there is a cost and often there is no immediate relationship between the cost of the innovation and the value to the business. Establishing a portfolio-based valuation of innovation will enable complementary innovations to express their true value. We talk about this more in the section of this chapter on reporting and measuring.

Aligning innovation to business strategy requires a knowledge of the business strategy, but innovators must also have an understanding of their expert domain. New technologies and IT processes should be evaluated as part of a constant search for business value. It is equally important to establish the cost of any business process change. The cost of business process change is also a cost of an innovation. You can think of the cost of an innovation being calculated by this formula:

Cost of IT implementation project +

Cost of business process change =

Total cost of innovation

The cost of business process change is the cost of all the evaluation, design, communication, education, and training that the changed business process requires. Some organizations ignore this part of an innovation with the subsequent problems of cost overrun that can ensue. CIOs introducing an IT-led innovation should not neglect business process change as part of their plan. The cost of the IT implementation is usually the major cost element in any business case. The business process change needs to be factored into the business case.

If the innovations are to be IT-led, then the technology-aware CIO has to be able to engage with the people most responsible for the business strategy. This means a deeper understanding of their cultural and mindset differences. For someone in a line of business, the most frequent driving force is quarterly performance. This is something that is alien to many innovative projects that need discussion, experimentation, and modification before they can deliver. It would be difficult to try to persuade someone with a line of business mindset to sponsor or support an innovation unless the value was readily apparent and the delivery was within their timeframe, normally a three-month period. Resolving this language/mindset barrier is the first step to aligning innovation efforts with broader business values.

How to Discuss Innovation Outside of IT: Learning to Speak CEO and CFO

Innovation is important for business growth. There have been a number of surveys of CEOs conducted on a regular basis, and these surveys often show that the majority of CIOs are innovating internally, either in IT itself or in the wider business. Few of these CIOs are innovating externally to produce market-facing or new market innovations. This is often expressed as an issue by the CEOs. Communication between the CIO and the CEO is one area that can help both in internal innovation but also in external innovation. The use of the right language, understandable by the target audience, often clears up misunderstanding and confusion. An understanding of the motivations and mindset of the different members of the C-level is a necessary part of selecting the right language. We have spent many years meeting and talking with business people and have identified that the CEO and CFO are the executives more generally interested in innovation across the company. Conversely the Chief Marketing officer and other members of the C-level are interested in innovation in their own domain. Understanding the audience for your innovative proposal can smooth the communication and ensure that the message is clear, concise, and presents your argument in a way that gains maximum acceptance:

- CEOs have a split focus. Part of their concentration is focused on the current growth of the organization, and the other part is on the future growth. Current growth is not normally a target for innovation since the timescales are too short for anything innovative that requires lengthy implementation. Innovation to drive future growth will capture the attention of the CEO as long as it is clear that your focus is on growth in the future. Once you have captured the CEO's attention, you don't have much time to explain the benefits and potential of the innovation. There is a challenge in this—CIOs tend to be detail-oriented and CEOs expect the big picture. If you are presenting a report, spend the majority of the time talking about the broad picture that should be part of your executive summary and leave the details for questions and background. CEOs are also invested with a sense of urgency. Your innovation may be a compelling idea, but will take time to deliver. CEOs may be driven to the more immediate innovative solution, such as a merger or acquisition to deliver the results faster. If the fastest way to deliver on an innovative idea is through M&A, you need to have an M&A strategy in place. Going to the CEO with a good idea, agreeing to buying a company to fill the skills gap, and then failing to integrate and support the acquisition is not a good scenario for success, as we noted in Chapter 8.

- CFOs are charged with maintaining and improving the financial health of the organization. CFOs tend to develop a risk-averse attitude to anything that has a cost. They are mostly interested in numbers—not outcomes. This can generate a misunderstanding between you and the CFO because innovations are not generally easy to measure and quantify. CFOs most frequently evaluate projects on the Return on Investment (ROI) measure. ROI on an innovation is not easy to establish, partly because the return from some innovations may take a long time to arrive. ROI is most frequently used to measure the success of a well-defined implementation of existing technology. If you have an innovative idea for a new product, you will need to develop the product, invest in marketing, and then sell the product. Depending on the maturity of the market and the sales cycle for the product, it could be three or more years before you get a realistic view of the return on your innovation. This would give a poor ROI measure compared with implementing an upgraded e-mail system. CFOs are interested in the future, but they have a clear preference for results and return-oriented milestones. The CFO will also appreciate cost-saving innovations. You should be cautious about overstating the cost savings to the CFO. Setting expectations too high will affect your credibility when you propose the next innovative project.

The CEO and CFO are likely to be the arbiters of the innovation budget. The CEO sets the vision, and the CFO sets the budget. Both of these executives will be valuable sponsors of innovation if you can gain their attention and engage their imagination. The two depictions given are stereotypical views of the mindsets and attitudes of these two members of the executive suite. They point out some of their most prominent attitudes and behavior. It is possible for you to establish their concerns and enthusiasms in your discussions with them.

If you want to engage with the CEO and CFO outside of your normal reporting and business discussions, you will need to pick a topic that is not a product or existing business process innovation but something more adventurous. One suggestion is that you take something that is new and interesting but is most likely something that has not been considered by either the CEO or CFO. In Chapter 8, we discussed the concept of ambient telepresence. This is not on the horizon for most executives at the moment. Discussing ambient telepresence with the CEO and CFO may generate interesting conversations and could show two different views. The CEO may feel that there are no communication problems that need to be fixed. After all, they can have face-to-face conversations with their leadership team when they want. The leadership may travel often, but they are generally co-located in company headquarters. Also most people come running if the CEO hints they need a conversation! The CFO, however, may view ambient telepresence as an innovation with a high potential for cost reduction. Any international or global business is likely to have a large travel budget. This is often one of the single most expensive items in the cost of doing business. Any CFO with a budgetary line item of travel will tell you that reducing the cost of travel is a major controllable priority. If you offer the opportunity to reduce travel and improve communication at the same time, it would be a surprise to me if the CFO did not become an immediate and enthusiastic supporter.

This assumes that an innovative project is successful. Communicating realistic estimates including a potential failure is just as important as communicating the potential for success. Many discussions and presentations focus on the advantages of success but seldom mention failure. This would be an error of judgment. Failure may happen, and the C-level can be unforgiving of a surprise failure. Unpleasant surprises can have a permanent effect on innovation and your own career. Carrying out a risk assessment on a proposal and communicating the risk is important. Total failure, where the whole innovative project crashes and burns, is something that has to be dealt with.

A risk assessment should also provide information about the remedial action that may be needed if a risk occurs as well as the probability of a risk happening. A good example of this is in the world of research. It is an accepted risk that a research project may fail to deliver all or some of the results anticipated. Even for complete failure, there remains the knowledge that something can't be done. This knowledge has value to a researcher. Innovation shares some of the characteristics of research, but if failure comes as a surprise, extolling the virtues of knowledge rather than success may not help the image of innovation in the company.

There are other members of the management team, particularly in the C-level, who may be potential supporters or sponsors of your innovations. They may have different attitudes and motivations than the CEO and CFO, but they can be relied on to support innovations that have a direct positive effect on their part of the business.

- Chief Sales Officer (CSO) or the head of sales will be interested in innovations that increase potential sales. The world of sales is driven by immediate or short-term returns. Therefore, implementing a mobile app that can improve customer relations will be appealing if the app can be shown to have a fast and significant effect on sales. Sales and LOB management are focussed on quarterly returns and year-end results since this is often the way they are measured and compensated.

- Chief Marketing Officer (CMO) or head of marketing has a view of innovation focussed on improvements in communication and messaging. Marketing and PR are heavy users of social media and communications technology. They often allocate part of their budget for procuring communications devices and software. This should not be seen as a problem of IT outside the control of the IT department—it should be seen as an opportunity. Marketing may consider using part of their budget to fund an innovation should they see an improvement in communication and messaging.

Sales and marketing staff are also skilled presenters of ideas and having them as sponsors will ensure that the innovation is seen in the best light, without techno-babble. Getting either or both of these stakeholders involved and enthusiastic can improve the chance of success of your proposal.

Beware of the Imitation Trap

In a meeting some time ago, I was told about the CIO of a firm of lawyers. The CIO said that innovating a business process in the firm was difficult. He could never get innovation funded unless he was able to mention that a rival firm of lawyers was making the same changes. This was the only tactic he could use to get an innovation approved, but he ran the risk of falling into the imitation trap. In the middle of the "noughties," there was a vogue for large and expensive customer relationship management software implementations. Many companies embarked on one- or two-year efforts to revolutionize their customer relations and improve sales and customer satisfaction. There was an expectation of unique insight into the customer base from applying these tools. The concern I have is the similarity of the solutions. If all the companies collect the same data, stored in the same CRM system with the same data structure and querying capabilities, what is the differentiator? Identical solutions will deliver identical results.

Imitation may be the sincerest form of flattery, but it is not a differentiator. Imitation does have a place in an innovator's portfolio if it is ensures that your company avoids commercial disadvantages. Figure 10-1 highlights that innovations can be categorized into four separate groups. The top two groups are strategic and disruptive innovations. They are responsible for competitive advantage, and neither of these two groups contain any imitative innovations. The lower two groups categorize innovations according to their area of influence. These groups are where the catch-up or imitative innovations can be categorized. If a competitor creates a disruptive or strategic innovation, it may alter the requirements for your products and services or your business process. The first organization to produce a mobile banking application for the phone created a disruptive innovation; it could also be described as a strategic innovation for that organization. If your company needs to offer the same services as a competitor, that may be classed as imitation, but at least it prevents you from being at a competitive disadvantage. This is similar to matching another organization's business process changes.

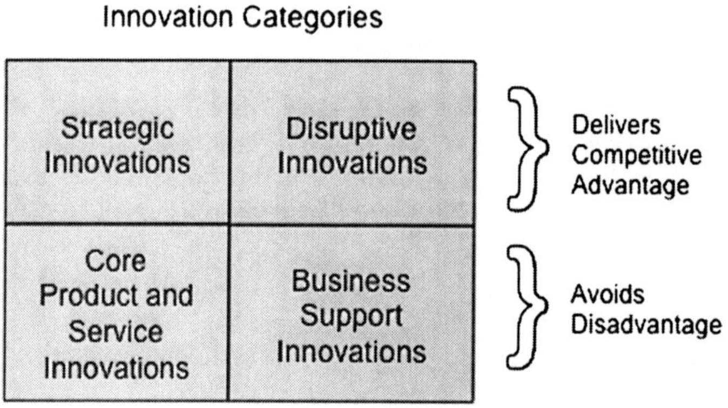

Innovation Categories

Strategic Innovations	Disruptive Innovations	} Delivers Competitive Advantage
Core Product and Service Innovations	Business Support Innovations	} Avoids Disadvantage

Figure 10-1. Four categories are included here for classifying innovation.

There is a good rule of thumb when considering if your innovation is merely imitation. If the innovation will ensure that your competitors lose their advantage, then it is valid. It the innovation does not make a significant contribution, then you should consider that it is an imitation and not follow the herd.

How to Persuade the C-level to Take a Chance on Innovation

We have discussed communications and creating a group of sponsors who will be prepared to be your allies when it comes to developing an innovation.

There are three key points to maintaining their support and making success more likely:

- *Developing your vision*: As we have mentioned several times, this is allied to the business strategy. The IT vision should be a business-focused vision, not a technology-heavy vision.

- *Communicating the change*: Poor communications are at the heart of resistance to change. As an innovative CIO, your job is to tell people what the change is, what it will bring to them and the organization, and how it will be implemented.

- *Embody a sense of urgency*: Good ideas stay as good ideas unless they are acted on. The sense of urgency for actions will ensure you are not playing catchup all the time, but that you are instead taking the lead.

These three areas are important in persuading the C-level to take a chance on innovation. The vision will demonstrate business-focused leadership. Communications will build confidence that the innovation is the right one and being implemented well. The sense of urgency will generate confidence that the innovation will be part of the immediacy of modern business. In the next section of this chapter, we will discuss how you can make innovation part of the company strategic planning and how to tell executives how well you are doing.

Persuading the CEO and other members of the C-level is not easy. The focus in any organization is growth, and the opposite is stagnation. Using these tools and the other methods in this book will help you create the strategic vision, have the necessary changes communicated, and if you add urgency into the mix, the arguments are likely to be compelling.

Making IT Innovation Part of the Strategic Planning

In Chapter 4, we talked about business strategy and its influence on IT. Many CIOs are faced with the challenge of implementing IT for a business strategy even though they were not involved in the decision. This can lead to frustration, but it also means that the strategic planning team has made decisions with an incomplete understanding of the relevant IT facts. The information about new and existing IT capabilities would be needed for the strategy team to be able to decide if their requirements are realistic. There is also the strong chance that a team without an IT leadership member would miss an opportunity to use strategic or disruptive IT innovations to lead a business innovation.

The results of the CA Technologies survey we mentioned in Chapter 4 showed that 64% of CIOs do not report to the CEO[1]. The CIOs who report to different C-level members are not often considered as part of the executive team for planning purposes. These CIOs only have the option to become influencers to the business strategy rather than having a direct input.

Influencing the C-level often requires more than a few suggestions and discussions. It is sometimes necessary to classify innovations into groups that are easier for the C-level to understand. This also helps you to explain the difference in emphasis that you may place on innovations that may not match the emphasis of other senior managers or executives with their own enthusiasm. Remember Figure 10-1 that showed the four different categories of innovation? You can regard this figure as a tool to help you to classify an innovation correctly. This tool will enable you to label an innovation as strategic, relating to the company strategy—for example, creating a mobile phone app to locate sales staff who are on the road. The innovation may be classified as disruptive—generating a fundamental change like enhanced reality displays. Updating a core product to include capabilities present in a competitor's offering, like adding a camera to a mobile phone, can be classified as a core product and service innovation. Making the move from telephone banking to Internet banking would be an innovation that fits into the business support innovation part of Figure 10-1. Core product and business support innovations are not part of the strategic planning process. Both strategic innovations and disruptive innovations must be considered as part of the strategic planning process.

Working with C-Suite and the Board to Bring IT into Strategic Planning

Being an influencer of senior management requires a different approach to developing innovative ideas. Legitimacy of the CIO is important, and there are several ways in which it can be demonstrated:

- *Legitimacy by stature*: This is often a feature of the expertise of CIOs and their prominence in the company, their length of tenure, and their expertise demonstrated outside the organization. CIOs in this position are believed because of who they are and what they know. CIOs who do not report

---

[1] "The Future Role of the CIO," CA Technologies, October 2011, www.ca.com/us/collateral/white-papers/na/The-Future-Role-of-the-CIO-Becoming-the-Boss.aspx, retrieved on May 2012.

to the CEO may not be seen as plausible because of their place in the reporting hierarchy.

- *Legitimacy by interest*: A competitor may be publicly implementing or embracing an innovation, and this makes it a potentially valid idea. This is one situation where you need to be aware of the imitation trap. Imitation in the core or support areas of Figure 10-1 is valid, but may fail to excite the audience.

- *Legitimacy by demonstration*: Here the legitimacy of the innovation is demonstrated by use of a prototype or mockup of the innovation. Often these prototypes can be achieved with a small amount of funding or through skunk works, but they are no less effective. There has been a lot of hype, in the past, about RFID and its potential to revolutionize retail and particularly the supermarket business. Several IT companies and supermarkets built demonstration stores that showed the use of RFID. These demonstrated contact free shopping and walk-through checkouts. These stores were relatively expensive demonstration sites. But in order to generate understanding and enthusiasm for an idea, it is sometimes important to help others visualize the concepts. You may think it trite, but in many cases a picture really is worth a thousand words.

- *Legitimacy by analyst*: Industry analysts frequently write papers that look to the future and make suggestions about new trends. These can either be gleaned from the web sites of analysts, meetings, or articles in the national or trade press. Some CEOs will ask what opinion makers think of an idea, even if you have developed a compelling case for the innovation. A regular scan of the trade press relevant to your organization will also ensure that you are thinking and talking the same language as your peers or CEO.

Each of these areas of establishing the legitimacy of an innovation is valid on its own. Alternatively you may find that a judicious mix of some or all of these methods may be needed to establish an idea as valid. One of the hurdles that you may have to overcome is the digital literacy of the C-level executive. There are a number of commentators who see an increase in the digital literacy of the general public increasing with the advent of consumer-driven IT. I was talking to a CIO recently who mentioned that this was an illusion. Understanding how to use e-mails and social networking tools to interact with people is different from being digitally literate.

In 2004, I met a customer—who was a senior executive—processing a huge pile of paper. When I asked what he was doing, he said he was reading his e-mails. He had a daily print out of e-mails done by his secretary. He would write comments and responses on the paper and give them back to his secretary to work on for the following day. At the other end of the scale, we have the digital natives who have difficulty with handwriting when they leave full-time education. It is true that over time the older executives will be replaced by a generation who has never known a world without the Internet or smartphones. Even then these new executives would not be expected to understand the world of innovative IT in the same way as the company IT specialist. Handling the lack of digital literacy in the rest of the senior management team is a difficult task, but it offers enormous opportunities for the CIO to develop into an essential part of the business strategy team.

Getting onto the Strategy Team

If you are not a member of the corporate strategy team, there are ways of infiltrating that group and becoming a trusted member of the team. While you may think it is obvious, the first thing to do is to review your IT strategy. If you haven't got one, get one. There are many ways to develop a strategic plan, but this topic is outside the scope of this book. Joe Peppard and John Ward, in their book on strategic planning for information systems, developed a strategic planning framework that you can use as a starting point[2]. If there is no IT strategy, then it would be difficult to discuss the strategy for the business because you would have no credibility as a strategist. Several times in this book we have made the point that there should not be a separate business and IT strategy—they should be merged into one. Merging the IT strategy with the business strategy is only possible if you have developed your IT strategy using a well-considered and clear process.

Orders for IT support from business strategists should be considered against an existing IT strategy. Having to adapt an IT strategy due to business demands is not a chore; it should generate a view of the IT department as a flexible, well-organized group.

The prevailing attitude of senior management is that IT is a cost of doing business. There is an understanding of how important IT is to the business, but many companies are not exploiting IT to the fullest extent to drive business growth. The CIO becoming part of the strategy team should change that, but only if the CIO is seen as open and flexible and capable of thinking strategically. We have suggested that having an IT strategy be the first step in

---

[2] John L Ward and Joe Peppard, *Strategic Planning for Information Systems* (John Wiley and Sons, 2002).

becoming a member of the corporate strategy group. However, this is not the only qualification. It is also important to understand the business needs and requirements of the company.

If you can, gain access to the business strategy. Understanding the business strategy will make it possible for you to review that strategy against the work you have done to build your own IT strategy. You may discover some flaws in the business strategy. It is often the case that a set of fresh eyes can see things that are hidden to insiders. You may also see that your IT strategy needs modification. In either case, it is important that you communicate your findings about the business strategy in a nonjudgmental way. Making suggestions where IT can improve the business strategy is the first step in gaining the trust you will need to become a regular member of the business strategy team.

Reporting and Measuring the Business Value of Innovation

Many commentators have mentioned that the more abstract an innovation idea is, the harder it is to evaluate. The hardest innovations to measure and evaluate are the most difficult to get funding or mindset for further work. Reporting and measuring the business value of innovation is generally acknowledged as one of the biggest challenges in developing and maintaining an innovative culture in a business. Innovators are almost universal in identifying the measurement of innovation as a problem of communication with the other members of the organization. Companies with little or no history of innovation have measurement that is seldom adaptable to measure innovation. Innovation is not the only situation where measurement is a problem. Estimation of project duration and cost is an issue across the whole industry. Some specifics fit the innovation case more closely. Scott Anthony, in his *Harvard Business Review* article "The Planning Fallacy and The Innovators Dilemma," makes the point that organizations often make exaggerated claims of the financial return on an innovation.[3] They also underestimate the project duration. Anthony notes that humans are bad at estimating how long a task will take. In his article, he put together an interesting sample of data about disruptive companies to illustrate his point that looking at historical data may give perspective and help develop more accurate estimates. He finally indicates that using an uninvolved outsider can counter a possibly unrealistic insider estimate.

---

[3] Scott Anthony, "The Planning Fallacy and the Innovator's Dilemma," *Harvard Business Review*, August 2012, http://blogs.hbr.org/anthony/2012/08/the_planning_fallacy_and_the_i.html, retrieved on August 2012.

We are not suggesting that you pull someone off the street to look at your plans, but someone from another part of the business, respected for their integrity, may be a good person to review your plans and offer constructive criticism. The bullet points below are from a conversation with a business manager that has bearing on this and other parts of the chapter. This manager recognized the problems with measuring innovative activites and the conflict between those activities and a quarterly-based revenue stream for mature products.

During the research for this book, I interviewed the general manager of a business unit in a Fortune 500 Company. This manager, who has a good track record for generating business from innovation, had a few things to say about getting an innovative product off the ground, including reporting and measuring innovation:

- Before you start building a team, make sure you have the support of the CEO—although that doesn't mean that other executives won't try and kill your project. They'll just find it harder.

- Recognize that you will spend more time on internal issues than promoting the innovative product outside.

- Corporate culture and business practices can kill an innovation before it has left the drawing board. Employees often see innovation as mere widow-dressing.

- You may encounter whispering campaigns across the company suggesting that the effort is failing. The only way to counter this is to communicate often and positively—press and analyst reports are very useful.

- Internal processes don't often fit your requirements. Your project may not fit the project management processes and won't get milestone signoff from other parts of the company. Ignore them or bypass them if you need to. Set up your own internal measures.

- Measurement is difficult. You have a lack of alignment on success metrics with the mature parts of the business, and you can't view progress and success through a mature business lens.

- Senior management doesn't have the appropriate "carrot and stick" to encourage their support for innovation. Their staff will focus on their own personal needs—not for the good of the project.

- There are unrealistic revenue-based measures placed on you that are always going to predict failure. Try and avoid these where you can or get the CFO onside so that the importance of these measures is reduced in the case of an innovative project.

Despite all the struggles, internal conflicts and constant vigilance, when he was asked if it was worth it, the general manager said that he was proud of the team's achievements. They were making steady progress and leading an emerging market. He also said that it continues to be enormous fun.

Approvals

The issues with measurement and reporting can be highlighted with an example from the approvals, project management, and benefits reviews typical in an organization with a well-established and mature product line. When this organization investigates an extension to an existing product, the first task is to create a business case. This is frequently used as a means to get investment approval. The benefits of the product extension are listed as the costs and the resources required. The business case may not be a stand-alone document but instantiated as data put into a project portfolio management tool. Either style of business case has a few problems for innovative projects:

- The benefits of an innovation may have a longer lead time before it reaches a level of benefit comparable with an existing project.

- The evaluation of the innovation business case may be conducted by executives who have a fixed formula for cost benefit analysis that does not match the cost benefit metrics expected for a mature product.

- Innovative product progress through the project management process may not be smooth. Project management gates will have to be negotiated, and innovations may not meet the mandatory requirements that will allow the innovative project to progress to the next stage in a development project.

- The development process may be too restrictive for an innovation but may work well for maintaining the correct level of control for extension or upgrade of an existing or mature project.

Approvals for an innovative project may be difficult, but having the CEO as a sponsor will often help. Although the benefits may not be fully understood at the start of a project, there needs to be a regular review of the benefits that are anticipated. The results of this review should be communicated frequently and as widely as possible.

Time Frames

Public companies have to report quarterly and annually on the financial health of the company. This leads to a short-term mentality in some parts of the company. Quarterly measurement and incentives do not generally match the progress of an innovative project. In the early stages of an innovative project, financial information may merely highlight cost rather than benefits. This is particularly true if the project involves the development of products to exploit a new marketplace.

An example here might prove helpful. If your organization is selling vacation packages on the Web and sees a new market for convention packages, there would need to be changes both to the web applications and the business processes. The initial research may have established the proof points of cost, potential profit, and market analysis for example. This has encouraged the CEO to approve the project. The project timeline and benefits need to be reviewed and firmed up. This review may lead to optimistic estimates of time-to-completion and project cost. There will be a time lag between approval of the project and the first implementation. In an extensive upgrade to software and business process, it may be more than a single quarter where investment is being eating up by costs and no sales benefit, which means no financial returns. If the reporting emphasis is on costs in the first part of the innovative project, other parts of the organization may become concerned about the lack of return on investment. This can often turn into pressure to review or even cancel the project, particularly if those other parts of the organization are feeling starved of resources, funds, or facing layoffs. Patience is always a quality that is in short supply in these circumstances. You need to make sure that the measure for the project focuses on benefits and not costs. You also need to report successes in the project—for example, on time, under budget, or creating interest in the company. These will allow you to communicate frequently while the expected results are being anticipated.

An innovative project for creating a new entry into a market has the additional timing issues of having to create marketing momentum to generate sales. Creation of a new product does not mean that it will find a ready market, particularly if the market itself is new. In these circumstances, more than one or two quarters will pass before the investments in the innovation make some impact. The longer the time before an investment starts to yield benefits, the more likely it is that there will be pressure to cancel the project.

The time frame of an innovative project can affect the perception of the project. A CIO leading the development of an innovative project should not neglect the frequent adjustments of any communications or progress reports. At each development milestone, there should be a re-evaluation of the benefits that are predicted and any adjustments that are needed. If the market for the new product is maturing and other competitors are validating the market, this needs to be communicated. CIOs from a technology background often fall into the development trap of concentrating on the IT development and communicating progress of that development. The CIO should give equal importance to the business process changes and include them. The benefits anticipated should be reviewed with increasing importance as the duration of the project extends.

Benefits Realization

There are a number of ways of describing benefits and linking them to the innovative vision, the IT development, and the business process changes they support. Joe Peppard, John Ward and Elizabeth Daniel have described how to identify, plan, and manage the benefits delivered as part of an IT investment. The Benefits Dependency Network (BDN) is a cause/effect network–based tool and is described in more detail in their paper written for *MIS Quarterly Executive*[4]. The BDN describes IT enablers, the enabling changes, business changes, benefits, and investment objectives as a set of linked objects. This network can be constructed in several ways, depending on how it should be applied. The important point is that building the network imposes a discipline on considering the relationships among benefits, IT, and business process change. It also creates a visualization of the project that can be used to describe the relationship. This network can be reviewed and refined to deliver an increasingly accurate picture of the innovative project's benefits and objectives. It can then form part of the reporting and measurement processes of an innovative project.

Measurement of Portfolio Innovations

Creating a value statement for an innovation may be difficult but achievable. There are often situations where there are several innovation-led projects that are at different stages of progress. Reporting on these innovations

---

[4] John Ward, Elizabeth Daniel, Joe Peppard, "Building Better Business Cases for IT Investments", MIS Quarterly Executive, Vol. 7, No. 1, 2008, 1–15.

individually may not lead to a full appreciation of the value of innovation. Some businesses have had to address this problem, and their approach can help in considering a portfolio of benefits. A good example of how a business reports value from each stage in a process is the metal pressing industry. It is common in this industry to need multiple pressings of a raw material to create a finished object. The raw material has a value—when the metal is cut and first pressed it has an increased value. At each stage in the production process, the value of the object increases until it reaches the value of the finished object. This object could be a button for a pair of jeans or a metal rivet. The value of the objects at each stage on the process is the work in progress value. It is common to add the value of raw material awaiting processing to the number of objects and their interim value, to give a value metric for the manufacturing process. This is part of the value reported as part of business management.

This approach can be used to report the benefit accrual for a set of innovative projects. You would need to establish the benefits already present for each innovation at a particular time. Some of the innovative projects may be nearing completion and have tangible benefits, sales, or performance improvements. If the benefits can be quantified, they can be added to the benefits accrued by projects at earlier stages of development. The benefits may not be as tangible, but each benefit may be reported. Even a new project may have a benefit—for example, training a member of staff in HTML5 could be a requirement at the start of the project but the benefit is that you now have a member of staff who has been trained. Summing up the benefits can offer a clearer picture of the total value of the innovative projects in progress and may refute some of the objections of other staff members to the investment in "unproductive" projects.

Overcoming Institutional Objections and Barriers

A key skill in shepherding any innovation to completion is how to overcome institutional barriers and objections. Objections tend to be personal, linked to company politics and personal concerns. Barriers are mostly organizational in nature and spring from a mismatch between the needs of innovation and the needs of the organization. Organizational barriers can be broken down into two further areas: organizational barriers that are a function of the organizational structure, management chain, etc. and operational barriers that are a function of the organizational business and management processes.

Organizational Barriers

Organizational barriers are manifested in organizational structures that prevent decision-makers, budget holders, and sponsors of an innovation from working together to implement the innovation. These barriers are often found in organizations that don't have an innovation infrastructure and a clear mandate to innovate. An organizational barrier can be as simple as isolating human resources needed under a different part of the management structure. The different parts of the management structure may have different priorities to your own. Marketing and PR in many organizations are handled in a centralized part of the organization. If an innovative project needs marketing or PR resources, they would be expected to apply to the corporate departments for resources. Responses from these departments may not be positive, particularly if they have already committed their annual marketing and PR budgets to promoting mature products and projects.

The only way of overcoming these barriers is to ignore them, with the blessing of the senior management sponsor. This may have a negative effect on your relationship with the affected department heads. This negative effect may be mitigated if you are careful in your communications with other department heads and use this as an opportunity to educate them in the positive values of your plans. In this circumstance, there may be a need to create a company within a company. Building a small multidisciplinary team can be the only way of ensuring that you have needed resources under your control. There comes a time when the innovative project has matured sufficiently that some resources need to be returned to the mainstream, and this can also present some challenges.

Operational Barriers

Operational barriers are those that are a function of the existing business processes, such as procurement, supply chain, human resources, and facilities. These processes are not likely to be flexible in a large or mature company with little or no innovative culture. Even companies who have a good track record of innovating mature products or exploiting mature markets often have business processes that cannot be adapted without disruptive risk to the existing business processes and operations. There may need to be an operational review before the innovation can be adopted. A good example would be a supply chain innovation promoted by IT, sponsored by resource management, but opposed by purchasing due to procurement rules that may need review or changing. Tools like BDN will help you to describe the situation more clearly with regard to the impact on process rigidity on an innovation's benefits. Operational barriers often become insuperable in a time of strict cost control. When a company is reducing operational budgets, for example in a time of recession, the innovative project that has not yet yielded a return on investment will come under pressure to reduce costs. Often an innovation has been allocated the minimum investment and may not have much excess budget to lose without a severe impact on development and benefits. These are the times that having the CEO and/or the CFO as a sponsor will pay off.

You may need to counterpressure for cost and staff reductions. The best way to do this is through communication and reporting. It is important to keep staff, particularly sponsors, informed on progress and achievements, particularly if there are complementary pieces in the trade press.

As an innovative CIO, you may have implemented an innovation by sponsoring it yourself, through skunk works, or a small internal budget realignment. If you have confidence in your investment, then it should be relatively simple to maintain the momentum. Telling people about the innovation and looking for investment are often hurdles that you can overcome with demonstrations and prototypes.

Overcoming Objections

Innovations can also fall foul of political and social group dynamics in a company that can make any proposer of a new idea quail. Objections are often unique to the individual and may not be easy to see or understand.

There are often seemingly valid objections to the implementation of an innovation. If these objections are clearly and openly stated, they can be discussed and resolved. Objections that are more difficult to counter are those that are hidden as part of a whispering campaign. The objection is never aired publicly, but the innovation does not get the support that was anticipated or needed. You may not even know that there are objections to an innovative project. The motivations for people to raise objections can be difficult to establish. Some objections can be attributed to the characteristics of the objector. Some habits of objectors have already been discussed under the term innovation killers in Chapter 2. We will expand on these habits and characteristics here in the context of innovation and business value. These characteristics may be stereotypes, but they are also valid despite being stereotypes.

The novelty of a proposal, particularly if it proposes significant changes, can be met with obstacles, objections, and resistance to change across the whole organization. Novelty alone is sometimes sufficient to generate objections. A frequently raised objection to innovation is expressed in the phrase "we have not done anything like this before." Another phrase that is often used in these circumstance is "That's not how we do things here." These types of objections are a symptom of a resistance to change and a desire to maintain the status quo. They are deeply rooted and as such will be difficult to move. They can also be the expression of a risk averse executive.

The risk averse executives will be concerned about the level of risk that is involved in an innovation. The results-driven executives will ask how much and how soon will the company see a return on investment. As we mentioned earlier, the measurement criteria of innovation are sometimes difficult to establish. We sometimes refer to these members of staff as "nervous nellies." They see only the downside—all risks are inflated and exaggerated because they are nervous about the outcomes. Nervous nellies can sometimes be won over by illustrating the past record of innovation and the ways in which the current plan is working well.

Personal pique is also sadly common in many organizations. If your innovation has been granted funding, other executives may feel aggrieved if their innovation has not gained funding. Professional jealousy can often undermine an innovation, particularly if it is supplemented by organizational or operational barriers. These barriers can sometimes be ignored, but ignoring a barrier is more difficult if there is an executive with an alternative agenda labeling you as a maverick who is ignoring company policy.

Managing Change

Managing change is one of the most extensive disciplines of management training. It has been recognized that any change will meet resistance. Resistance can often kill or restrict change, hence the emphasis on change management in management training. Many of the tools and techniques for managing change and overcoming resistance have been well-documented in books, articles, and, of course, management training. There are many authors writing on this subject, including John Kotter. Kotter has identified an eight-stage process for creating major change in his book, *Leading Change*.[5] This process has suggestions that can help the CIO overcome barriers and objections. One relevant point he makes is that creating a guiding coalition can deliver a group with the power to create change. Managing change is one of the main tools in connecting IT innovation with business value.

To help you consider the fellow employees that you are working with, we have identified a number of different stereotypes of people who will raise objections about an innovation:

---

[5] John Kotter, *Leading Change* (New York: Harvard Business Press, 1996).

- *Devil's Advocate:* This is a person who persistently looks at the downside of every project and seems to get pleasure from forecasting disaster. When they are right, they are often ignored because their good call is is discounted. Frequent predictions of disaster that are proven wrong may discredit all their predictions. Sometimes they are right more than they are wrong, and in that case they become a key influencer. The only way to counter these people is to take their first set of objections seriously, review the project against their forecast, and if they have a valid point, it will need to be addressed. The drawback to this approach is the amount of time it can consume. In our experience, this requires an "answer-once-and-then-ignore" style of solution.

- *Confused Employee:* There may be a genuine reason for the confusion of this group. This may also be a subset of the group who complain "we have not done this type of thing before." It could be a lack of understanding of the objectives, a confusion about the "how" of what you are trying to do, or just a general confusion about why there needs to be an innovation. Before dismissing this group's objection, it is always wise to review what you have already said about the project. Is it as clear as you think? Often this group can highlight a flaw in project communication and sometimes in the reasoning. You should take an unbiased view of the group's objections and perhaps pass them on to a third party for review. If this group is still confused after relevant changes to the project or the communications, you will have to consider ignoring them. Before finally dismissing any new confusion they exhibit, you may want to take a last look at any points they raise. If these employees are still among the few who are confused about some aspect of the project and they don't have concrete points to make, they may lose their influence and cease to be significant as objectors.

- *Change-phobics:* There are people like this in most organizations—one executive I met referred to the middle management permafrost who were determined that things would not change in their organization. The change management tools mentioned earlier should be brought into play to overcome their resistance to change. If the change-phobic is a senior executive, overcoming the objection can be difficult. However, the CEO may be enlisted to provide persuasion. Not all change is good, but the rapid and frequent changes in many organizations have helped them to adapt to changing market and financial pressures. These objectors are often driven by fear of change and the impact of change on them.

- *Politician*: These are people who are intent on developing personal or departmental success rather than considering the organization as a whole. This is a common type of person in large organizations, and they can be destructive to the entire organization. They sometimes live by this maxim: it is not enough for me to succeed, someone else has to be seen to fail. They are generally smart people, and this is where the issue lies with handling them. The innovative CIO may be making suggestions and planning innovations that affects their area of business. If they are onboard one of the guiding coalition or the sponsorship group, then you will have every chance of succeeding. They will see your success as being their success. Our advice in this circumstance is to get the politician on your side if possible, unless you are confident of the support of the CEO and other members of the C-level. The politician is frequently the main objector to projects that remain untouched during a period of cost-cutting or during a critical evaluation of their department's performance.

These are not scientifically determined groups of employees but groups that we have identified in our long careers. Often an individual can be in one or more groups and their group membership may change over time and circumstance.

Overcoming these objections and barriers is a time-consuming and almost full-time job. It cannot be neglected, for just expecting everyone to see the benefit of your innovation will not save the project. If your efforts in innovation have not been aligned with business value, they may be dismissed as a nice option, not really worth the investment, and ultimately the first casualty in any cost-cutting. Establishing this link between business value and innovation is one of the key skills for any CIO who wants to become innovative.

The Dirty Little Secrets of Innovation

The path to becoming an innovative CIO can be a rewarding one, but it may not be an easy one. While we see hundreds or thousands of volumes, articles, and speeches extolling the virtues and beauties of successful innovation—and of famous innovators—we rarely get insight into the ugly side of innovation. We see the triumphs and successes, but we rarely witness the blood, sweat, and tears; the road bumps and detours; and the failures of innovation and of innovators.

In this chapter, we will highlight some of the less obvious challenges you will face, and expose the darker side of innovation. Some of these hazards will be readily apparent, but many will not. Some of the hidden challenges will be avoidable, but most will not. Worst of all, some of your biggest obstacles will be deliberately put in your way, not by your competitors, but by your own colleagues.

These are some of the "dirty little secrets" of innovation.

Most Innovation Will Fail

First and foremost, you must understand that innovation is not a sure thing. Indeed, you should go into your innovation program realizing that most innovation will fail to deliver the results you want, let alone the results you expect.

You can do everything right—set up the right organization to foster innovation, establish a culture of innovation, allocate staff and resources to innovation programs, ensure executive sponsorship and support—and still get innovation wrong. Perhaps you simply do not have the right ideas or the right people; perhaps the wind is blowing the wrong way on the day you release your innovation to the world; perhaps the competition was working on the same idea and beat you to market.

The fact is, innovation is not predictable, and it is not assured. On any given day, any number of factors, many of which are not yours to control, can undermine your chances of success.

For example, many people would cite Google as one of the most innovative companies on the planet. From its early days as a slimmed down web search page to its current incarnation as a massive conglomerate of technologies, Google has innovated in Web, mobile, publishing, communications, collaboration, e-commerce, news, advertising, media, social networking, and other technologies. Google has a reputation for encouraging innovation, building its workforce and culture around innovation, and delivering some of the most highly regarded innovations in recent years.

However, most of even Google's innovations have failed to be a success, in commercial terms at least.

In 2011, Google spent 13.6% of its total revenues on research and development (R&D), slightly up from 2010 (12.8%) and 2009 (12.0%). In 2011, Google's total revenues were $37 billion, so this works out to around $5 billion annually spent on R&D—a substantial amount in anyone's terms.

Yet, Google depends on what more or less amounts to a single revenue stream—paid advertising—for more than 95% of its total revenue. Indeed, most of Google's other innovations (organic and inorganic)—e-mail, chat, video, maps, etc.—have added very little directly to its reported revenue (although many of them do support a growing captive market for its revenue-generating advertisements).[1]

Moreover, many of Google's innovative services have been completely or partially abandoned, sometimes very publicly. Here are a few examples:

- *Google Wave:* the company's high-profile communication and collaboration tool was given up for adoption to the Apache

---

[1] Financial data from Google Inc., "United States Securities and Exchange Commission Form 10K, for the Fiscal Year ended December 31, 2011," www.sec.gov/Archives/edgar/data/1288776/000119312512025336/d260164d10k.htm, retrieved on July 2012.

Foundation in just less than 18 months. This was despite wide and generally positive media coverage and substantial uptake by customers.

- *Google Buzz*: the company's attempt to compete with other social and collaboration networks like Facebook and Twitter lasted a little longer, but was shut down just two years after it debuted to broad fanfare (ultimately replaced with Google+).

- *Google Knol*: the company's attempt to counter the huge popularity of the free online user-contributed encyclopedia, Wikipedia. This service certainly included a number of important competitive innovations, but was nevertheless abandoned after four years as it failed to attract the popularity of its better known rival.

These are just three well-known examples in a long list of shuttered Google projects, including Google Checkout, Google Answers, Google Code Search, Google Desktop, and many more.

Similarly, the history of Apple, another frontrunner in many people's minds for title of "the most innovative tech company on the planet," is strewn with failures like The Quicktake, the Lisa, the "hockey puck" mouse, and the Pippin.[2,3] Perhaps few examples are more symbolic of this than the Apple MessagePad, running the Newton operating system—one of the first in a long line of mobile devices then known as PDAs.

The first Newton was released in 1993, but by 1998 Apple had killed off the product line, as its reportedly poor functionality and high prices[4] led to under expected product sales and poor reviews.[5] After initially being spun off as a separate entity, then reabsorbed into the Apple mothership, the Newton platform that had shown so much promise was also eventually abandoned.

---

[2] Andy Greenberg and Rachel Rosmarin, "In Pictures: 10 Apple Flops", October 2011, http://www.forbes.com/2008/10/29/apple-product-flops-tech-personal-cx_ag_1030apple_slide_2.html?thisSpeed=30000, retrieved on September 2012

[3] Bryan Gardiner, "Learning From Failure: Apple's Most Notorious Flops", January 2008, http://www.wired.com/gadgets/mac/multimedia/2008/01/gallery_apple_flops?slide=7. retrieved on September 2012

[4] Andy Greenburg, "When Apple Failed", Forbes.com, October 2011, http://www.forbes.com/2008/10/29/apple-product-flops-tech-personal-cx_ag_1030apple.html, retrieved on September 2012

[5] "PDA (handheld computer)," Encyclopedia Britannica, last updated February 25, 2010, www.britannica.com/EBchecked/topic/1581618/Newton-MessagePad, retrieved on September 2012.

Similarly, Apple's first foray into cloud computing was also rife with fits and starts, and it too was eventually abandoned. Initially released as iTools, then renamed to .Mac, Apple attempted to penetrate the personal cloud storage and application space with what would become better known in its later incarnation as MobileMe. However, even after these multiple iterations, MobileMe was cancelled, having never reached the level of success that had been expected.

However, this regular and almost predictable tendency for innovation to fail is not always a bad thing.

Failure is an inherent part of the innovation cycle, and can even be the basis of valuable learning to drive further (and successful) future innovation. For example, Google leveraged its failures in collaboration and social networking (Wave, Buzz) into another new innovation, Google+. This innovation introduced many new and popular capabilities like "hangouts" and "circles," which were competitive differentiators against other social networks.

Similarly, Apple eventually leveraged its failures in the cloud market to transform MobileMe into a more successful cloud storage service, iCloud. And there can hardly be a starker example of turning failure into success: Apple went from the disappointing Newton-based mobile devices to ultimately releasing its phenomenally successful and truly revolutionary iPad tablets.

The real secret here is not that innovation fails, but what to do when it does—as it almost certainly will. Rather than simply updating your resume and abandoning ship, look to analyze the failure and learn from it, so you can make a conscious (and rapid) decision whether to conclude, remediate, or end the innovation project. The adage here is to "fail fast" (and fail cheap), so you can either prove or disprove your innovative ideas.

In relative terms, "fail fast" is what Google did with Google Wave, which allowed Google Buzz to fail fast, which then allowed Google+ to come to market just over two years after the initial release of Google Wave.

By contrast, Apple "failed slow" with the MessagePad and Newton OS, taking more than five years to pull the plug. While this did not hurt Apple in the long run, there were times soon after the Newton platform was cancelled when the company's very existence was in jeopardy. It took Apple more than ten years to recover and find success in the handheld device space with the introduction of the iPod, iTunes and the iTunes app store business model, and eventually the iPad. It is almost hard to believe that its earlier attempts in mobile device innovation almost destroyed the company.

Innovation Will Cost You Money

Perhaps this goes without saying, but intentional innovation can be very costly. It often takes a substantial investment, from the cost of staff and other human resources to the cost of development systems, cloud services, physical space for desks and equipment, testing, pilot procedures, necessary equipment, and much more. In the software business, for example, some of the most innovative companies spend up to a quarter of their revenues in R&D, with companies like Microsoft, IBM, and Cisco spending more than $5 billion a year on R&D (as shown in Figure 11-1).

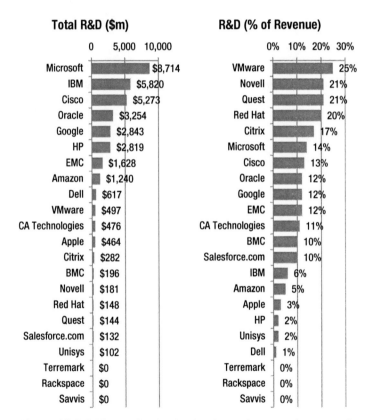

Total R&D ($m)

Microsoft	$8,714
IBM	$5,820
Cisco	$5,273
Oracle	$3,254
Google	$2,843
HP	$2,819
EMC	$1,628
Amazon	$1,240
Dell	$617
VMware	$497
CA Technologies	$476
Apple	$464
Citrix	$282
BMC	$196
Novell	$181
Red Hat	$148
Quest	$144
Salesforce.com	$132
Unisys	$102
Terremark	$0
Rackspace	$0
Savvis	$0

R&D (% of Revenue)

VMware	25%
Novell	21%
Quest	21%
Red Hat	20%
Citrix	17%
Microsoft	14%
Cisco	13%
Oracle	12%
Google	12%
EMC	12%
CA Technologies	11%
BMC	10%
Salesforce.com	10%
IBM	6%
Amazon	5%
Apple	3%
HP	2%
Unisys	2%
Dell	1%
Terremark	0%
Rackspace	0%
Savvis	0%

Figure 11-1. R&D spending by cloud and virtualization software vendors is shown in this figure. Data was taken from SEC filings from respective companies.[6]

---

[6] Google Finance, http://www.google.com/finance

Unfortunately, a lot of that money is lost, if not wasted, because as we have seen, a great deal of innovation effort fails to deliver commercial results.

Even ostensibly successful innovation may actually end up losing money. To start with, it can be very difficult to link revenue and profit definitively back to a singular innovation. It is clearer in the case of a blockbuster product like the iPad and its antecedents in the Newton platform, but even then it may not account for the losses incurred by previous failures, even if they ultimately informed the innovation success.

It may also be difficult to show the results of innovation in financial terms when the return on investment (ROI) spreads out over multiple products and services. An innovative capability may attract more customers and broaden the revenue base, yet still be difficult to attribute because it does not drive revenue to a single product. For example, Google continues to grow revenue through its single core revenue stream, undoubtedly fed by the increasing engagement with its customer base through a range of innovations. Yet it does not identify these innovations explicitly as sources of new revenue in their own right, at least not in its official SEC filings. It is therefore very difficult, especially for an outsider, to allocate new revenue specifically to the innovative services that Google has added to its portfolio.

It may be that your innovation efforts pay off once in a blue moon. If you are lucky, the return on that unitary success will cover the costs of your many failures. However, it is also possible that your innovations may simply never pay off.

This was clearly the case with webOS, a handheld operating system designed by Palm, Inc., released on a handful of proprietary devices. Despite many innovative features and being from the one-time market leader in the mobile device market, it was never as successful as intended. Ultimately, webOS proved to be no competition for other successful platforms such as (perhaps ironically) Apple iOS. Palm was eventually acquired by Hewlett-Packard (HP) for $1.2 billion in 2010, with webOS being a centerpiece of the deal,[7] before HP effectively abandoned this investment, and several webOS-based devices, as they failed to meet financial targets and internal expectations.[8] In 2011, HP finally turned over the core OS to the open source development community,

---

[7] Richard Waters, Chris Nuttall, "Hewlett Packard to Buy Palm for $1.2bn," Financial Times, April 2010, www.ft.com/intl/cms/s/2/0aa1ef6e-5303-11df-813e-00144feab49a.html, retrieved on September 2012.

[8] Hewlett-Packard, "HP Reports Third Quarter 2011 Results and Initiates Company Transformation," August 2011, http://h30261.www3.hp.com/phoenix.zhtml?c=71087&p=irol-newsArticle&ID=1598003, retrieved on September 2012.

while selling off remaining inventory of webOS devices for as little as 20% of their original retail prices,[9] presumably at a substantial loss.

Similarly, Research In Motion (RIM) attempted to compete with the emerging tablet market (substantially dominated by the Apple iPad) with the PlayBook, a tablet device that was criticized as a copycat. In the second quarter of 2011, the PlayBook had underachieved its estimated sales by a ratio of 10:1. After initially estimating sales of 2.4 million units, RIM soon revised that estimate to 800,000 units[10] before finally reporting actual sales in the quarter of just 200,000 units.[11] As a result, the PlayBook almost certainly failed to recoup its investment, and in fact forced RIM to take a $485 million write-off to account for the losses the company incurred as it heavily discounted the device in an attempt to generate sales.[12] Although the complete history of the PlayBook has yet to be written, it is certainly true that it has cost RIM a substantial amount of money, and to date it cannot be viewed as anything but a high-profile, high-cost failure to capitalize on innovation.

Innovation Can Be a Career-Limiting Move

While almost everybody would jump at the chance to be a Wilbur or Orville Wright, how many would jump at the chance to be a Samuel Pierpont Langley?

Already I can hear you asking, "Samuel who?"

An older contemporary of the Wright brothers, Samuel Pierpont Langley (seen in Figure 11-2) was an award-winning scientist, a respected inventor, and a self-styled innovator who struggled unsuccessfully for years to find the secret to manned aviation.

---

[9] Nathan Olivarez-Giles, "HP TouchPad Mania: TouchPads Selling Out in U.S. at $99.99," *Los Angeles Times*, August 20, 2011, http://latimesblogs.latimes.com/technology/2011/08/hp-touchpad-mania-touchpads-selling-out-in-us-at-99.html, retrieved on September 2012.

[10] Lance Whitney, "Report: RIM Axes PlayBook Sales Target," C|Net, June 2011, http://news.cnet.com/8301-1035_3-20073637-94/report-rim-axes-playbook-sales-target, retrieved on September 2011.

[11] Research In Motion, "Research In Motion Reports Second Quarter Fiscal 2012 Results," September 2011, www.rim.com/investors/documents/pdf/pressrelease/2012/Q2_press_release.pdf, retrieved on September 2012.

[12] Research In Motion, "Research In Motion Announces Third Quarter Provision Related to PlayBook Inventory and Confirms Commitment to Tablet Market; Provides Update to Q3 and Fiscal 2012 Guidance," December 2011, www.rim.com/investors/documents/pdf/financial/2012/Dec-2_press-release-FINAL.pdf, retrieved on September 2012.

Figure 11-2. Samuel Pierpont Langley (right) is shown here with his chief mechanic and pilot, Charles Manly. (Photo courtesy of NASA)

Despite a number of innovative attempts, including catapulting an unmanned prototype off a barge anchored in the middle of the Potomac River in 1896 (as seen in Figure 11-3), Langley never did find the secret of manned flight in a heavier-than-air craft.

Figure 11-3. This is a modified houseboat on the Potomac, showing the launching machinery for Samuel Pierpont Langley's manned flight experiments. (Photo courtesy of US Library of Congress)

But to the victor goes the spoils, so while everyone remembers the Wright brothers as the inventors who succeeded in the first manned flight in 1903, few remember Langley and his failures, even though he was actively experimenting with manned flight until just nine days before the Wright brothers' historical first flight. With a history of failure, including multiple crashes, Langley died just three years later, without contributing anything more of substance to the history of aviation, or indeed to the history of innovation.

For Langley, this was not exactly a career-limiting move (CLM)—his career was already well-established when he started his research of manned flight, and he was, after all, 71 years old when he died. However, following his failures, he was forced out of this research primarily because he could not gain additional funding to continue his endeavors.

This stands as an object lesson in the risk of establishing yourself as an innovative CIO. When most innovation ends in failure, and much innovation ends up costing money with little or no attributable ROI, the risk of being labeled a failure is very real and can have severe consequences. Taking up the position as an innovative CIO, and embarking on such a path, can easily result in this turning out to be the feared CLM. Do you really want to be the chief of a program known for cost and failure? This could well be the harsh reality of a bent toward innovation.

Moreover, it is not just failure that can make innovation a CLM—ironically, you can also be the victim of your own success. Radical innovation can upset the existing regime so much that you effectively invent yourself out of a job.

Take automation as an example. Automation allows IT administrators to document, standardize, and automate their day-to-day work processes. In doing so, it eliminates much of their work, and in some cases eliminates it all. As a direct result of this innovation, IT administrators or operators can easily innovate themselves out of a job. Even as a leader, this can be true. For example, cloud computing has the potential to replace a large proportion of the tradition IT establishment, and in some cases may even replace it entirely, leaving very little for a traditional CIO to do.

There are ways around this, of course. Transitioning from Chief Information Officer to Chief Innovation Officer (or any of the other I's we discussed in Chapter 3) is just a start. You may end up becoming the Chief Digital Officer or Chief Technology Officer for your organization, rather than the CIO.

Such an evolutionary transition is, after all, a proven path in what today we call "IT." Remember that before Information Technology (IT) there was Information Systems (IS), before that it was Management Information Systems (MIS), and even before that we had Data Processing (DP). Going forward, some pundits predict the replacement of "IT" with "BT"—Business Technology—and further into the future it could be something different again. This is simply another step in the ongoing evolution and regeneration of this industry.

The trick for you as an innovative CIO will be to identify the impacts of innovation before they happen; get ahead of them with a new focus, new skills, new capabilities, and new contributions; and maintain your value to the business as a leader in technology and business, regardless of your title.

Good Innovation Sets a Bad Precedent

Ironically then, even successful innovation is clearly not always a personally positive outcome. In fact, successful innovation can set such a high expectation for *future* innovation that it is impossible to be as successful a second time. Not every innovation will be golden, but you will be judged against those that are.

It is true that some people and organizations have the uncanny ability to innovate continuously and successfully, delivering products and services that are increasingly better, more functional, more attractive, more profitable, and more successful.

Look at organizations like Xerox PARC, inventors of many revolutionary and successful innovations, including the graphical user interface (GUI), the laser printer, Ethernet, WYSIWYG editing, and object-oriented programming (OOP).

Or individuals such as Nikola Tesla, who was substantially responsible for a string of radical innovations, including the principles (and many patents) behind alternating current (AC) power, X-rays, bladeless turbines, cryogenic engineering, and the modern transistor.

In the tech world, we see a few similar examples of innovative entrepreneurs who continue to deliver successful inventions, including Niklas Zennström and Janus Friis (Skype, Kazaa) and Jack Dorsey (Twitter, Square).

However, history is also littered with inventors, both corporate and individual, who never managed to deliver success beyond their first and most famous invention, no matter how good their subsequent ideas actually were:

- Dean Kamen made his multimillion dollar fortune when he sold his first invention as an adult, the autosyringe, to an international health care company. By contrast, after investing $100 million developing the now famous Segway, only 30,000 units were sold in six years, well short of its hype and of the success of the autosyringe.[13]

- Ernő Rubik is famous as the inventor of the eponymous Rubik's Cube, a smash-hit toy which became the world's fastest-selling toy when it was released in 1980 and by some measures is the most successful puzzle toy in history.[14] Despite attempts to replicate this success, with subsequent toys like Rubik's Magic, Rubik's Snake, and Rubik's 360, Ernő Rubik never did achieve the same level of success.

- Alexey Pajitnov was the man behind one of the most successful video games in history, Tetris. However, despite his invention being named "Greatest Game of All Time," becoming the best-selling mobile game of all time,[15] and working on or with almost 20 different video games since the

[13] Douglas McIntyre, "The 10 Biggest Tech Failures of the Last Decade: Segway," *Time Magazine*, May 2009, www.time.com/time/specials/packages/article/0,28804,1898610 _1898625_1898641,00.html, retrieved on July 2012.

[14] Alastair Jamieson, "Rubik's Cube Inventor is Back with Rubik's 360," *The Telegraph*, January 2009, www.telegraph.co.uk/lifestyle/4412176/Rubiks-Cube-inventor-is-back-with-Rubiks-360. html, retrieved on July 2012.

[15] Tetris Holding, "History," www.tetris.com/history/index.aspx, retrieved on July 2012.

release of Tetris, Pajitnov has never replicated his initial success.

Clearly then, *successful* innovation does not guarantee *ongoing* innovation. This is perhaps never as apparent as the many one-hit wonders of the 21st-century technology boom. In so many Silicon Valley success stories, such as Napster, PayPal, Netscape, and more, their creators—including famous names like Marc Andreeson and Peter Thiel—never repeated the same level of success. Many of these innovators have gone on to fund others' new innovations by contributing to or running venture capital funds, but have not reached the high bar of expectation that they set for themselves with their first successful innovations.

This is not to say that any of these inventors are known as failures *per se*. Marc Andreeson, for example, has had substantial success with other ventures of his own, including LoudCloud (rebranded as Opsware and subsequently sold to HP for $1.6 billion), though clearly not as groundbreaking as his earlier innovation with Netscape.

Nor is it to say that one major innovation cannot set your organization and yourself up for a long career of success. Mark Zuckerberg, the founder of Facebook, barely created a single idea himself (at least according to allegations from Tyler and Cameron Winklevoss that he stole their idea, resolved when Facebook settled with the Winklevoss twins for $65 million[16]), yet he has parlayed that into a multibillion-dollar company and personal fortune.

However, they do provide a clear lesson that you cannot always live up to the expectations set by prior successful innovation.

As an innovative CIO, you will be responsible for setting a path to continued success. Using the advice in this book, you will need to develop the management understanding and institutional knowledge to maintain and sustain growth through innovation. As we have seen, it is clearly not impossible to put in place organizational structures and processes to enable continuous and successful innovation.

However, you must also be prepared for the possibility that you and/or your team may end up being marked as failures, simply because you did not live up to the initial expectation you set with others by virtue of early success.

---

[16] Steven Musil, "Winklevoss Twins Drop Facebook Lawsuit," C|Net, June 2011, http://news.cnet.com/8301-1023_3-20073512-93/winklevoss-twins-drop-facebook-lawsuit, retrieved on September 2012.

Not All Innovation Is Good Innovation

As we explored in Chapter 2, innovation is not always useful in your "day job." Good innovation requires immense discipline. It is not enough just to forge forward with innovation programs, processes, and structures even in the face of difficult or poor results. You must also reject some ideas that come from innovation programs even when they seem to be unique and exciting.

Just because it can be done, does not mean it should be done. Just because you come up with a new idea, does not mean it is a good one. Just because you can develop an idea, does not mean you should put your resources into that idea.

To adequately develop and take advantage of innovative ideas, you need to apply resources to that development. Modeling, prototyping, testing, piloting, trialing, producing, marketing, and all the other effort needed to take an idea and make it real requires specific allocation of finite resources.

This recognizes the well-known economic principle of "opportunity cost"— the resources you devote to one innovation are no longer available to develop another, so at a figurative level the cost of developing one innovation is often the lost opportunity to develop another.

Like many business opportunities, you need to prioritize your resources into the projects and innovations that are most desirable for your organization. Sometimes, perhaps often, this will mean that many ideas, even good or great ideas, will never get the resourcing they require to take them to fruition.

And this dirty little secret is also, surprisingly, a good thing.

Retaining focus is critical, especially in a business setting. Your owners and shareholders will hold you accountable if you lose your way. You should understand your organization's vision and mission, and be sure that any innovation you pursue aligns with that vision and mission.

Even brilliant ideas may not suit your vision and mission, and will not advance your corporate goals. Even an unquestionably visionary idea can be beyond your ability to capitalize on, for any number of reasons:

- It may require too many resources to adequately develop.
- It may need capabilities outside your current competencies.
- The risk of failure has a high probability, high impact, or both.
- The ROI is not high enough or will take too long to achieve.
- It will not deliver enough of a competitive advantage.

As an innovative CIO, you must set the bar on what to pursue and what to abandon, carefully deciding according to the business opportunity and benefit, and stick to that bar. You must have the will (and the support) to not only identify "good innovation" but also to identify "not good enough innovation." Understand that you simply cannot execute on every good idea, and therefore be prepared to throw away ideas that do not meet your bar. Otherwise, you risk diluting your ability to innovate effectively and becoming "a jack of all trades, but a master of none."

Apple cofounder and CEO Steve Jobs, ever-quotable on the topic of innovation, was also a strong proponent of having the discipline of focus. He was well-known to reject innovation that did not fit his organizational vision, even to the point of rejecting good innovation simply because it was not right for the business, the time, or the need:

> People think focus means saying 'yes' to the thing you've got to focus on. But that's not what it means at all. It means saying no to the hundred other good ideas that there are. You have to pick carefully. I'm actually as proud of the things we haven't done as the things I have done. Innovation is saying 'no' to 1,000 things.

—Steve Jobs, Apple Worldwide Developers Conference, May 1997

Conversely—and somewhat confusingly—there are times when persistence is as valuable as focus. This is exemplified in the now-famous history of the 3M Post-it Note. As the story goes, the original inventor of the glue used on these repositionable notes, Dr. Spencer Silver, initially found very little use for it. His invention was, in effect, a glue that did not really stick things together, barely usable, let alone a good innovation.

A focus on usable innovation may have caused Silver to abandon this as simply a failed invention, but instead he pursued a use case for this unusually nonadhesive glue for years. It was six years before Silver and his 3M colleagues figured out a use for this "failed" innovation, and 12 years before 3M released Post-it Notes to a commercial market and to phenomenal success.[17] His determination to find a commercial use for the innovation paid off eventually, perhaps the exception that proves the rule.

Similarly, though on the other side of this coin, it can also be difficult to determine that an innovation is actually good, not bad. Take the case of Kodak and the digital camera. It is perhaps not well-known that an engineer at Kodak,

---

[17] 3M, "About Post-it® Brand," www.post-it.com/wps/portal/3M/en_US/Post_It/Global/About/About, retrieved on July 2012.

Steve Sasson, was actually the first person to invent the digital still camera.[18] Unfortunately, the executives at Kodak were unable to recognize that this was a good innovation. Instead they tried to understand how this radical and revolutionary technology could fit into the then-current paradigm of taking, storing, and viewing print photographs. In hindsight, it is easy to see that this viewpoint was flawed. Often the best innovation completely disrupts and even destroys current approaches, but you need to be able to see the possibilities, not just the difficulties, of a new approach.

The key to both of these stories is that you need to be able to look beyond "how we do things" and be able to see "how it could be different"—which is not always easy to do.

Innovative Ideas Are Not Enough

Good ideas, no matter how innovative they may be, do not guarantee success. How many times have you had an inspiring idea without acting on it, only to later see that idea translated into a phenomenally successful product or service? How often have you seen such an offering and thought to yourself, "That was *my* idea. If only I had done something with it!"

The truth is, good ideas alone do not ensure successful outcomes. They are certainly necessary, but not sufficient.

A promising new product or service does not just become a phenomenal success overnight, especially in a larger enterprise. It needs executive backing, financial investment, production facilities, resource allocation, marketing strategy, training and education, go-to-market execution, demand generation, sales activity, logistics, and organizational support to drive an idea to fulfillment.

A good innovation also needs to exist at the right time and in the right place. Externalities including market readiness, competitive positioning, cost of production, economic situation, infrastructure availability, technology maturity, public policy, and more can all make or break an innovative idea. This means that even with the best idea and the best internal support, it is not always up to you.

Innovation also needs to be able to scale, and do so at the right pace. As a new technology service or capability is taken on, and it grows even with an internal customer base, it will likely follow the same growth pattern identified by Everett Rogers in the theory of "diffusion of innovations,"[19] extended and

---

[18] Steve Sasson, "We Had No Idea," Eastman Kodak Company, October 2007, http://pluggedin.kodak.com/pluggedin/post/?id=687843, retrieved on July 2012.

[19] Everett Rogers, *Diffusion of Innovations* (Glencoe: Free Press, 1962).

made popular in Geoffrey Moore's *Crossing the Chasm*.[20] This pattern can be seen in Figure 11-4.

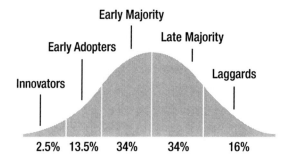

Figure 11-4. This graph depicts Everett Roger's Innovation Adoption Life Cycle.[21]

That is, you must hit the right scale at the right time, from just a 2.5% take-up among innovators and enthusiasts, to a larger scale with early adopters, and then to the additional 34% that make up the early majority. Plan how to make your innovation, as Moore puts it, "cross the chasm" from the early adopters to the early majority so that you can get to a sustainable scale. Also plan on how to scale your innovation for when you achieve that goal. If your service does not cross the chasm, it will be hard to sustain it. If it crosses the chasm without being sustainable, then it will fail to satisfy demand. Ultimately, it does not matter how good the innovation is—without the right scale at the right time, chances are it will not be successful.

Even if your innovation team creates the right ideas at the right times, gets the internal support they need, has alignment with the external environment, and achieves the right scale at the right time, the rest of your organization may not be ready to take it up. It may be the wrong time for them. You may have the wrong people on the program or in the audience. Or you may have an insurmountable cultural challenge. There may be internal political issues, or even intentional sabotage. Some organizations are simply not good at leveraging new innovations or accessing new markets. Other organizations, pushed by Wall Street expectations, are too worried about quarterly returns to commit to long-term innovation success.

Something as simple as having the wrong organization chart can also get in the way of your good ideas becoming successful innovations. As we have seen in Chapter 9, there are ways to set up an organization and establish supporting processes to enable intentional innovation. However, you cannot always

---

[20] Geoffrey Moore, *Crossing the Chasm* (New York: HarperBusiness, 2002).

[21] Wikipedia, http://en.wikipedia.org/wiki/File:DiffusionOfInnovation.png, retrieved on July 2012, reproduced under Creative Commons Attribution 2.5 License.

predict where innovation will come from, so a fantastic innovator or innovation from the wrong part of the organization will have substantial barriers from the start.

As we have noted, executive support and vetting is key. Not every organization can function well with a powerful, charismatic, and/or hands-on leader making firm decisions. However, over-reliance on executive support and approval can also kill off even the best ideas. Every additional person who can support an idea can also probably veto it, adding one more roadblock, and one more way to fail, even for the good ideas.

Therefore, it is important to manage this uncertainty as you would any predictable risk. Continue to encourage and evaluate good ideas, but understand their chance for success. Consider how they relate to the internal and external environment, whether they align with organizational objectives, how and when they can scale, how to gain the right level of executive support, and how to mobilize the organizational support to move from good idea to successful innovation. And understand that even with all this in place, sometimes the best ideas still will not produce positive results, regardless of what you do.

People Will Want You to Fail

By definition, innovation means doing new things, doing things in new ways, or both. Unfortunately, that works against a very common human emotion—a fear of change and a desire to maintain predictability.

As an innovative CIO, you will be actively planning to upset the day-to-day lives of many of your people, at least some of whom may not want to consider radical new ideas. They are comfortable in their roles and responsibilities, able to deal with everything in their jobs every day, without any risk or challenge. They consider this to be a successful way to work because every day they do the things that got them to where they are. They believe this is just what is expected of them. To do new things in new ways is to undermine not just their routine habits, but their fundamental belief systems.

You may also find political ramifications to innovation. Changes that disrupt existing organizational structures, staff levels, budgets, and other sources of institutionalized power structures will threaten people's positions and power bases, which can drive resentment and resistance. Even senior executives may be looking for you to fail in order to protect their empires and power bases, so you may find these threats are no less true of your bosses than your staff or your peers.

From their perspective, innovation will threaten many people's worlds. It could be as simple as innovation meaning they cannot do the same things they used to, so you are upsetting their rhythm by making them adapt their processes. Perhaps your innovation is creating additional work for them, which is almost always unwanted. Or it could be exactly the opposite—your innovation could be reducing or even eliminating their work, which is a much more existential threat. If you are making roles obsolete and people redundant, drastically changing jobs that have been the same for many years, and gutting departments or even entire business units (such as in the example of Kodak and digital photos), then in the best case you will struggle to gain support for your ideas. In the worst case these affected people will actively work against the success of your agenda, willfully or otherwise.

Unfortunately for you and your innovation agenda, this means that many people in your organization—including your own staff, senior IT managers, staff and executives from other business departments, and even other C-level executives—will be actively trying to undermine your efforts. Perhaps they do not consciously want you to fail, and almost certainly will not talk about their intent in such explicit terms, but ultimately that is what they want to happen.

Therefore, be prepared to see your own staff and your business peers actively looking for and espousing many different reasons why your innovation will not work. They will throw out objections and highlight barriers. Hallways and e-mails will echo with the sounds of "Yes, but . . ." Staff and executives will show negativity and skepticism, albeit couched in concern for the business and its success. Important innovation projects will get bogged down in process, external support for your programs will be understaffed and reprioritized, your requests will go to the bottom of the queue, and important prerequisite tasks will slip through the cracks—intentionally or otherwise.

Of course, shedding light on potential barriers to innovation is not in itself necessarily destructive. After all, as we have already discussed, many innovations will fail, so there are clearly many valid barriers and objections that will cause this failure. For the most part, such objections are not just made up and mostly do reflect real barriers, though they may not always seem significant. When raised as a way to detect and overcome potential risk, raising objections is actually very positive, and a necessary part of acting on innovative ideas. It is important to understand risks and actively manage them, and plan to overcome obstacles. For this risk management to work, you need to dispassionately identify and accommodate the very real potential for failure.

So the naysayers may well be right, but that does not mean they are helping.

When objections are raised as an excuse to *impede* innovation, rather than as a way to *facilitate* innovation, they can quickly put the brakes on your plans to do new things in new ways. It is all too easy for an innovation jam to become the "downer dog pile" we described in Chapter 2, with multiple people piling on why something cannot be done.

In addition, you may be blocked by the challenge of inertia and the path of least resistance. It is simply easier to do the same things tomorrow as you did today. It is easier to do nothing than to learn how to change. It is easier to resist change than to support it. It is easier to point out a barrier than to figure out how to overcome it.

Brace yourself for this resistance, whether passive or active. Never underestimate the human issues involved with innovation, and especially the natural human inertia against disruptive change.

Innovation Is an Art, Not a Science

It may be late in our book to say this but, despite all the ideas in this book, and in many other notable and scholarly writings on the topic, innovation is not a science.

There is no definitive formula for successful innovation.

Innovation is, rather, a rarefied and exquisite art.

This really should be apparent in the ongoing mantra throughout our writings that much innovation will actually fail—and this is a good thing. Of course, we have tried to outline for you a number of keys to success and some important ways that you can help to avoid or mitigate failure, but at its heart innovation remains fragile and unpredictable. Innovation is as much the result of trial and error, fortuitous accident, hard work, or sheer luck as it is the result of intentional activity. In this regard, it is clear that innovation is more like an art than a science.

A corollary of this particular dirty little secret is that measuring innovation—like measuring any art—is not always helpful. It may be possible to measure some outcomes of innovation with empirical data, such as the number of patents filed or granted, new products delivered, positive recommendations received, new sales closed, existing customers served, or new customers acquired. Moreover, you absolutely should measure the success of your innovation, not just for the sake of reporting, but also to catalog and document what works for you and what does not. However, you should not be tricked by the many useful and viable metrics surrounding innovation into believing that this makes innovation a measurable scientific endeavor.

Because it is not always possible to measure innovation. Indeed, it is not always even desirable to measure innovation. Sometimes the benefits and improvements of innovation are recognizable more in qualitative terms than quantitative terms. You may be able to readily understand what it means to be "better," to improve your competitive or market position, and to generate excitement in your customers and staff, but such outcomes are frequently difficult to measure. Like the investor said while looking for a good painting to buy, "I don't know what art is, but I know what appreciates!"

There are no hidden secrets to successful innovation, no "silver bullets," even though article after article will tell you they exist. Just search the Internet for the phrase "secrets of innovation" and you will find tens of thousands of results—but then again, if it is on the Web, how "secret" can they be? Books like ours can give you a framework, a starting point, a foundation, and a vision. We can show you examples and explain where they went right or wrong. We can give you ideas and help you develop strategies and tactics, all proven to help you drive successful innovation.

Nevertheless, no one (ourselves included) can guarantee you will be successful, even if you do everything in this book. It will ultimately be up to you to paint your own picture, author your own guide, sculpt your own progression, sing your own praises—and deliver your own success.

Not Everyone Can Innovate

Sorry to say, it does not matter how smart, funded, resourced, committed, inventive, or supported you and your team are, it is not always possible to innovate. There are a number of external issues, beyond the secrets we have already discussed, that will hold you back if you are not careful to avoid or overcome them.

One key external issue that will affect your ability to innovate, over and above these other mechanistic qualifications, is the personal capabilities for innovation within you and your teams. How individuals respond to new ideas is always difficult to predict. With a number of very real reasons for your staff and others to reject and resist change, as we have noted earlier, this is potentially a major barrier to your success.

Another key external issue is your corporate appetite for innovation. If, as we noted in Chapter 2, "culture eats strategy for breakfast,"[22] then it could also be said that it comes back to eat innovation for lunch. You should always beware of phrases such as, "That's not how we do things around here," or, "That's how we've always done it," as they do not bode well for any innovation

---

[22] Generally attributed to management consultant Peter Drucker, popularized in 2006 by Mark Fields, president of Ford Motor Company.

program. Watch out for politics too, especially the old guard in your organization who may not be predisposed to your new ideas. Whether they are invested in the original (although now perhaps obsolete) decisions about process, tools, products, and services; or they are invested in the status quo because of their empire or the recognition they have garnered or the power base; or they simply cannot see the same future that you can—these cultural forces can be difficult to surmount.

Then there is the question of whether the market and your customers (internally as well as externally) have given you permission to innovate. You must gauge the perception of your organization and determine whether your market will allow you to be innovative.

Some organizations or companies are almost expected to innovate. Think of Apple, for example. Rightly or wrongly, it is expected to be innovative, and when it fails to deliver that innovation it is actually punished for it. This was the case when it released the incremental iPhone 4S, rather than the expected innovation of the iPhone 5, causing its share price to drop substantially.[23] However, many organizations not only lack an expectation of innovation, but even lack permission from the market to be innovative.

We see this regularly when "old favorites" try to change, only to be faced with a lukewarm, if not downright hostile, reaction from their customers.

One example of this (albeit outside technology) happened in April 1985 when the Coca-Cola Company introduced a new (arguably innovative) formulation of their market-leading beverage of the same name. Despite extensive market testing that predicted its success and a substantially positive response from some customers in major markets, "New Coke" (as it came to be known) created an uproar among Coca-Cola's customers. In certain key markets, it was so roundly rejected by the customers that in July 1985 Coca-Cola reintroduced "Coke Classic" and by 2002 the company had ceased to produce the new formula at all, renaming "Coke Classic" back to "Coke."[24] Ultimately, while accepting many other innovations (including Cherry Coke, Diet Coke, and Caffeine-free Coke, for example), the market fundamentally rejected the ability of Coca-Cola to change one of its core products.

Another key constituent in your ability to innovate, over whom you have almost no control, are your shareholders (for private enterprises) or your citizens and politicians (for public sector enterprises). Many businesses are

[23] Rory Cellan-Jones, "Apple Unveils Refreshed iPhone 4S, but no iPhone 5," BBC, October 2011, www.bbc.co.uk/news/technology-15172238, retrieved on July 2012.

[24] The Coca-Cola Company, "Coke Lore: The Real Story of New Coke," www.thecoca-colacompany.com/heritage/cokelore_newcoke.html, retrieved on September 2012.

rated on their quarterly results, and may not be intrinsically set up to support the longer-term vision that is essential in an innovation culture. It is very difficult to contemplate innovation in an organization that is laser-focused on a three-month return. Even annual reporting can be deleterious. Public sector organizations can find more leeway in expectation (there is a reason many long-term "public good" innovations like the Internet were undertaken by government, not private enterprise). However, even these organizations can face anti-innovation pressure as they are asked to deliver results in a single election cycle, and often much less.

The reality is that you are not always in control of your own innovation destiny. Customers, shareholders, constituents, other executives, and more can all too easily undermine your innovation efforts—despite your best efforts.

Innovation May Cannibalize Your Business

As we have explored, innovation definitely upsets the apple cart. It can undermine individuals and teams, and reduce the power base and empire of otherwise well-positioned executives. It can fundamentally change the way people work and the outcomes they are expected to achieve. Sometimes innovation is so radical that it may even threaten to cannibalize your core business. It can decimate or make obsolete anything from individuals to whole departments or business units and even to entire companies.

And neither you nor your organization is immune from this same radical disruption.

To be a true innovator, you should be looking for the next development that will revolutionize and/or dominate your industry. You should be looking to find what will disrupt your competitors and erode their advantage, what will drive your market to significant change in purchasing, what products and services will drive a substantial change in your business opportunity.

Sometimes you will discover innovations that will not just undermine your competitors, but will undermine your industry. You may find innovations that will undermine your own staff, your department, or even your own job. When the point of innovation is to do new things new ways—and to do existing things in better (new) ways—then sometimes you will find that innovation means the need to disrupt yourself or your business. This may mean that you find ways to cannibalize or undermine your own business.

The problem is that once you see these disruptions, you cannot simply ignore them. If you can find these innovations, it is a good bet that eventually someone else will. If you do not take advantage of these disruptions, you run the risk that someone else will. So you may need to do it first, even if it may kill you. You may need to disrupt yourself before others disrupt yourself for you.

Examples of this in technology form the stuff of innovation legends. You can look at IBM, which dominated the typewriter market with the Selectric but eventually killed off the typewriter by embracing the personal computer—in effect cannibalizing their business by embracing this innovation.

By contrast, we have already noted the history of Kodak, which has suffered significant market pressure as it failed initially to embrace its own innovation in digital photography. We can also point to bookstore chain Barnes & Noble, which for too long failed to embrace digital publishing, allowing Amazon and its Kindle e-reader to erode Barnes & Noble's market position. We can also see how Blockbuster continually rejected efforts to dismantle its bricks and mortar business model, allowing innovators like Netflix and Redbox to do exceptional damage to its business with new delivery methods like mail order, self-service kiosks, and online streaming, all of which Blockbuster was late to embrace.

There is also the immediate threat from cloud computing, which many say will make the traditional IT department obsolete. Cloud will likely change your personal job in the business of IT, and without significant change in your own role, may even make you redundant. Yet you cannot ignore it, as that will only lead to an inevitable atrophy in your role as your business counterparts demand new approaches, and adopt cloud services directly. Like King Canute, you cannot turn back the tide, and must instead figure out how to embrace these changes—even if it may damage your department, or even your own prospects. Putting your head in the sand is simply not a viable option when faced with the opportunity of radical innovation.

Of course, these are just a few examples of factors outside your control that will affect your ability to innovate. Difficulties satisfying the requirements of other business executives, channels, and partners; an ecosystem that relies on your products and services, backward compatibility, standards and interfaces; and many more factors can get in the way.

In the end, to be a successful innovator you will need to accommodate and manage the conflict that cannibalization can create. There is no one correct approach, but you must recognize, acknowledge, and react to this threat when it appears. In some situations, you may be able to simply accept and mitigate the risk. In others, you may be able to ameliorate the threat. In a best case, you may be able to take advantage of the new opportunities this threat creates.

However, one thing is for sure—you cannot simply close your eyes and hope the threat of cannibalization goes away, because it will not. You must accept it, make a plan to deal with it, and move forward.

What's Next for Me?

Few things are impossible to diligence and skill. Great works are performed not by strength, but perseverance.

—Samuel Johnson

If you have gotten this far, you have read a lot of practical advice based on the experiences of the authors. This practical advice has been written to help you take action. After all, as we have stated many times in the previous chapters, good ideas without related action are nice but will have no impact on the organization. You have the opportunity with the help of this book to develop a strategy that will improve the use of IT in your organization. This can lead to growth, new products and services, or hopefully the rewards that come with them.

It is time to decide on your priorities for innovation. These will be different for each reader of this book. The first stage in this process is to use your personal experience and what you have picked up from this book so far. At this time, you will need to ask some searching questions:

- Does the culture of your organization support innovation?

- Who are the innovators in the business?

- Can you improve your relationship with them?

- Is the business growing?

- Is it possible to develop growth to improve your position in your market without radical innovation?

- Can you move into new markets with innovation?

- Is there an appetite for change in your IT organization or in the business as a whole?

- Who are the most likely sponsors for innovation?

- Do you have the nerve to promote innovation?

- Do you have the patience to stick with an innovative project until you see results?

- How well does your company use technology now and could you do better?

All of these and more questions need to be considered before creating an innovation strategy and an action plan from that. You will notice that we have not mentioned technology in any of these questions. Detailed technology is outside the scope of this book, and we are assuming that you already understand the capabilities of the technology you provide to the organization.

So what is next for the innovative CIO? Can you develop a "nose" for innovation? This chapter will look at some of the qualities of an innovative CIO. We will encourage you to be—or continue to be—adventurous in your promotion of innovation. We will also discuss the reality that not all innovations deserve to see the light of day. Some innovations need to be terminated before they cost too much in resources or reputation.

What Is an Innovative CIO?

We have discussed the role of an innovative CIO in previous chapters. The CIO is responsible for supplying IT to the business. This is the day job and the expectation of senior management. Many CIOs see IT maintenance as their sole responsibility. Keeping the lights on is what they believe is the highest single priority for the business. CIOs with this mindset see IT excellence as about performance, uptime, and cost control. These are, without dispute, important parts of the role. But we hope that we have persuaded you that CIOs should be doing more beyond their core business.

A continual theme of this book is that innovation is needed to add value to the business and this value-add should be IT-led. Keeping IT costs low is important, but cost reduction does not add value to the business. Value is what IT leaders will be measured on in the future. At some stage in our discussions with senior business executives, they tell us that IT is the heart of the business. They say things like the following:

"We couldn't run our business without IT."

"IT is critical to our business success."

"IT enables business innovation and is core to our strategy."

These firmly held views are often at odds with answers from the same executives when you ask if IT is fulfilling their expectations. Their answers to this question frequently indicate that IT is still not as effective as the business needs. These views were gathered in informal discussions but also supported by a survey into the changing role of the CIO[1]. When CIOs were asked how closely they believe their view of the CIO role matches the CEO or other C-suite executive's view of the role, only 29% of the CIOs said the views were identical. Further insight into the attitudes to the CIO came from asking if their respective companies use IT to the extent the CIO would expect. The result of this question was 37% of CIOs responded "no." The responses of the CIO to these survey questions indicate that there is a continuing disconnect between the expectations of the CIO and the expectations of others in the company with regard to the effectiveness of CIO and IT.

The conflicting views cannot be reconciled by communication alone. You need to ask yourself about the senior people in your organization. Do they know what is happening in the IT domain—what new technologies and what new services are being promoted or developed? Increasing numbers of people in their thirties are entering the senior management ranks. These people have not known a world without personal computers. There is an assumption that the digital literacy of the executive team will increase as these "digital natives" become more senior in organizations. At the current time, this is still not the case, although we are watching the next ten years with interest! The evidence from the CIO survey shows that 59% of senior management is not considered digitally literate by the CIOs in their organizations. As an innovative CIO, you will have to manage the expectation of people who are not as digitally literate as you are, but who sometimes think they are. You will also have to overcome the doubts of people who know IT is important, but think that they are not getting the best from IT.

You should also consider the velocity of technology change and introduction. There are a number of commentators who argue that technology is moving too fast for a single executive to keep pace with. The increasing number of

---

[1] "The Future Role of the CIO," CA Technologies, October 2011, www.ca.com/us/collateral/white-papers/na/The-Future-Role-of-the-CIO-Becoming-the-Boss.aspx, retrieved on May 2012.

new advances, and more particularly, the understanding of the potential impact of those advances are overwhelming. The role of the CIO is to be an IT specialist. More and more frequently, the expectation is for a business expert who has special responsibility for IT. This would be the IT equivalent to the COO who is the business expert with special expertise in logistics. You are fortunate if you are in the position of being regarded as an IT-savvy business expert. The Future Role of the CIO survey also highlighted the previous experience of the CIOs we questioned. The sizable majority of the CIOs had an IT background with only 5% having experience in finance, logistics, or sales and marketing. This shows that the "home-grown" CIO promoted from within the organization is most likely to come from an IT background. In our view, this is the reason that few CIOs are regarded as business experts. Many large organizations hire in CIOs with a business background. The progression from business expert to CIO is not easy but is valued in many cases for the credibility it gives to the CIO's innovative business suggestions.

This seems to imply that only CIOs from a business background will have credibility to talk about innovation to the business. IT people who want to make it as a business expert need to have some additional business experience, not just experience keeping the data center's lights on. There are a number of ways to gain the required business experience. Training or education is one way, such as part-time or on-the-job MBA degree courses or courses for other qualifications. The important thing is to develop a business focus and equip yourself with the language of business. As we have stressed in many places in this book, leave the technology chats for the IT department. Talk business and capabilities to the business people.

During the writing of this book, we have had some interesting discussions about the changes that a CIO would need to make to convert from a technology to business focus. One of the comments most frequently made is that the changes and opportunity to convert are not fully within the CIO's control. A CIO may be driven to be innovative, but it is not possible for them to go it alone. In Chapter 10, we talked about how the CIO can work with sponsors. Gaining an executive sponsor and capturing the imagination of the decision-makers is often the key to getting things rolling.

Often the IT department and the CIO are spending all their time maintaining their existing infrastructure. This is a demanding task. You should take a few minutes to look at your daily workload. How much of your workload is running to stand still? What did you do that was innovative in the last working day? If the answer is nothing or near nothing, then you have some work to do to generate the energy to innovate. Innovative work is not concerned with maintaining the status quo. Consider the structure of your department. Are you notified of all problems or only the most serious ones? Have you delegated correctly? Does that give you time to plan or even review any innovations?

If you consider yourself a pragmatic manager rather than an innovator, do you have someone in your department who is an innovator? Can you structure your department so that it will foster innovation?

Recently I came across an IT department that was generating some interest in their innovative suggestions for the business. When I spent some time discussing this with them, I found that the one thing that had generated the suggestions was moving the IT department desks into the same physical space that some of the other departments occupied. Just moving outside of the isolated IT offices started to get conversations going. Adding some sporting events and the occasional afterwork social event ensured that contacts made at work carried over. This was just good management, fostering a united workforce. It did get people talking across departmental boundaries.

While these changes may be influential, developing an innovative culture and habit may require a "rethink" of the whole organizational structure. While this is not normally something within the scope of the CIO, it is worth your thinking about new structures and being able to discuss them when the CEO asks about innovation, particularly if innovation has not been successful.

Creating an Innovative Organization

The previous chapters of the book have emphasized the difficulty in measuring and managing innovation with the same measures and in the same way as mature products and services are managed. We have discussed tactics for avoiding some of the negative effects of innovating in a company that is not geared up for innovation. A Fortune 500 general manager told us that he has had to treat an innovative project as though it was a startup company. He set up a separate team to duplicate every function he needed, keeping the team small and focused. This was the only way that he could get the project off the ground. His problem was that each quarter other parts of the company were asking when there was to be a return on the investment, and any return he stated was always perceived as lower than expected.

One way of avoiding these problems may seem obvious—create a completely separate startup. Acting as a venture capitalist for a separate startup creates the emphasis on agility and innovation and removes the bureaucracy of a large organization. Creating a separate company may lose some of the economies of scale and the support that being part of a larger organization can give. There are other methods of creating the separation between innovation and core developments through changes in organizational structure. Creating an "emerging business unit" as a separate entity, only reporting to the CEO or general manager is always a possibility. Again this would duplicate all the functions, on a smaller scale, of the larger organization. This has many of the advantages of a startup, but gains little from being part of the larger organization and has little management support except at the highest level. This structure creates a climate of functional duplication, where even the HR or office facilities may be duplicated. Another possible solution is the creation of an innovation team within an existing core business unit. This team would have separate goals from the other parts of the unit but the same management. Inevitably this may lead to conflicts of objectives where neither part of the organization thrives.

Acceptance is growing for an alternative organizational strategy. This strategy will encourage innovation and still enable the existing business to function optimally. The strategy is to create an ambidextrous organization. This organizational structure creates a separation between the core, mature business, and innovation. The innovative business can still use the skills, HR, and cash of the larger organization but not be measured in the same way. The innovative part of the business will not have to follow processes and corporate rules in the same way as the mature part of the business. This may look like all the advantage goes with the innovative part of the business, but in fact it removes the issues with innovation from the mature part of the business and allows this mature part to focus on sales, marketing, and product development needed to keep it healthy.

Charles O'Reilly and Michael Tushman call this type of organizational structure an ambidextrous organization in their 2004 paper for *Harvard Business Review*[2]. This is not a new concept. Ambidextrous organizational structures have been discussed in many papers over the years dating back to 1971. The main feature is the two separate domains in an ambidextrous organization. There is the core products domain, where products and services are mature and exploiting a mature market. Secondly, there is the innovative products and services domain where new products and services are being developed to expand into new markets.

Both core and innovative domains are important to the company, but they have different goals. If this level of separation is maintained with different marketing, sales, and development goals, both parts will succeed. A critical success factor is that the integration of the two domains is at the higher level of management of the organization. Both domains should have separate management structures and budgets. For example, the innovative part of the

---

[2] Charles O'Reilly and Michael Tushman "The Ambidextrous Organisation" 2004, http://hbr. org/2004/04/the-ambidextrous-organization/ar/pr retrieved on November 2012.

organization should have their own HR function that has a dotted line report to the HR executive to ensure that HR policies are in-line with regard to legal and ethical considerations. Innovative HR can use different processes and goals for recruitment but use the advice and experience of the HR executive as well.

This brief discussion of a management theory is needed to demonstrate that organizational barriers are the concern of the CIO even if the CIO has no direct influence on them. We spent some time on reviewing operational and organizational barriers to innovation in Chapter 10. The points mentioned here are for further consideration. Once you have established yourself as a trusted IT advisor to the business, you may have the opportunity to suggest alternative management or organizational structures that are worth considering. A story from the past may illustrate the point about gaining the confidence of the business executives.

One of the companies I worked for had very tight operational controls on each of its business units. The complexity of the business, staffing ratios, and delivery mechanisms meant that there was little flexibility for managers to develop any innovative programs. After several attempts to persuade the executives that the company needed a new service offering, my colleague and I discussed new services in management meetings and informal communications. We were initially told to concentrate on the day job but over a period of months the ideas gained supporters and we were invited to present to the chairman of the board. The chairman listened for about ten minutes and then gave the green light, informed the operations manager to set up a separate team, instructed the finance director to make budget available, and told my colleague and me to prepare a more detailed plan for implementation starting the following week.

Five months later we were demonstrating the pilot version of our idea. This pilot enabled the company to enter a new market and for a while the company made a lot of money until other organizations entered the market and innovated beyond our entry. Getting the buy-in from the chairman and major shareholder and setting up a separate team were crucial to success. The only problem was that this was not the development of an innovative culture in the company, just a one-off innovation. We were lucky that we had patience so that we gained support in the company, and we were lucky with the timing. We had made our pitch just at the time that the chairman had been considering the future of some software packages that had been developed. He had concluded that he needed some new hook to sell the packages to a larger market, and we provided the opportunity.

In this war story, success depended on luck but there are two other points to consider. First, we put our head above the parapet. We made the point that there was a new opportunity; we didn't accept the initial knock back and persisted with our idea. Second, we suggested an organizational change that was accepted, but not made permanent. Both points were crucial to the success, but alone neither of the points would have made success possible. To create a lasting innovative culture, you need to consider how an innovative organization should look and how it will relate to the existing organization.

Why Would You Stick Out Your Neck to Innovate?

The number of failed IT projects is legion, and they range in size from big to small. Failure is one thing that most managers and executives don't want their names associated with. Some corporate cultures are so risk averse that they are almost static. Something new and untried does carry a high risk. Innovation brings with it a high risk of failure. So why would a CIO want to be associated with innovation?

The most compelling reason for CIOs to innovate is that it is expected of them. Most executives see IT as the innovative factor that will drive growth. Examples of innovative uses of IT fire them up. They expect the IT department to come up with suggestions and projects that will revolutionize their business. Sadly, this expectation has generated frustration with the IT department. Expectations are sometimes inflated by a review of competitors and their use of IT. If a competitor has launched a new product and is starting to corner the market for that offering, this would be seen as a disadvantage to your company. The questions then asked of the IT group in this circumstance are this: "Where is our innovation? Why aren't we doing this?" A good example of competitive advantage was displayed a few years ago. A bank had developed a mortgage offering that reduced the amount owing by the monthly payment plus any interest accruing on other positive balances. This offering caught the public imagination and was popular. Other banks soon came into the market for this product but were disadvantaged by being late. Because some banks had relatively inflexible IT systems, they were unable to enter the market until later and lost business. Some were not able to make IT changes at all and were never able to compete with that offering.

A common characteristic of many businesses is impatience. If they get a great idea of ways to drive revenue, they won't want to wait for a long time. When I first started in the IT business, IT projects had tens or even hundreds of programmers, analysts and systems programmers working for many months, sometimes years. With agile development and continuous release strategies, the IT world is continually reducing time-to-release software changes, sometimes down to days and weeks. Imagine the expression of the business leaders if you come to them to talk about the extra delays on your already delayed project. Ensuring that you have a flexible and agile infrastructure is a valid IT innovation, but it still needs to be placed in a business context. This is what the business leaders will expect of an innovative CIO.

Lack of growth leads to stagnation, and stagnation in business will eventually lead to the demise of the business. If you only have a year to retirement, lack of growth may not be an issue. The likelihood is that you want to continue being employed, unless you have just won the lottery. Investing in innovation-led growth is part of the "keep paying me" plan, which can meet with some resistance from the established lines of business. In a company that has a core group of mature products, there may be resentment that investment is going into the new products or initiatives. It is frequently said by the core business managers that the core products are supporting the waste of resources on innovation. This is certainly the case if allocation of resources to innovation might reduce resources available the core product business.

So, if innovation has a high risk of failure and may discourage employees from considering innovation, we should first look at some of the reasons for failure:

- Failure is often the result of management impatience. The expectations have been high and time frames have been reduced. If the innovation has failed to deliver in those time frames, no matter how promising the project, it gets killed by senior management. One additional effect of failure is that the employees may get fired as well.

- Has the innovation suffered from mission creep? An innovation to improve the user interface for one application suddenly becomes a complete redesign of the other user interfaces, costs more than the original estimate, fails to deliver, and the redesign is seen as a failure.

- Failure can come from not focusing on the growth potential of an innovation. The other innovations in your portfolio are under pressure to release budget or resources, so this project should release resources. You should always look at each innovation and evaluate the level of market disruption it will cause and its growth potential before deciding to alter budget or resources.

The potential to fail should not discourage CIOs from innovating. There are ways of mitigating the risk of failure, as we discuss later in this chapter.

Innovation is a strategic direction that the CEO should be expected to support. However, there are managers who see the status quo as the optimal mode of operation. This "head in the sand" attitude is often the default mindset of middle management. Without growth, the organization may stagnate and fail. We have mentioned the business conflict between Netflix and Blockbuster. Blockbuster was complacent, had shops that it needed to support, and failed to see the impact of high-speed broadband on the movie download community. Blockbuster had stagnated and instead of leveraging its name and market presence, it allowed a new organization to take its market. We can speculate that Blockbuster was not worried about movie downloads because there had been several organizations who had entered the movie download market while Blockbuster was riding high and these companies had all failed to catch the imagination. Download or streaming speed was one reason for their failure, but also there was little understanding of the potential of movie streaming from the movie distributors. The distributors wanted to protect their revenue from DVD and tape hires rather than threaten this with streaming initiatives. Once broadband, streaming speeds, and distribution and demand had all lined up, the days for tape and DVD rentals were numbered. I haven't rented a movie from a store in seven years or bought a DVD for two years. The then CIO of Blockbuster should have been focusing on new delivery methods and not the efficiency of POS (Point of Sale) terminals.

As an innovative CIO, you are expected to embrace the idea of new tools and technologies—being late in the game may be a company killer and cost you and the department dearly. You should not let corporate stagnation deter you from developing and delivering innovation.

How Can You Develop a "Nose" for Innovation?

Developing a "nose" for innovation is part of a CIO's personal development. It takes time and needs practice. It is easier to learn a new language in small bites. In the same way, this skill needs to be practiced little and often. Most innovators are curious. Asking questions and trying to find out answers, solving puzzles—this is the lifeblood of innovation. Innovators are always interested in the new and novel. They store each fact away and often make surprising connections between facts. There are even tools that can do this like DEVONthink. This database has a query engine to create associations between what you write and content you already have stored or read. These connections can illuminate an idea or expand it into something unique. Trying to bridge the gap between the IT and business world may require unusual connections before it can result in something new. When Facebook started, it was a college project. The business connections were not made until later. Businesses may have cautiously decided to use Facebook for communications but they are all familiar with the potential. Twitter is another personal communication tool that has also become a business tool.

There are other ways that you can gain insight. You may consider a refresher course on business management if that is your experience or background. If you came into the role of CIO through the IT route, you may consider business as a new area of study. We mentioned earlier in the chapter that there are a number of online or part-time MBA courses that will expand your business experience. If you don't have the time or inclination for study, you may be able to join in with some of the business managers, particularly when they are discussing new business strategy and sales approaches.

The IT world, new directions, and technologies are all considered the primary area of expertise of the CIO. Keeping up to date in the IT domain should be a given. Magazines, papers, books like this one, blogs, online articles, and industry analysts are all good sources of information and opinion, and we are sure that you are already well-versed in their use. However, just reading the articles is not enough. Each article or blog should be evaluated against your current IT situation and the business you are in. Does this new technology have potential for your business? If you only have Microsoft tools and operating systems, you should not restrict your reading and reviews of that technology base alone. There may be something in the Linux or mobile worlds that can be applied to your business. As we just stated in the previous paragraph, you need to have a broad view of technology. Making the connections between what you have, what the business needs, and what new IT stuff is happening is the source of a lot of innovative thinking.

If you are evaluating the potential impact of new technology, indulging in "what if" sessions with your staff can help you in your evaluations. Develop a way of handling the information that you receive. Like most people, we expect that you are suffering from information overload. You will need to be selective, and every piece of information needs to be evaluated for its potential. The only problem with filtering information is that you may miss the one key thing that starts a train of thought.

In our discussions with CIOs of leading companies, we have been given some reasons for their difficulty in innovating. A frequently mentioned reason is "the day job.".As a CIO you cannot neglect this area, but even in the most difficult circumstances you also need to take time out to consider growth and innovation. You may even find that you return to the current system's problem with a fresh approach that saves the day. Watching the ways that competitors are using IT is another way of expanding your knowledge; however, you may need to consider if you can "leapfrog" over the competition with innovative uses of IT.

In addition to these ways of generating a nose for innovation, there are more organized ways. Creating a more formalized way of generating innovation may require a cultural change. We will look at that later in this chapter but from an individual perspective, creating a more formal nose for innovation may require considerable effort and some cost. We have talked to a CIO who tells us that he spends two weeks a year in Silicon Valley, meeting with venture capitalists and small companies to discuss developments. Another CIO has developed a complex database of technology that contains details of new technology, the vendors' offerings, and analysts' reports and opinions. This work may result in a more formal cultural change, but will require time and effort and again, support from the other executives. These CIOs have built a knowledge base that can be continually updated and expanded to help them to gain a good overview of the IT landscape. Knowledge is the way to develop the nose that you need for innovation.

Is Innovation in Your Title?

This is a politically tricky question to ask. If you search the Web, you will find a number of thinkers and analysts who are convinced that announcing the creation of an innovation department or the role of a Chief Innovation Officer indicates a company that is not innovative. How true that would be in your case we will leave to you to answer, but you should consider the following points:

- An innovation department will generate some visibility that there is somewhere for all those good ideas to go.

- Chief Innovation Officers only have innovation to focus on— they would not be expected to focus on other operational considerations.

- It will be expected that a Chief Innovation Officer need to come up with good ideas and processes to improve the innovative standing of the company.

So, it is not always the kiss of death. It is sometimes the knee-jerk reaction of the CEO to a perceived lack of innovation in your company. If you have followed the advice and points in the rest of this book, you should not be in a position of standing on the sidelines waiting for the appointment. You should already be considered the Chief Innovation Officer as well as the Chief Information Officer.

If you have joined an organization that has already put an innovation department in place or has created a chief innovation officer, you will have to work within that structure. It does not mean that you have no innovation role, but in the early days you may have to get approval for innovations that you are promoting from the innovation team. An innovative CIO buzzing with new ideas and enthusiasms may be seen as a potential threat to the Chief Innovation Officer or their department. You should be aware of this, but innovation is too important to your organization to allow politics to obstruct it.

Can You and Your Culture Adapt to Become More Innovative?

Earlier in the book, we mentioned how a company can change to become more innovative and generate high levels of growth. We also outlined some of the organizational changes that may smooth the way for innovations by removing or ignoring some of the operational and organizational obstacles. Many of these changes will have a positive effect, but they won't generate an organization that is focused on innovation for growth. That requires a cultural change, not just in the department that is innovating, but also in the wider organization to develop an understanding and appreciation of the value of innovation. Cultural changes are always difficult to achieve. A cultural change does not happen by dictate, just because the CEO says so. There are underlying attitudes and behaviors that will need to be modified before a cultural change becomes more than a plan. Management that is intent on maintaining their power base or employees who only see change in a negative way can undermine the best-intentioned cultural changes. Cultural changes take time to occur.

Often a company will announce a new mission statement that will not work without cultural change. A year later when the company performance against the mission statement is reviewed, there is often surprise that there have been few real changes and developments. There must be a real drive and focus on change to see progress even three years down the line. Trying to change the behavior and mindset of employees is a long-term task. Trying to develop an innovative culture will take just as long.

We have talked to a number of CIOs who want to create an innovative culture in IT. They have researched innovative companies like Google and have noticed that Google and other companies allocate time for employees to innovate. We have discussed the Google case more fully in Chapter 9, but other companies also have the concept of innovation time. The time allocated to innovation ranges from 10 to 25% of the employees' working time. Some executives believe that telling employees they have 20% of their time for innovation will generate innovative ideas; however, just allocating time will not increase the innovative potential of the team. One executive in a Fortune

500 company told us that despite a change to the working time to include innovation time it was undermined by middle management who didn't change workloads and priorities. Employees still could not get the time to innovate, but there was still an expectation of an increase in innovation. It took time for the problems to filter through to senior management. There needs to be a unified process supporting the allocation of time for innovation. We have outlined some of the process changes for idea creation and measurement in other chapters. It is clear to us that creating a cultural change in a team or a department is a complex, long-term exercise. It can be even longer if it is a cross-organizational change.

Measuring cultural change is as difficult as measuring innovation. Some people are happy to measure innovation and cultural change using the Justice Potter Stewart method:

During a judgment in an obscenity case Justice Potter Stewart said that hard-core pornography is hard to define—*but I know it when I see it.*[3]

Others need to measure the impact of innovation and of cultural change by trying to associate increases (or decreases) in revenue or profitability with the changes. One area that has been used to measure innovation is the patent measurement. Innovative ideas can be patented. Some parts of the world only allow a patent to be awarded to a technology; others allow business processes to be patented as well. Registering a patent is costly and time-consuming, but there are a number of analyses of US patents that place average values of $9,000 on a patent, although some are worth much more. One reason for placing some emphasis on patents is the leverage that a company gets when they are holding patents. This is particularly important when negotiations to sell or buy licenses and franchises are underway. If your company does not have a well-established patent process, then creating a culture that emphasizes patent production as a way of measuring innovation will not deliver results. In this circumstance, a discussion with the company legal department may generate a change in attitude to patents.

---

[3] Judith A. Silver "Movie Day at the Supreme Court or "I Know It When I See It," FindLaw, 2008, http://corporate.findlaw.com/litigation-disputes/movie-day-at-the-supreme-court-or-i-know-it-when-i-see-it-a.html, retrieved on November 2012.

Do You Have the Attention Span to Be Innovative?

It's always nice to get some quick wins, particularly when you can use them to validate an approach. Whenever you engage in a project that is new or has potentially unknown benefits, you need to look for the quick win or validation that your approach is working. A balance needs to be achieved between quick wins generated by impatience for results and the need for patience to allow project results to be realized. This balance needs to take into account projects that are not fulfilling early promise.

Once a project has been given the green light, there is a great enthusiasm that can be maintained by communication of progress and early wins. Early wins can be a milestone met or an endorsement from someone influential, for example, an analyst or the press. An influential quick win is a commitment to purchase on project completion or an agreement to join a project pilot study. We have already stressed the need to communicate to ensure that the project is seen as a real project and worth continuing. There may come a time when the communication and wins start to tail off. This is the most critical part of an innovative project. The doubters and "nervous nellies" start to make their presence felt when things are not going well. You may be urged to cut your losses, close the project, and move on to something more viable. How do you know when the time is right to pull the plug or increase your drive to continue the project?

There are many examples of innovations that have been killed early and as many that have stayed the course but failed to make it to market. Consider this example. Gardening is a popular pastime and during the last 30 years more and more products have been created to tap into this enthusiastic market. In the 18th century, gardeners in the employment of large households looked for ways to force plants to grow faster in the cooler times of the year or to protect delicate plants from frost and predators. They often used bell cloches (large glass domes). These were put over plants for protection or to encourage growth. In the 1970s, a plastic version was designed. It would fit a large circular plant pot like a miniature green house—it could be used like a bell cloche and was designed with small holes in the top so that plants could be watered without moving the cloche. The holes were drilled precisely, after a lot of experiment and calculation, to enable the optimal amount of water for the plant without too large a drop of water that would damage delicate plants. This was marketed under the name "Ploche."

Why are we discussing garden equipment in a book for CIOs? In our view, this is a good example of an innovation that had been overdeveloped. With the Ploche, there had been market and sales analysis and advertising material prepared. But despite all the investment and work, the product failed to sell in any great numbers. It was an innovation; it had been engineered precisely and people were initially enthusiastic. So why did it bomb? After a lot of discussion, the producers discovered that cheaper alternatives were considered "good enough" and precision engineering of this type of item did not have a premium value.

The Ploche also suffered from being so well made. After you had bought three or four, you did not need to buy any more for years so there were few repeat purchases. The Ploche didn't break easily and again the opportunity for future sales faded away. The development should have ended earlier than it did, cost less, and got out onto the market earlier. There was no need to spend weeks and months creating a perfect article that would fit onto an eight-inch pot when sales depended on purchasers owning or buying additional pots. The project should have been reviewed at each stage and this vital question should have been answered: "Will the public pay enough of a premium to recover the investment in each innovative change?" If the answer was negative, then the development should have been stopped or modified to create a "near enough" product that would sell.

There is another good example of a technically good product that didn't sell well because of a mistaken development direction, the Psion 5. Back in the 1990s, the Psion 3 handheld computer was released. You could use it to write notes and letters, and it would store diary entries, notes, tasks, and contacts. It was one of the first best replacements for the day planner or Filofax. As a standalone tool, it was excellent—it was compact, had good battery life, and there was a limited integration with PCs. It was never intended to become a peripheral for the PC, and so the integration was a little clunky. The rival was the Palm Pilot that came out with much better integration with PCs but no keyboard. Many people were happy using the Psion and had no plans to replace it.

At this time, companies started to deploy Microsoft tools for e-mail and appointments. In these environments, the Psion became more awkward because of the lack of simple integration. Needing to rekey diary entries into the Psion from Windows applications was a common problem users experienced. Psion released a new version, the Psion 5 with a touch screen and marginally better integration. Users of the Psion 3 had become frustrated with the lack of integration and PC tools, although the Psion 3 had simpler data entry and better-looking applications than the Palm Pilot. If the PC integration had been of the same quality as the Palm Pilot, customers would have been happy. But the new Psion 5 was more a hardware and user interface upgrade. Psion missed the point. Most of the commercial world was starting to use Microsoft tools as their internal standard. The developers of Psion would have been better served if they had concentrated on software integration rather than touch screens. The Psion 5 is another example of an innovation that should have been tested at each stage rather than developed, as we suspect, inside a bubble.

There are a number of key indicators to help you decide if you need to kill off a project. The adage is "fail fast," and is often extended to "fail fast, fail cheap." If you look into the two examples we have given, both of them should have identified the point at which the cost of completion would be less than the value of success. The Ploche could have been put to market faster without the extra design tweaks and the Psion 5 could have been a Palm killer if the Microsoft integration had been perfected. The indication that you may need to kill a project can come from a number of questions:

- What does the market expect from you in terms of innovation? If you are in a stable market, then there may not be much demand for innovation. It is a different matter if you are breaking into a new market area. Look at your competitors. Their innovation activities may tell you that you should put your innovation money into another area.

- Is there anything on the market that is "near enough" that you can only compete on cost? There is no point in over-engineering if there is something that is cheaper and fulfills 80 or 90% of the market requirements. Will the market sustain a premium for perfection?

- Is your innovation different enough? To make a real difference, an innovation has to be different. You should consider the disruptive effect of the innovation. The more disruptive potential an innovation has the more you should persist with the project.

- Are the early pilot studies getting the traction that justifies continued investment? A prime advocate of the fail-fast adage is Google. If you used the first versions of Google Wave, you would have been impressed by the potential but depressed by the number of people using it. Google announced that it was ceasing support for Google Wave a short time after opening it up to all users because the user uptake was not as significant as Google expected.

These questions, the answers, and this section of the chapter can be reduced to three rules that will enable you to decide on patience or the axe for an innovative project:

1. Talk to your critics. They often highlight areas that you have not thought about or had hoped no one would notice.

2. Microfailures are better than macrofailures. If you are planning to "fail fast, fail cheap," the microfailure is your friend. You should set up measures for all the critical components of the project and a plan for the possible failure of that component. If your risk assessment and risk management plan is good, you should be able to continue with the project without a macrofailure.

3. Trust your gut instinct. Sometimes you just know that things are not going right without being able to point to anything obvious. Use your gut feeling to tell you to review the microfailure risk assessment before deciding to kill off a project or to continue with investment.

Being innovative is not a one-off. Being innovative is an attitude or mindset that uses curiosity and interests to improve things. By using these rules, you should be able to develop innovations that will change things for the better in your work.

Summary

Although *innovation* may appear to be the latest hipster buzzword, innovation itself is and always has been important. All types of innovation matter, as well. For evidence of how even apparently simple innovations can be of remarkable value, we need look no further than to the use of clothing as a simple water filter in the prevention of guinea worm disease.

The value of a specific innovation is not always obvious to everyone—sometimes not even to the inventor. And when the inventor does realize its value, others still may not see that value. Sometimes innovation happens but is not captured. Sometimes innovation is temporarily forgotten. Sometimes it is lost altogether.

However, one truth remains: in today's business climate, every company must innovate, lest it put its future at risk.

Part of your role as the innovative CIO is to recognize all innovation when it appears, regardless of its source, and to divine its potential for adding business value. This is why it is so important to acknowledge the many types of innovation and how each can be of value. Whether you drive innovation in use or in process, whether it's incremental innovation, fortunate innovation, deliberate innovation, or desperate innovation, you should not overlook or discount the value these different approaches can bring to your organization. Furthermore, innovation need not involve invention. Even simple ideas can fundamentally change your organization and help it achieve core business goals. Indeed, innovation can come from anywhere, from anyone, at any time.

Not all innovation will be valuable to *your* business, despite the best efforts of your people, even though it may be of value to others. So, another aspect of the innovative CIO's job is to channel your team's creative energies toward the innovation that matters, without crushing their innovative spirit. One key approach is to suppress those negative views that can kill innovation as it occurs—or keep it from occurring. There are many innovation-killers, such as culture; organization; styles and personalities like The Perfectionist, The Innovative Authoritarian, or The Protector; attitudes like the downer dog pile; as well as constrained thinking, timing, and communication. Each can have a profoundly negative impact on team morale, innovative spirit and output, and overall productivity. Innovative IT leaders must face these innovation-killers head on.

These are just a few of your immediate challenges. As we have seen from the other I's in "CIO," there are many pressures, both positive and negative, facing innovative IT leaders. For example, you must learn to respond to and minimize the "I-Negative" pressures while fostering and leveraging the "I-Positive" pressures. There will always be opposing forces in almost all human endeavors; shifting the balance in favor of the positive is the key to building an innovative team. Shifting the balance of work time to favor employees' passions and strengths can also be key to success. In fact, this can help you increase the "innovation time surplus"—the amount of time you can free up for each team to focus on innovation.

As we have discussed, even if you master these I-Negative and I-Positive pressures, it is not enough to foster innovation; that innovation must align with your strategic business goals. Unfortunately, as an innovative CIO you will face so many challenges to producing innovation that maintaining a focus on alignment will be difficult.

Only a minority of CIOs are involved in building their organizations' business strategies; the reasons for this may be personal or organizational, but it means that it is a bigger challenge for a CIO to generate business innovations than to produce IT innovations. However, if you want to gain funding for innovation, you will need to develop a strong business case, using business terms, that concentrates on the "why," not the "how." You need to tell the time, not explain how the watch works.

Your ability to be successful will, therefore, depend highly on developing and improving your business communication skills. Using business-centric tech-niques and guidelines, adopting the correct language, focusing on the business value, and describing IT innovations as business imperatives—all these methods will make your business case much more compelling.

Innovation is even more compelling when it is not only described in business terms but also linked to business direction and strategy. This will be easier for a CIO who is part of the corporate strategy team, but as mentioned above, this C-suite engagement is sadly rare for all but a few CIOs. However, you can still participate in business innovation with some level of access to the corporate strategy, and by using tools such as the innovation funnel. You can also influence corporate strategy by using IT expertise to deliver business-aligned IT innovation, as well as educating business leaders so they can recognize the strategic value of technology in achieving business goals.

This, alas, sets up the potential conflict between the "business pull" and the "IT push" of innovation. But do not assume that there is only one, right way to drive innovation. Many organizations focus on building, enabling, and responding to the demands of business users as a primary source of innovation. Indeed, most business leaders perceive this as the most appropriate source of innovation. Others view the voice of the customer to be the only legitimate source of innovative ideas. Of course, business users often are more connected to your customers and the demands of your market, and customers often are a significant source of new ideas—but they are not the only, or even the best, sources of innovative ideas.

As a technologist, you know that a great deal of innovation comes from technology drivers, not just from business users and customers. But when business leaders try to innovate without understanding how the technology landscape is changing, and what the new possibilities that these changes enable, they are effectively operating with one hand tied behind their backs. Moreover, while customers and markets may sometimes drive good innovations, they frequently do not demand the innovations that will ultimately be the most successful. As we have seen from several examples, sometimes all a customer *wants* is a faster horse, but what she really *needs* is a new mode of transportation.

In fact, neither business nor IT has a monopoly on great innovation. It is, instead, a pairing of technology expertise (and the ability to exploit it) and an understanding of business goals (and the market demands that drive them) that drives the best new ideas. This combination of business and IT opens up many more possibilities to be truly innovative, to drive radical rather than incremental change, and to move the needle measurably toward meeting your organizational goals.

Even without radical new ideas, there are incredible opportunities to innovate today using currently available technologies. We have seen how IT leaders can adopt, adapt, or repurpose common technologies to accelerate innovative business opportunities. From virtualization and automation, which have been around for over 40 years, to relatively new concepts such as big-data analytics and gamification, there are some clear paths for driving business innovation.

Consider, therefore, how you can consolidate IT, improve process, accelerate development, and give your business peers the opportunity to try more new ideas faster, cheaper, and more efficiently than ever before. Use existing technologies like NFC, RFID, or GPS to improve your existing products and services, create greater efficiencies, open up new market opportunities, or drive competitive differentiation. Understand how you can use the information from Internet-connected devices and sensors to expand capabilities for your organization, optimize operations and logistics, and create new markets.

More specifically, look at the consumer-driven technologies that are rapidly permeating the market, including current and future customers, to see what is now possible. In some cases, you will not even need to drive innovation—your employees and customers will do it for you. As internal and external users adopt new technologies and bring their own devices to work, they will help you uncover new ways to address key corporate goals.

CDIT and related technologies (including mobile devices, social media, personal networks, unified communications, and set-top boxes) also open up many immediate opportunities for intentional innovation. For example, you can increase mobility for your employees and services; improve your ability to attract, retain, and satisfy your customers; or uncover new sales opportunities that deliver better market attachment and increase revenue.

On the other hand, you will find that future opportunities for innovation are difficult to predict. As an innovative CIO, you will need to match knowledge of world markets with an instinct to differentiate between valuable innovation and uncontrolled innovation. Still, some more structured approaches will help. Innovation may happen in spite of what an organization does or does not do; but there are intentional activities that will dramatically increase the likelihood of success and the quality of innovation.

For example, finding the right innovation may require networking with your peers and others. We have identified the importance of alignment with the C-suite to gain their trust and explicit support for innovative programs. Unfortunately, the intangible nature of IT value makes it difficult to establish it as a quantifiable business value. Indeed, many people in business believe that IT just happens—unless it fails, and then only a major failure brings home the true value of IT. It is up to the innovative CIO to actively promote an understanding of IT's innovative value among the C-suite members and other business leaders.

Executives attach different significance to innovations, based on their organizational roles and experience. A social-networking campaign may delight the head of sales by generating interest in certain products. The CFO concerned with quarterly balance sheets may view the same campaign as a waste of money. Thus, CIOs need to ensure that the IT innovation message is variously adapted to appeal to the different motivations of C-suite members.

However, C-suite support and promotion are not enough. You also need to network with other IT and business leaders, and with non-IT and junior staff, both internally and externally. There is no harm in creating top-down slogans and posters, but these alone will not make a company innovative. Encourage an innovative culture and make innovative habits pervasive throughout your organization. Move your teams beyond the institutional objections and barriers (including the innovation-killers we have described) and ensure they recognize the positive and negative influences on innovation while striving to keep innovation moving forward. Explicitly train your managers and leaders, especially newer employees, in your innovative culture. Since they are in the trenches, they are often the first to be exposed to new, innovative ideas.

Developing good innovations can also require physical networking, from instrumentation of the physical world based on the Internet of Things and smartphones, to gathering information that will expand your knowledge of future IT. You can also leverage mergers and acquisitions to deliver innovation by bringing in either new staff with different cultures and ideas or new technologies and processes.

While instinct and judgment are important, reconciling the potential sources of future innovation benefits most from establishing a process for achieving success. The best results come from structured activities that deliver innovation. For example, we have seen how SWOT analyses, idea competitions, speed rounds, and other intentional approaches help capture innovative spirit, foster innovative teams, and escape an innovative funk. Some other best practices include the following:

- leveraging your inexperience
- listening to your customers
- being socialites
- embracing rogue innovation
- lowering your artillery and not permitting belittling
- being intolerant of negative behaviors and innovation-killers
- providing adequate time for innovation
- investing in innovative activities
- taking a longer view
- being prepared to spin off innovative teams
- getting innovative products in front of customers

Practices like these will help you foster, generate, and recognize good business-focused innovation. However, you may find that your organization is unable to effectively capture and harvest its value. Innovative leaders must be aware of this possibility, and always be on the lookout for ways to reliably leverage the value of innovative ideas. It takes a lot of work to make an innovative idea a reality. First, it requires explicit ownership and defined simplicity in approach and delivery. Second, it needs streamlined business processes, good habits, and an appropriate level of diligence.

We started out this book by demonstrating the value of innovation—in curing disease, spreading knowledge, and connecting friends and family. Similarly, we have noted that, to be successful as an innovative CIO, you must demonstrate the value of innovation. This means reporting the business value of innovation, using business metrics. It requires monitoring the business benefits of innovative programs throughout their lifetimes, not just at the delivery point. It means looking beyond IT measures and including business measurements like market penetration, customer satisfaction, and financial returns. Even then, you have no guarantee of success. As time goes on, you will become familiar with the "dirty little secrets" of innovation.

In a world where most innovations will fail, you have to be determined and committed to becoming an innovative CIO. Innovation can be very costly for your organization even when it succeeds, but it's especially costly when it does not succeed (regardless of how fast it fails). You may find that innovation is barely wanted at your organization, especially if it may cannibalize current business or splinter burgeoning empires. Yet if you do not identify the potential impact of innovation, you cannot manage that impact, and may instead cede new markets to new competitors while losing existing markets to obsolescence.

Innovation can also be very costly for you personally. You may find that a focus on innovation could damage your career progression and burden you with expectations that you simply cannot meet. You could find yourself pigeonholed in a role with limited resources and given little chance of success. Even when you have organizational support, innovation is hard to manage; when others in your organization deliberately undermine your efforts, it can be literally impossible.

Moreover, you will find that innovation success is difficult and elusive. It is not enough to have a great idea; you or your organization need the structure and positioning to give that idea support, resources, and priority. It is insufficient to voice support for good innovation; you have to show the impact that innovation will have on your organization. You must be realistic and understand, first, whether your organization is even capable of innovating. Even then, you may be unable to predict when you will be successful and when you will not.

And, finally, there is the need to internalize innovation, to manage the organizational, cultural, structural, process, and personal changes that innovation demands, both within IT and without. As mentioned earlier, CIOs often view the value of IT differently from other executives. Many executives consider IT of critical importance to the organization, but they do not feel that the IT department is delivering the maximum value. Often, CIOs feel that the low level of IT literacy among other executives prevents them from exploiting IT innovation to its best advantage.

Culture change is, therefore, a prerequisite for building an innovative organization. But culture change is not a short-term exercise. As much patience is needed to bring about organizational change as to develop innovation itself. Nevertheless, organizational structures can be changed to foster innovation; an ambidextrous organization is one structure that can have a positive effect on innovation.

CIOs and their executive peers need the courage and patience to innovate. Courage is often required when an innovation fails to deliver its anticipated value. One failure should not close an innovative program; it should be viewed as a gain in knowledge and experience. Rather, having too few innovation successes should be the measure of overall value. Remember, innovation can lead to personal and cultural growth, and with foresight, patience, and perseverance, it will deliver new processes and products that strengthen the CIO's organization.

***

The bottom line is that, despite all the challenges and caveats, becoming an innovative CIO is not just a goal worth pursuing but also an imperative for any modern IT leader (and his or her business) to thrive—or, in many cases, simply to survive. If today's organizations look to the past and treat innovation as arcane magic that can be unleashed only through rarified incantation, or as some fortuitous accident that no one can predict or control, or as something for other organizations to lead, then they will lose market, lose customers, and ultimately fail.

On the other hand, if IT leaders leverage new technology developments in cooperation with their business leaders; if they approach innovation intentionally with structure and discipline; if they exploit the complex interconnections of people, process, and technology to do new things in new ways; if they describe, deliver, measure, and prove business value, then they will be able to open new markets, beat their competition, improve their value proposition, and thrive in a modern marketplace.

Perhaps most important, becoming the innovative CIO is not a pipe dream; it's an achievable reality, both today and in the future. Here, we have shown how many CIOs have not only driven technology innovation to improve the IT environment, but also to improve the business environment.

Summary

The choice today is to "innovate or die"—and this is the choice that you now have as an IT leader. Do you look to drive innovation intentionally to survive and thrive? Or do you keep doing what you have always done and let the chips fall where they may? In this book, we have given you the starting point you need to recognize the opportunities in front of you, to try new things and make them successful, and to make a real and fundamental difference to your organization. We have provided a launching point for your new career as an innovative CIO.

The rest is up to you.